THE TALENT POWERED ORGANIZATION

Strategies for Globalization, Talent Management and High Performance

Peter Cheese, Robert J Thomas and Elizabeth Craig
with a foreword by Don Tapscott

KOGAN PAGE

London and Philadelphia

Publisher's note
Every possible effort has been made to ensure that the information contained in this book is accurate at the time of going to press, and the publishers and authors cannot accept responsibility for any errors or omissions, however caused. No responsibility for loss or damage occasioned to any person acting, or refraining from action, as a result of the material in this publication can be accepted by the editor, the publisher or any of the authors.

First published in Great Britain and the United States in 2008 by Kogan Page Limited
Reprinted in 2008 (three times), 2009 (twice)

120 Pentonville Road
London N1 9JN
United Kingdom
www.kogan-page.co.uk

525 South 4th Street, #241
Philadelphia PA 19147
USA

© Peter Cheese, Robert J Thomas and Elizabeth Craig, 2008

The right of Peter Cheese, Robert J Thomas and Elizabeth Craig to be identified as the authors of this work has been asserted by them in accordance with the Copyright, Designs and Patents Act 1988.

ISBN 978 0 7494 4990 2

British Library Cataloguing-in-Publication Data

A CIP record for this book is available from the British Library.

Library of Congress Cataloging-in-Publication Data

Cheese, Peter.
   The talent powered organization : strategies for globalization,
talent management and high performance / Peter Cheese, Robert J.
Thomas, and Elizabeth Craig.
        p. cm.
   Includes bibliographical references and index.
   ISBN 978-0-7494-4990-2
1. Personnel management. 2. Creative ability in business. 3. Ability.
4. Success in business. 5. Organization. I. Thomas, Robert J. (Robert Joseph),
1952– II. Craig, Elizabeth. III. Title.
   HF5549.C4446 2007
   658.3'14--dc22
                                                        2007031113

Typeset by Saxon Graphics Ltd, Derby
Printed and bound in the United States by Thomson-Shore, Inc

Contents

Foreword

If you are not yet a believer, this book will convince you that talent has become the single most important force creating strategic value for your organization. And it will give you a new framework for doing something about it.

Under industrial capitalism, the key corporate assets were physical resources, physical plant and financial capital. Today physical resources are relatively unimportant in most industries. Even in the steel industry it's not the iron ore that counts but the people, knowledge, systems and processes that count.

In yesterday's economy, workers contributed their brawn, not their brain. Companies invested in big factories with production processes and sophisticated machinery that required little decision-making or skill from the operator. General Motors 50 years ago did strength tests for prospective factory workers. Physical labour was a commodity sold by workers and organized by their unions to increase its value. Time at work was pretty much time taken away from your life – and working people sought their personal fulfilment through leisure.

No longer. Today, the only meaningful assets are knowledge assets and the only meaningful form of capital is intellectual capital. This is why former Citigroup chief executive Walter Wriston once noted that 'Information about money has become almost as important as money itself'. The revolution in information and communications technologies is at the heart of these changes. The internet and other technologies enable thinking and the communication, management and sharing of knowledge like never before. And workers derive a great deal of their sense of self-worth from the work that they do and the intellectual contributions they make.

This book amply documents that today's organizations need to be able to learn and teach if they wish to be competitive. In the authors' words, 'the key factor in determining the success of any organization is its ability to use human talent – to discover it, develop it, deploy it, motivate and energize it. Human talent – the combined capacity and will of people to achieve an organization's goals – is a productive resource like no other.' A company remains competitive only if it acquires, develops and uses knowledge faster than the competition. Any firm can have the same technology as another company; any product can be copied. Competitive advantage is ephemeral as firms constantly seek new ways to create value. Marketplace success hinges on the knowledge and creative genius of the product strategists, developers, and marketers. Peter Senge was right to note many years ago that organizational learning becomes a critical competitive advantage.

Coupled with this corporate transformation is the arrival of a generation of workers with a completely new approach to the workplace. Today's youth are the first generation to come of age in the digital age. Computers and networks are transforming business, entertainment, government and every institution around them. Unlike their parents, they have no fear of the new technology because it is not technology to them. I call them the Net Generation. Their arrival is causing a Generation Lap – they are lapping their parents on the info track. For the first time ever children are an authority on a central innovation facing society.

This has profound implications for corporations. Although the Net Generation is savvy, confident, upbeat, open-minded, creative and independent, they are a challenge to manage. To meet their demands for more learning opportunities and responsibility ownership, instant feedback, greater work/life balance and stronger workplace relationships, companies must alter their culture and management approaches, while continuing to respect the needs of older employees. Properly cultivated, this generation's attributes will be a critical source of innovation and competitive advantage to the organization.

But while the demand for knowledge workers grows, the domestic supply is shrinking. Enrolment in science and technology faculties is declining in the US and other western countries. The upshot is that companies increasingly conclude that it makes more sense to locate new research facilities in countries where there is a larger supply of science and technology graduates. This usually means opening offices in China or India. Any job that is not confined to a particular location has the potential to be performed anywhere in the world. If the job activities do not require physical proximity, local knowledge, or complex interactions with colleagues, then location is immaterial. Such jobs may be performed wherever a company deems most attractive.

Furthermore, human capital is becoming networked as organizational boundaries become increasingly porous. In 1937 the Nobel laureate economist Ronald Coase asked why corporations exist. After all, the marketplace was theoretically the best mechanism for equalizing supply and demand, establishing prices and extracting maximum utility from finite resources. So why weren't all individuals acting as individual buyers and sellers, rather than gathering in companies with tens of thousands of other co-workers and effectively suffocating competition within the corporate boundaries? Coase argued that the answer was transaction costs, such as searching the marketplace for the right product and negotiating its purchase. The upshot is that most corporations concluded it was more cost-effective to perform as many functions as possible in-house.

That was then. Today is now. The new information and communications technologies centred on the internet are slashing transaction and collaboration costs. The result has been that vertically integrated corporations have been unbundling into focused companies that work within what I call business webs. The mantra 'focus on what you do best and partner to do the rest' is serving most leaders of the global economy well. In the past a company would outsource functions and ask for weekly or monthly status reports. Today the status reports are 24/7 as companies integrate their networks. Rather than offloading a process, companies now collaborate.

Take the most complicated product you can think of – a new generation jumbo jet. Rather than creating a specification for its supply chain, Boeing co-innovated the 787 Dreamliner with thousands of partners around the world in a new form of mass collaboration. Boeing views the companies who design and make non-trivial parts of the aircraft like the engine, fuselage, interiors, electronics and entertainment systems as peers, not suppliers. Rather than shipping massive specifications to an old style supply chain, Boeing built a global ecosystem that co-innovated the new aircraft with it.

The next step? Companies are beginning to tap into huge pools of talent outside their boundaries. Consumer goods giant Procter & Gamble is a performance example. Until recently, P&G was notoriously secretive, and about as closed as a company can get. It didn't look outside its walls for anything and it was failing, punctuated by a stock collapse in 2000. New CEO A G Lafley led the company on an ambitious campaign to restore P&G's greatness by sourcing 50% of its new innovations from outside the company. Today P&G searches for innovations in web-enabled marketplaces such as InnoCentive, NineSigma, and Yet2.com. These eBays for innovation have contributed to hundreds of new products on the market, some of which turned out to be hits. In the process Lafley and his managers transformed a lumbering consumer products company into a limber innovation machine. Five years after the stock implosion, P&G has doubled its share price and now boasts a portfolio of 22 one-billion-dollar brands.

Today, smart firms recognize that not all innovation will occur within the company. Much will begin at the fringes and beyond. Companies such as Yet2.com and InnoCentive enable people to participate in value creation without being part of a traditional firm. These services enable individuals to work with a wide array of firms by organizing them into highly liquid global markets for innovation and high-end human capital. Such 'ideagoras' are transforming the way many firms innovate and manage their intellectual capital. These firms turn to collaborative self-organizing business web models in order to accelerate innovation, increase growth, cut costs, and engage deeply with customers.

Firms are also embracing an array of new tools, such as wikis, social networks, blogs, and jams to harness the power of talent inside their boundaries. New models are slashing the collaboration costs – within companies and amongst companies – associated with meetings, telephones, travel and even email. The result that leading companies are building high-performance work systems based on 'wiki workplaces'. And evidence is mounting that peer collaboration among employees that cross organizational silos and hierarchies are beginning to change the nature of hierarchies, power and management itself.

In this new context, the traditional model of recruiting, managing and retaining employees is outdated. The over-riding factor today is engagement. Organizations must build a positive presence in the minds of employees and dynamically engage them throughout their employment years. Companies should encourage those who need a change of scenery and exciting new developmental opportunities to work for business partners, while continuing to maintain ties through alumni groups and other types of networks that can provide ongoing feedback and support for corporate initiatives.

Engagement is a two-way street and a merging of the well-defined needs of the employee and the company. 'What's in it for me?' and 'What's in it for you?' are questions that must be clearly addressed. Then it is up to both the employee and the organization to deliver on their commitments.

As you will see from this book, organizations must adopt new work styles, workflow models, time horizons for the workday, and career paths. New and old employees alike will show up to work with energy, enthusiasm and dedication if mentored and coached to contribute to business performance. *The Talent Powered Organization* is an exceptionally articulate and example-laden contribution to understanding the new corporation and the new employee.

Don Tapscott is chief executive of New Paradigm, a technology and business think tank, and the author of 11 books about information technology in business and society, including *Paradigm Shift*, *The Digital Economy*, and *Growing Up Digital*. His recent book *Wikinomics: How Mass Collaboration Changes Everything* is a *New York Times* bestseller.

Acknowledgements

Books like this don't come together by accident. We are very grateful for the support, encouragement, and input of a number of people. We have drawn on our own experience, but also shamelessly on the experience of others, and we would like to thank a number of colleagues for their support in pulling together the many references, case studies and points of view that we have drawn together.

Staff across the Human Performance practice of Accenture who have played a particular role in assimilating our knowledge and experience include Terry Corby, Darcy Lake, David Smith, Rodney Bergman, Peter Farrar, Jim Benton, Karen Wolf, Prithvi Shergill, Aimie Chapple and Fran Adenis, who helped on many occasions to organize critical logistics and meetings.

Staff of Accenture's Institute for High Performance Business played a valuable role in supporting the research and analysis at the core of this book. In particular, thanks are due to Chi Pham for her diligence in identifying talent management best practices in a wide variety of organizations (public and private), to Susan Cantrell for her creative thoughts and writings on the 'workforce of one', and to Amy Burkhardt and Karen O'Brien for their unflappable reaction to a never-ending series of tedious but critical assignments. We also thank Roland Burgman of AssetEconomics Inc. for his important work on the strategic value of intangible assets that has shaped our thinking on the subject.

A special thanks should go to Richard Heller and Rupert Morris from Clarity. Richard had the at times thankless task of making sense of many hours of ramblings and thoughts from us and turning it into readable draft scripts as our key supporting writer. Rupert did master-ful work as an editor as he worked valiantly to keep us in line and disciplined, working together with Kogan Page. Along with Rupert and Richard, our editors at Kogan Page, Charlotte Atyeo and Helen Savill, were instrumental in getting the book over the line and providing a lot of very pragmatic advice and structure for us.

Finally, we thank our families who endured competing with piles of books and drafts of manuscripts, and the inexorable draw of the PC during the months of drafting and editing. This book is dedicated to them.

Introduction from the authors

PETER CHEESE

As head of Accenture's Human Performance practice for the last several years, my job is to help organizations get the most from the human talent that is available to them – to source the talent, manage it effectively, develop and align it. I have a great passion for these issues, and I also work on these first hand within Accenture, a global business that is wholly dependent on its talent and aims to be the archetypal talent-powered organization.

We serve a range of clients which are immensely varied, in size, ownership, geography, and the nature of their business; and our work with them has pointed to some inescapable conclusions. These conclusions are supported by our own extensive research on the issues facing businesses today and the practices they follow.

First, the key factor in determining the success of any organization is its ability to use human talent – to discover it, develop it, deploy it, motivate and energize it. Human talent – the combined capacity and will of people to achieve an organization's goals – is a productive resource like no other, with a unique capacity to add value to an organization.

Second, for that very reason, talent issues need to be handled strategically. They are too important to be assigned only to specialist functions and regulated by specialist processes, however well designed in themselves. They need a holistic approach, in which every part of an organization, every individual within it, is connected and animated by the need to foster talent.

Third, the conditions faced by every organization in the search for talent are changing with astonishing rapidity in every part of the world. Familiar talent pools are shrinking, new ones are emerging; new technologies are transforming the nature of work, the skills demanded at work and the ways in which people can work; new elements are arriving in the global talent mix with new attitudes and ambitions. All these trends are making talent an ever more critical and complex issue for every organization.

Fourth, although the modern world tells us repeatedly how vital it is to use talent well, there is precious little guidance on how to do this – particularly on how to do it in an integrated way across the wide range of possible interventions or investments, and how to look at talent more strategically.

This book is a first attempt to achieve this, drawing on our collective experience of talent issues with clients and our own firm. It sets out a common journey for any organization to achieve high performance through the use of talent. The book is itself a truly talent-powered enterprise, drawing not only on my hands-on experience, but also on the research and academic work of my co-authors Bob Thomas and Elizabeth Craig, from the Accenture Institute for High Performance Business. Our thinking comes from many different disciplines, not only management science, but also finance and economics, human development, sociology, psychology, international business studies, marketing and supply-chain management. We see it as imperative to widen the thinking that is being applied to the issues of talent, given its complex nature and the need to raise collective understanding of the subject.

I have travelled all over the world meeting clients and our teams working alongside them, and it is remarkable how these issues and concerns around talent now resonate. Globalization is having a huge impact everywhere, but the globalization of work and talent has become the defining theme of this new era. There are so many examples of this in all industries and sizes of organization. I was reminded on a recent trip to India that Accenture's workforce in that country is now the largest single geographic workforce in the firm. This is almost incredible when one reflects that it has reached this position in a mere seven years.

Things are moving so fast in India that the country's leading manufacturing and engineering companies are struggling to recruit the people they need. How can this be the case in a country with a simultaneously booming economy and ever-growing population – and where engineering and manufacturing industry has traditionally been the mainstay of the economy?

When you understand the overall environment there, the explanation makes perfect sense. For of course the boom in IT services and the rocketing demand for associated talent has not been especially good news for India's traditional industries, which have suddenly become desperately unfashionable. Why would India's brightest young graduates want to go into industry when they can rise rapidly in the future-oriented world of IT and telecoms?

So this is the first 'whammy' to have hit traditional Indian industry. Then there is the fact that these traditional industries have never paid much attention to talent management in the past – leaving them sorely ill-equipped to cope with a sudden shortage of the kind of skilled marketers and managers they so desperately needed. What made it a triple 'whammy' was that the best HR people who might have been able to help them sort things out had all been snapped up by the booming IT and telecoms sector.

I may have put the difficulties of India's traditional industries in somewhat stark terms as an example of the complexities of talent markets around the world, but business in the early years of the 21st century is moving faster than ever before, and there is no doubt that these talent challenges can undermine whole economic sectors in a very short time, if leaders and organizations fail to adapt to the new realities. The global competition for talent between organizations and even between countries now has major economic and political implications. It concerns governments and lobby groups; it is redefining organizations; it is changing the way we live.

There has been no shortage of analysis of the organizational issues associated with talent, particularly from the HR perspective. But I do not believe that there has yet been a book that takes the necessary strategic and holistic view of the talent issue, then applies it to organizations root and branch, providing the necessary conceptual frameworks and practical examples of how to apply them. That is what we have tried to do in this book, and if it helps your organization to compete successfully in this new economic world, it will have achieved its mission.

I should add that we have been conscious of the danger of putting too much of Accenture in this book. Various mentions are inevitable given that we are in part drawing on our own research and experience, as well as our practical observations in the course of our work for the firm. We have made a scrupulous effort to eliminate any references that are not justified by their context. However, the fact is that few organizations are as definitively talent-powered as Accenture, and if we consequently make reference to this 'insider' experience, then we make no apology for that.

BOB THOMAS

My role as head of Accenture's 'think and act tank', the Institute for High Performance Business, gives me an exciting challenge: to search the horizon for developments in business practice, technology and geopolitics that are a year to three years away, and to position Accenture and its clients so they can ride the waves of change. The research and thinking that went into this book represents one of three thrusts that have occupied the Institute for the past several years. A word about each is in order since they all contribute to the point of view embedded in the book.

First, the overall High Performance Business (HPB) initiative in which Accenture has been involved for the past five years has enabled us to examine closely the winning mindsets and practices of companies that have proven capable of out-competing their peers across business cycles, technological disruptions, and changes in leadership. In total, we have studied 500 high performers globally. The HPB research has given us a unique opportunity to isolate common features (what we refer to as an organization's 'performance anatomy') across organizations from very different industries, technologies and cultures.

Second, Accenture and Institute researchers have concentrated significant energy over the past several years on the challenge of measuring the role of human capital development in the creation of shareholder value. As we point out at the very beginning of this book, the overwhelming majority of organizational leaders and managers are quick to argue that people are their greatest asset. But standard accounting conventions and executive compensation practices routinely treat training, management education and non-technical workplace innovation as an expense: something easily cut when earnings or share-price ratios are being squeezed. To counter this tendency, while retaining organizational responsiveness to market fluctuations, we developed an approach to measuring returns on investments in intangible assets – human capital, brand and reputation, capacity to innovate being principal among them – that more clearly demonstrate how they can support business strategy. This approach, called the Human Capital Development Framework, is described in some detail in Chapter 6. Implemented in over 70 organizations worldwide, the Human Capital Development Framework provides a much-needed guide to investing in people that is driven by business objectives, not by loose rules of thumb whose only justification is organizational inertia.

Third, Institute research over the past decade has spotlighted the role of top leadership teams in creating a talent mindset – or what we call in this book a 'talent multiplier'. Starting with a study of global leadership requirements for the 21st century in the mid-1990s, then the publication of *Geeks and Geezers* (with Warren Bennis), which chronicled the changing as well as enduring qualities of effective leaders, and finally with *Crucibles for Leaders* (to be published later in 2007), which introduces an experience-based approach to leader development, we have both argued and demonstrated empirically that talent management has to be one of the top two or three agenda items for senior executives.

I am immensely grateful to senior executives like Peter Cheese, Tim Breene and Bill Green for giving me and my colleagues in the Accenture Institute for High Performance Business the opportunity to study such complex problems, work with clients to understand their practical implications, and partner with senior executives and managers to formulate truly creative solutions.

ELIZABETH CRAIG

The notion of multiplying human talent to create talent-powered organizations is as exciting as it is timely. This belief is grounded in my experience researching a wide range of talent management issues. While completing my doctoral studies at The Wharton School, I examined topics ranging from executive retention to employee alignment to young workers' career expectations. In my time as a member of the Boston University School of Management faculty, I also investigated the changing role of HR in organizations and trends in career development practices. And now, at the Accenture Institute for High Performance Business, I am writing about the evolution of talent management as well as the promise and challenges of employee engagement. Having spent more than a decade studying talent management, it has become quite evident that no issue is more urgent and complex for every business – indeed, for every organization that relies on talent to achieve high performance.

We are witnessing a revolution in talent management philosophies and practices as human capital becomes an ever more valuable source of competitive advantage. Organizations large and small are grappling with enormous strategic and practical challenges as markets and competition become increasingly global and new technologies change not only how, but also when and where, work is done. New and varied types of work, modes of working and employment arrangements are emerging, accompanied by an increasingly demographically diverse and global workforce. In responding to these important challenges, many organizations are developing more strategic approaches to talent management.

The challenge for today's leaders and managers is to build engaged, productive and committed workforces for their organizations. Indeed, engaging talent in creating value for the firm is now a critical organizational capability. This is an enormous and important task for every organization, especially those in businesses and sectors where employees' valuable knowledge and skills are the primary source of competitive advantage.

In my role as a research fellow with the Accenture Institute for High Performance Business, I have the opportunity to research and report on how high-performing businesses leverage their employees' strengths, capabilities and career aspirations as a source of competitive advantage. One lesson is quite clear. The most successful organizations have a deep understanding of the strategic value of their talent. These talent-powered organizations build and nurture distinctive capabilities in multiplying talent which unleash the energy, creativity and collective contributions of their workforces. This book is an effort to explore and explain how these organizations generate talent power. It has been exciting to be involved in developing these important ideas. I join Peter and Bob in hoping that the research, theory and practical experience distilled into this book will help you to create a truly talent-powered organization.

1

Talent Imperatives for a New Economic World

When the winds of change blow, some people build walls and others build windmills.

Chinese proverb

The world is changing at a bewildering pace. Everywhere new markets are opening up, new workforces are emerging, and new ways of working are challenging our thinking. We are in a new stage of globalization where talent and brainpower are becoming the predominant currency.

The traditional management paradigms which focused on productivity and efficiency were designed for the 20th-century economy. Enabled by technology and process engineering, they derived from the need to obtain high productivity from a workforce whose costs were rising. This narrow focus made sense for the world's developed economies at a time when more than half the world was effectively excluded from the global marketplace. In the past two decades, politics and technology have changed the world beyond recognition: with a total world population of 6.4 billion, fewer than 100 million people are excluded from the new global economy.

The first phases of globalization in this new era focused on the movement of production from the developed world to the developing world as a means to reduce costs – working cheaper. Now we are emerging into an era which is about working everywhere – a truly multi-polar world – going where the talent is, where the resources are, and where the markets are, connecting up people and processes globally and breaking down traditional barriers.

The famous 'war for talent' has gone global, or as Jonas Ridderstrale and Kjell Nordstrom observed in their book *Funky Business* (2002), 'The war for talent is over and talent won.' We want to explore what this means, especially for how we think about talent and workforces and manage them, and what new disciplines and capabilities we shall need to do this a lot more effectively – as we must.

In this first chapter we shall consider some of the remarkable changes in the global marketplace, people demographics and the ways in which we work. Understanding this context and its many apparent paradoxes is crucial for understanding what to do about it.

A NEW CONTEXT

The task of finding and managing talent has become more complex, turbulent and contradictory than ever before. Once-familiar talent pools are drying up as new ones are rapidly opening – rich and seething but often full of cross-currents and hidden rocks. This is creating great challenges for managers and leaders of organizations large and small.

Talent managers today must cope with a world of change and contrast:

- global abundance but local scarcity of talent;
- fewer young people and more older people, many heading rapidly towards retirement;
- rising demand for new skills aggravated by demographic pressures and educational shortcomings;
- new methods of working and new relationships between users and suppliers of talent;
- more diverse and remote or even virtual workforces, with different attitudes to work across the generations;
- steady change in the nature of work, with more and more of us working in the fuzzy world of information.

Overlaying all of these trends is the challenge of engagement. Finding talent is not enough if it is not aligned and motivated, yet the evidence suggests that many of our workforces are less and less engaged. Attitudinal differences to work across the generations make it harder to understand how to deal with this. But without that understanding, business growth is unsustainable.

All these trends have propelled talent issues to the top of the corporate agenda. They have brought with them a mix of new opportunities and challenges which must be met with new thinking. When all taken together, they represent an extraordinary level of change – almost the 'perfect storm'. We are reminded of a remark by Harold Macmillan, British prime minister in the late 1950s. When asked about the hardest thing about his job, he replied, 'Events, dear boy, events.'

THE CURRENT CHALLENGE

Although many organizations have begun to recognize the important role talent plays in their success, few are managing talent strategically. Leaders need to identify and invest in the critical talent that provides a platform for success, growth and new opportunities, but they must do so in a world of constraints – on time, money and especially talent. The increasing fluidity of global labour markets, shifting workforce demographics, and changes in the nature of work itself make it more difficult to attract, engage and retain the critical talent that creates value for organizations.

Moreover, companies are confronting the realities of competing in a multi-polar world in which organizations from both the developed and the developing world seek to take advantage of new markets, new opportunities and new sources of growth. Talent has become a precious resource fought over by competitors in a global war for talent.

But firms cannot effectively compete or create lasting competitive advantage by just focusing on winning a war for talent. Simply securing the best talent will no longer ensure competitive success. The secret to sustained competitive success in the new economic world is to build a talent-powered organization that sustains and builds all the skills needed to compete.

THE TALENT-POWERED ORGANIZATION

What is a talent-powered organization? It is an organization that invests in building distinctive capabilities in managing talent to produce extraordinary results for the organization. Talent-powered organizations are adept at defining talent needs, discovering diverse sources of talent, developing the organization's individual and collective talents, and deploying talent in ways that engage and align people around a compelling set of objectives. When these talent management capabilities are highly integrated, aligned with the organization's business strategy and embedded in its operations, they constitute a distinctive organizational capability and a source of lasting competitive advantage.

Talent-powered organizations nurture this distinctive capability in talent management alongside the other distinctive capabilities that underpin the organization's formula for success, allowing talent power to propel the organization to high performance. For example, the very successful US-based consumer electronics retailer Best Buy began transforming itself into a talent-powered organization when it moved to a customer-centric business strategy five years ago. CEO Bradbury Anderson's intent was to transform Best Buy 'into a talent-powered, customer-driven enterprise' focused on enhancing customers' enjoyment of technology. 'As a retailer, the secret today isn't how you invest capital,' says Anderson. 'It's how you invest in your employees, so that they can deliver superior service to customers.'

The shift in Best Buy's formula for competitive success, from efficient operations and low-cost products to outstanding customer service and innovation, demanded that it build capabilities in defining, discovering, developing and deploying employees' talents to create extraordinary value for the company. The customer centricity strategy 'invites employees to contribute their unique ideas and experiences in service of customers'. Best Buy recognized that, even as it committed to nurturing and developing its distinctive capabilities in outstanding customer service and innovation, it also needed to build distinctive capabilities in managing talent to 'unleash' employees' talents and propel the company to high performance.

Other organizations such as Starbucks, Google, Marriott, Microsoft, Tata Engineering, CEMEX, UPS and Accenture have also figured out how to build and leverage talent power to achieve extraordinary success. In this book, we explain how every organization can build the talent power necessary for success in the new economic world.

We will examine five talent imperatives – which have emerged as critical to sustained business success for all types of organizations today and for the future:

- **Talent is a strategic issue, and a human capital strategy is an intrinsic part of any business strategy.** This means understanding the value of talent, and recognizing the critical components of business strategy that require us to think through the talent and organizational implications and options.
- **Diversity is your organization's biggest asset.** Your ability to attract and work with diverse talent is a critical competitive advantage.
- **Learning and skills development is one of the most important capability for the talent-powered organization.** Development needs to be focused and built around a clear understanding of the specific skills and competencies your organization needs to succeed.
- **Engagement is the mystery ingredient that can transform business performance.** Aligning and motivating people will enable you to multiply talent in your organization and improve its performance.
- **Nurturing and developing talent is everyone's concern in your organization.** The HR function is a key enabler, but best practices and a talent mindset and culture must be embedded and sustained throughout your business.

We will begin by reviewing the range of issues which have given rise to these imperatives, and in the ensuing five chapters we will deal with approaches, processes, and innovations that are helping truly talent-powered organizations to address these imperatives.

THE STRATEGIC IMPORTANCE OF TALENT

Converging economic, societal and technological forces have all elevated the importance of talent for 21st century organizations. Talent-powered organizations anticipate and take advantage of the rapidly changing talent landscape, shaped by sustained worldwide growth, the rise of new economic sectors, and the increasing role of human capital in creating value for organizations. In an increasingly talent-dependent world, talent-powered organizations understand the strategic importance of talent, and view talent management as a critical organizational capability.

THE NEW PARADIGM OF GROWTH

We are living in times of sustained worldwide growth. GDP growth is expected to continue at average rates of 3.5 per cent for the foreseeable future, with virtually every country in a growth cycle, although the rates of growth are unevenly distributed, as shown in Figure 1.1. The fastest-growing economies in 2006, India and China, both far exceeded the average with GDP growth rates of 8 per cent and 10 per cent respectively. The Indian minister of finance, P Chidambaram, was recently quoted in the *Economic Times of India* as saying that India had to sustain growth rates in this range for the next 10 years to remain competitive, in particular with China. The growth rates in Figure 1.1 are across the whole economy, and in reality new sectors such as IT services and communications are growing at a much faster rate.

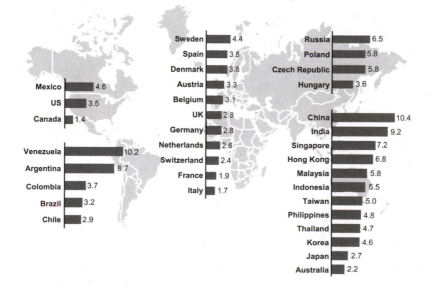

Figure 1.1 World GDP growth rates, fourth quarter 2006
Source: adapted from Garelli (2006).

The pace of growth at the moment seems relentless. Within the next 20 years, by most projections, India and China will be the largest economies in the world, followed by the United States and the European Union. A whole new 'middle class' is emerging today, based on over 600 million people with spending power estimated at US$4 trillion. The only constant now is change – adapting to new market opportunities, new competitive pressures, and new operating models for workforces and businesses. Organizations must respond, and they must have the right resources and capabilities.

The idea of talent as the force that powers companies is taking centre stage. Without the people, you cannot succeed, and people are emerging as the prime source of value, sustainability and, in most companies, of cost. Yet business understanding of how people add value, how to invest in their development for best effect, and even how they work and what motivates them, remains surprisingly limited.

ECONOMIC REVOLUTION: THE CHANGING NATURE OF WORK AND VALUE

Over the last 20 years, along with the opening of new markets, the economy of the developed world has undergone a revolution in the type and nature of work, and where and how value is added. The prime engine – still at full throttle – is the growth of services. It has propelled fundamental changes in methods of work, the nature of production and value creation.

Modern organizations own and employ fewer of the basic inputs of production – land, materials, capital and support services – than they did 20 years ago, and they generally produce a much smaller proportion of their output directly, in their own facilities. The twin forces of globalization and new technology have produced a decisive shift away from centralized production with repetitive methods to a more devolved system, in which production is shared between many different units and partners, often scattered round the world, and often independent of the producer of the final output.

As a result of this transformation there has been a massive shift in the sources of value in modern businesses. Twenty-five years ago, 80 per cent of a typical company's market value was based on its tangible assets, such as machinery and facilities, and how effectively it was generating returns from these. Only a small part of its value was attributed to intangible assets, which were largely residual and unrecognized. But today those proportions have been reversed. On average across all industries, only around 20 to 30 per cent of value is attributable to tangible assets. By far the greatest part of a typical company's value now comes from intangibles – such as its unique knowledge of production, service and delivery methods, its knowledge of markets, its relationships with customers and suppliers, its brand value and reputation, and of course its workforce capabilities. Almost all of these intangible assets are driven, in one way or another, by human talent.

Figure 1.2 illustrates the changing nature of value among major US companies. It shows the decreasing relevance of accounting-book value among S&P 500 companies between 1980 and 2002. It shows the market-to-book ratio: how much of a company's market value can be accounted for by the traditional accounting assets on the balance sheet. It has been argued that intangible assets, especially intellectual capital, can explain much of the premium between market value and book value. Whether this is a total or partial explanation, there is no question that companies have become more and more reliant on intangibles and intellectual capital at the same time as market value has come to dwarf book

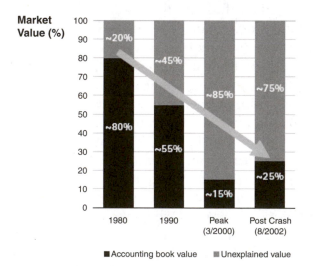

Figure 1.2   New sources of value
Source: Ballow *et al* (2004).

value. This suggests that managing intangibles may be the key to increasing market value.

The shift to intangible sources of value reflects a fundamental change in the nature of competitive advantage. For any enterprise, even in traditional manufacturing, competition has shifted from owning fixed assets such as land, buildings and machinery, to knowing how to produce goods and services in the most efficient way and bring them to market more successfully than do competitors. In this new economic world, it is less valuable to own a piece of land than to know when to sell it and relocate activity somewhere else. It is less valuable to own a factory than to know how to produce something in the most efficient way possible, less valuable to own a piece of technology than to know how to use it – or to think of a better means of production which may make that technology valueless. All of these forms of essential competitive knowledge – and many more – derive from human beings.

Recognition and measurement of these types and sources of value are very inconsistent and incomplete. There are no commonly agreed standards, and we persist in focusing measurement of enterprise value on predominantly tangible assets and backward-looking accounting measures. Attempts to improve this situation have not taken off, particularly attempts to get agreement on how to value human capital, such as the UK government-sponsored Accounting for People initiative some years ago. We shall return to this important theme in later chapters and offer frameworks and measures that shed more light on these 'unexplained' types of value.

But first we look at the issues that have brought about much of this change in underlying values, and raised the importance of understanding and managing talent to new levels. Added together they look like they are creating the perfect storm in this new economic world.

THE NEED TO EMBRACE DIVERSITY

Global demographic shifts and dynamic labour markets have made identifying and accessing talent vastly more complex for every organization. Talent-powered organizations build capabilities defining critical workforce skills and anticipating talent needs, discovering new sources of talent in diverse and dispersed talent pools, and managing a global, ethnically diverse, multigenerational workforce. In an increasingly diverse world, talent-powered organizations use demographic and geographic diversity for competitive advantage.

SHIFTING POPULATIONS AND AGEING WORKFORCES

The world's population continues to grow, although at a rate that has been slowing since the 1970s, and is now at 1.2 per cent a year, according to the US Census Bureau. Fertility rates have dropped by half since 1972, from 6 to 2.9 children per woman, which is an extraordinary decline. There is now significant variation in rates of population growth, and a general trend of populations starting to shrink in the developed world. The rate of population growth in developed countries is now five times lower than in less developed countries. The causes are not surprising: better education, availability of contraception, higher survival rates for infants and children, and pursuit of improved living standards have all contributed to the reduction in births.

A fertility rate of 2.1 children per woman is needed to maintain population numbers, yet Europe's fertility rates have been dropping below this for years – France and Ireland being the highest at 1.8, Italy and Spain the lowest with 1.2 (UN, 2002). Germany at 1.4 is at the average for the whole of Europe. At this rate, Germany will lose a fifth of its 82.5 million people over the next 40 years – a loss of population unknown in Europe since the devastating Thirty Years War in the early 17th century. Elsewhere across the continent is a similar story – Estonia will shrink by 25 per cent, Romania by 27 per cent, Bulgaria by 38 per cent. Russia is losing 750,000 a year, enough for President Putin to call it a 'national crisis'.

In other more developed countries of the world, the same thing is happening. Japan, having had a low fertility rate for many years and today averaging 1.3, has become the first industrialized nation to move into population decline. In 2006 the official statistics showed that it had a net reduction of almost 20,000 people, and from this point the reduction will start to increase. The average age there is now 42.3 years, up from 30.4 years in 1975. Populations continue to grow in many parts of the world, mostly in regions such as Africa and the poorer parts of India, but also in areas like the Middle East, where the United Nations expects the population to double by 2050 to 650 million people. China stands out among emerging economies, as its birth rate has declined from 5.8 in 1970 to 1.8 today owing to its stringent birth-control policies. In the longer term this will cause problems with an ageing population.

Never in the last 650 years, since the time of the Black Plague, have birth and fertility rates fallen so far, so fast, in so many places, according to Ben Wattenberg in his book *Fewer* (2004). Figure 1.3 shows the range of decline in many countries in the youth population expected over the next 10 years.

Other significant demographic changes are taking place at the same time. People are moving to the cities to take advantage of the new economic opportunities and jobs. By 2007 more than half the world's population will live in cities: in China there are now more than 160 cities with populations in excess of 1 million.

Immigration patterns continue to shift as movement across borders becomes easier. This may well offset population decline in some countries but can exacerbate population decline in others, particularly amongst the young, which is a challenge currently for many Eastern European countries. However, political and social barriers in many countries continue to make it difficult to close the demographic gaps through managed immigration. By contrast, the United States is expected to continue to grow through immigration by 100 million in

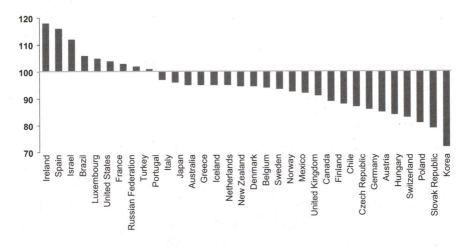

Figure 1.3 Expected changes in the size of youth population aged 5–14 between 2005 and 2015 (2005 = 100)
Source: OECD (2006), Chart A11.1, p 160.

the next 45 years, while Europe will lose roughly the same amount (according to Ben Wattenberg). So on current trends the United States will be the only modern nation that will grow.

At the other end of the population age scale, the postwar baby-boomer generation in most Western countries and Japan is approaching retirement and is expected to live longer than any previous generation thanks to improved healthcare, diet, and general improvement in economic conditions. Hence the much-quoted ageing workforce phenomenon. Some of the statistics can make for startling reading:

- The United Nations estimates that by 2050, one in five of the world's population will be aged 60 or older, compared with 1 in 10 now.
- According to the United Nations, China will have a median age of 44 by 2015 (compared with a median age of 30 in 2000), and can expect to have 349 million people aged 65 or over in 2050 – more than the entire current US population.
- Within the US federal government, 30 per cent of the entire workforce will be eligible to retire in five years, and in some US states this figure rises to half.
- The European Union's working-age population (aged 15–64) is set to fall from 307 million in 2004 to 255 million by 2050 – from 67 per cent of the total EU population in 2004 to 57 per cent by 2050 (European Commission, 2005).
- By 2009 the size of the youngest cohort of the EU working-age population (aged 15–24) will drop below the size of the oldest cohort for the first time (European Commission, 2005).
- If current migration and employment patterns continue we could lose more than 12 million employees in Europe, or close to 8 per cent of the workforce, by 2030 (Ederer, 2006).

Figure 1.4 shows graphically that the fastest-growing segment of the US workforce is older workers, especially those aged 55 and older.

Aside from the impact on workforce size and availability, the economic burden of these changes is becoming apparent. China will have major problems because of the lack of a social safety net for its ageing population. The Center for Strategic and International Studies (CSIS) estimates that less than a quarter of the population has pension cover, which will put a big burden on the current generation of only

The graying of the factory floor

US workforce by age group, % change 2000–100

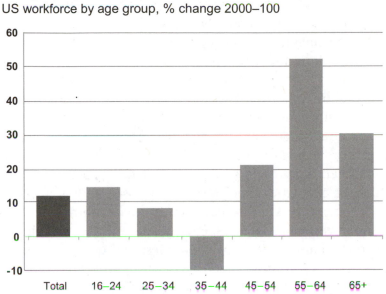

Figure 1.4 Changing age profiles in the United States
Source: Bureau of Labor (2004).

children – the so-called 4–2–1 problem, with four grandparents, two parents and one child supporting them. The United States will also have significant challenges in affording the costs of the ageing generation – costs of Medicare and Social Security will rise from 4.3 per cent of GDP in 2000 to 11.5 per cent in 2030 and 21 per cent in 2050, according to the Congressional Budget Office.

The situation is perhaps most critical of all in Russia, where the population has been shrinking at about 700,000 a year, prompting the United Nations to warn that without drastic action it could fall from 149 million today to less than 100 million by 2050. Worse still, the ageing of the population means that on current trends there will be four dependants for every Russian worker by 2025. No wonder President Putin has doubled child-support payments, improved maternity benefits, and introduced cash incentives for women to have second children.

Japan is already innovating to address the problem. As *The Economist* recently reported, the Japanese are taking production automation to the limit with so called 'dark factories' which have no human labour at all. Further automation is being introduced in areas such as healthcare, where the shortage of manual labour is already acute. We can expect technology to enable more and more creative responses to demographic developments.

Looking at all these demographic trends collectively, we can see the shift in the key working age groups across the world in the next 20 years in Figure 1.5. The US is projected to have a shortage of 17 million skilled workers while India will have a surplus of 47 million.

Within certain industries, the ageing workforce issue is becoming acute as they have more of a tradition of long-serving employees and have not been bringing in younger talent to compensate. These are typically the industries that young people see as less attractive or 'cool'. The trends are mostly common across countries. Particularly prone are government agencies, energy and utility companies, heavy engineering, non 'eco-friendly' industries, and even, in some countries, industries like insurance. The ageing workforce problem in government in the United States is now well documented, and has prompted state and federal governments to introduce a range of programmes, albeit with varying degrees of urgency. Figure 1.6 illustrates the problem dramatically.

Surplus or shortfall is calculated keeping the ratio of working population (age group 15-59) to total population constant.

Figure 1.5 World demographic trends and labour supplies (projected shortage/surplus in millions)
Source: US Census Bureau, IBM.

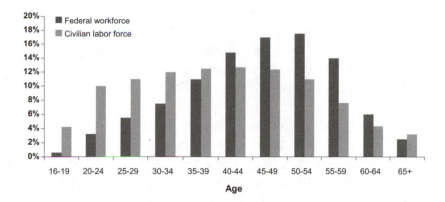

Figure 1.6 Ageing US workforces
Sources: Conference Board; US Bureau of Labor Statistics (2005).

Even at the National Aeronautics and Space Administration (NASA), surely a bastion of youthful talent, a survey by the newspaper *Florida Today* in 2004 found that nearly 40 per cent of its people were 50 or older. NASA employees over 60 outnumbered those under 30 by almost three to one.

This prompts an obvious question: how we can attract new workers and retain them for longer in the workforce in the countries and industries most affected? We shall explore this question further in later chapters, but to give a sense of the magnitude of the issue: in Germany by 2030 the average retirement age would need to move up to 66 from 60 today to neutralize the effect of this demographic change. The good news is that this generation of baby-boomers looks set to reinvent retirement, just as they reinvented many social phenomena now commonplace around the world.

GLOBAL ABUNDANCE, LOCAL SCARCITY

As the working population in the developed world shrinks in size and grows older, globalization has given us huge pools of new talent else-where, and organizations around the world are trying to tap into them wherever possible. In 1980 the workforce available to the free-market economies of the world was approximately 960 million, but by the year 2000 that figure had risen to about 2.9 billion with the political changes and opening up of countries formerly closed (Freeman, 2005). Of this increase, about 0.5 billion came from increased population, principally in poorer countries. The opening up of China, Russia and Eastern Europe in the last 20 years, and the strong emergence of India, have dramatically increased the available talent pool. The entry of these countries has added millions of new workers to the global labour force. They are not only cheaper than their counterparts in advanced economies, but in some areas they are equals or superiors in education, skills, productivity, mobility and ambitions. It is no surprise that organizations in advanced economies have been eager to hire them.

New technologies and methods of working have made this global talent more accessible, and opened up opportunities to make use of previously excluded or marginal sources of local labour. There are many millions eager to embrace new skills and new opportunities, and gain access to the products and services the developed world has enjoyed.

But there is a paradox here, for despite the huge numbers theoretically available as part of a globalized workforce, there are critical shortages of skills in organized labour almost everywhere. The huge working populations of India and China account for more than 1 billion people, dwarfing any other countries, but less than 10 per cent of these workforces have the education and background for organized work: the great majority still work in unorganized tasks, or in agriculture, or live in poverty.

To complicate the paradox in the supply of labour, there is intense demand for new skills, created by the accelerating pace of change in products, technologies and markets. New skills are needed in modern economies just when there are fewer new people to learn them. The growing attractions of the talent markets and consumer markets of India and China and many other emerging economies have led multinational companies to descend on them and stoke up local battles for talent.

In India, the IT services sector in particular is growing at an incredible rate. Local Indian IT services companies have grown from almost nothing in six or seven years to tens of thousands of employees. They include firms like Infosys, Satyam and Tata Consulting Services, which now employs 85,000 people in India. Accenture is one of the global multinationals competing for the same talent, and its workforce in India has grown from a few hundred to over 25,000 in the space of six years. In 2007 India will overtake the United States to become the largest single geographic workforce in its firm of 160,000 employees. IBM has announced that it expects to have more than 100,000 employees in India within the next two years.

All of this has prompted the National Association of Software and Services Companies in India (NASSCOM) to predict that the IT sector will face a shortfall of 500,000 professionals by 2010. Shortages are also projected among call centre workers in India. The government in India says that the demand for offshore call-centre workers there may outstrip the supply by some 260,000 workers by 2009. The call-centre industry has already absorbed many of the most highly skilled operatives, causing recruiters to settle for workers with less than ideal credentials (Gartner, 2005). The same concern is being expressed in the IT services and technology sectors.

China too is suffering from acute shortages of key talent, especially management and leadership talent, and these are becoming a major constraint on its rate of growth. Two-thirds of companies in China in a 2006 *Economist* survey reported difficulty in filling senior posts, and several leading companies had to hire American CEOs. Attrition rates at manager level are reported to be 25 per cent higher than the global average (SHRM, 2005), and it is reported that as many as 75,000 managers who can work in global environments will be needed over the next 10 to 15 years – today there may be as few as 5,000 (McKinsey, 2005). A recent report from executive search firm Heidrick & Struggles gives several reasons for the shortfall in qualified executives in China: the education and work opportunities of many of those now aged 50–60 were disrupted by the Cultural Revolution, the local talent pool was depleted by the 'brain drain' of the 1980s and 1990s, there are few strong business schools in China, and local Chinese executives often lack global know-how.

Many Chinese and multinational companies have also sought to address the issues through bringing Chinese talent from overseas back to China – the phenomenon of the *hai gui*, or 'sea turtle', the Chinese term for those who left China to study and work overseas but are now 'swimming home' to take high-level positions at multinational companies. These returnees are sought after by large companies not only for their fluency in Mandarin or Cantonese, but also for their understanding of China's complex history, political system, and cultural and social traditions, which can mean the difference between success and failure in one of the most important markets of the future. This group is in a privileged position.

Nor should we forget Central Europe. It has been more than 15 years since the collapse of the Iron Curtain opened up Central Europe, and its 10 countries have survived some painful transitions. Most of the region's economies have managed to thrive, as shown by the continued accessions to the European Union. Today, Central Europe is a major source of talent and capability in support of the rest of Europe. These countries have the obvious advantages of proximity to the rest of Europe as well as a wider range of European language skills.

Surprisingly, the region is drawing in foreign investment at a rate of US$37 billion annually, which places it second to China in the international competition for capital, and ahead of India (*Business Week,* 2005). Most of the region's countries have tax rates as low as 15 per cent for corporations, which is also a strong incentive. Multinationals from Hewlett-Packard to SAP, from GE to IBM, have been moving in. Accenture is also opening centres across the region to support global clients with IT skills, call-centre and back-office operations from Riga to Bucharest, and is being forced to look continually at new locations as popular centres like Prague show increasing signs of overheating.

Few anticipated that the once-bankrupt economies of Central Europe would move up the industrial food chain so quickly, and attract research jobs in knowledge-driven industries ranging from telecoms to autos to pharmaceuticals. Now, thanks to their growing ranks of high-skilled workers, these countries are growing fast as havens of outsourcing for engineering and software development, just behind China and India (*Business Week,* 2005).

In the Czech Republic, investments in such sectors as software and customer-service centres rose 150 per cent in 2004. According to IBM, Hungary, Poland and the Czech Republic ranked among the top 10 global destinations for research and development jobs in the first half of 2005. In Europe, only Britain attracted more R&D work. Some 67 per cent of the Polish economy already consists of services, according to the OECD. There is a strong entrepreneurial culture and spirit, demonstrated by people's appetite for work – Poles work an average of 1,984 hours a year, well above the 1,777 hours clocked by

US workers and far more than the 1,362 hours Germans work, according to OECD figures.

THE KNOCK-ON EFFECT

The demand for talent in new economies has had important consequences. In both India and China, local and multinational companies face significant challenges of retention, wage inflation, and battles for new graduates which are as fierce as anywhere in the world. Despite graduating 2.5 million college students with strong English skills annually, the campuses of the top business and technology schools when the potential employers roll into town have to be seen to be believed, with students being given multiple lucrative offers of employment on the spot. Turnover is high, and people in Chinese and Indian companies where talent shortages are greatest are quite prepared to leave a company to bump up their salaries. At PepsiCo's 400-strong sales team in Guangzhou, turnover was about 50 per cent in 2000. After setting up better systems for staff feedback, the company halved attrition over three years, but that still left turnover at close to 25 per cent.

Employers have responded by raising salaries, with some sectors experiencing annual wage inflation over 20 per cent. As a result, the lucky few can command high salaries. Pay packages for top-level managers in China are comparable to those of their counterparts in the United States, easily running into hundreds of thousands of dollars. Meanwhile, leading Indian companies are increasingly inclined to bring in Western CEOs, and good middle managers are so rare that wage increases for project managers have averaged 23 per cent for the past four years. Wages for software/IT middle managers in India were 5 per cent of US wage levels in 1998, but by 2003 had reached 15 per cent and rising.

In Eastern Europe, wage rate variations are indicative of where talent shortfall is the greatest. Manual workers' wage rates are around 20–30 per cent of those in Germany, but salaried workers' pay in the more competitive sectors is only around 30 per cent below the rest of Europe, and still three to four times higher than in India at the moment.

If these rates of wage inflation were to be maintained, it would negate most of the labour cost advantage from these countries within five to seven years. But this is a facet of the global talent marketplace, where wages for certain categories of talent will become more comparable as real and virtual mobility increase. Consequently, many organizations are now seeking to improve their people management, to increase their attractiveness as employers along with their ability to retain the talent they recruit. The IT services sector in India has been developing some of the best people and talent management practices in the world – because it has to.

The frenzy for talent in IT services and the communications and hi-tech industries is having a knock-on effect in all industries. For companies in less appealing industry sectors, and those that cannot pay at the same rates, attracting and keeping talent is becoming increasingly difficult. Many companies in the engineering and manufacturing sectors are finding it difficult to recruit and retain people, despite being the bedrock of economic growth in all of these countries for the past several decades. We are seeing more and more of the hourglass shape in organizations, where people who join at the bottom are leaving within three to five years to pursue opportunities elsewhere, while the loyal older generations of company men and women stay on.

Cities like Bangalore have become overheated since the world beat a path to their doors during the later 1990s. Infrastructure is creaking and the cost of living has soared, while real-estate prices are rising at 10–15 per cent annually. So firms are already looking for cheaper places in India – cities like Cochin, Jaipur and Pune. According to NASSCOM, about 30 per cent of India's outsourcing revenues (US$12.5 billion in 2003) will move to smaller cities in the next few years. This is not just a question of money – officials at IT firms say the employees are more loyal in the smaller cities since competition is so fierce in the larger cities, resulting in a lower attrition rate of more like 5 per cent compared with as much as 30 per cent in Delhi and Bangalore. The shift is good for these smaller cities, where unemployment among young people can be as high as 30 per cent. Accenture operates services and support from six cities in India today, and that will doubtless increase.

The same phenomenon is happening in China, and in Central Europe where new cities and regions are opening centres supporting multinational companies almost every month. According to the Conference Board, productivity continues to grow in the private sector in China, with an incredible 17 per cent annual improvement between 1995 and 2002. Costs have continued to fall in the face of competition, and Chinese companies are moving to cheaper cities and locations. Other countries such as Brazil, Malaysia and Vietnam are also becoming wired in to this new world, and are attracting multinational companies in search of talent and resources.

As basic infrastructure and support are becoming stretched, companies are sometimes taking matters into their own hands. For example, the acute shortage of hotel rooms in cities like Bangalore has led to Infosys building its own accommodation – so much that it will reportedly become the largest 'hotelier' by numbers of rooms in India. Such a development was unimaginable only a few years ago.

These issues create enormous challenges for companies seeking to 'globalize' and extend their workforces to incorporate more diverse sources of talent. Even for those in sectors where global expansion is more difficult, such as government, the issues cannot be ignored, as ultimately we are all competing in the same talent pool. We shall return to these points in Chapters 2 and 3 as we discuss strategies and approaches to meet these challenges and take advantage of the changes they are creating.

Figure 1.7   Panic time
Copyright 2005 by Randy Glasbergen.
www.glasbergen.com

In many countries the skills shortage for employers has been aggravated by powerful special factors such as:

- underperforming education systems which fail to match skills and expectations of school leavers and college graduates with those needed and valued by employers;
- pensions policies which penalize older workers who want to continue working or take up new positions in their organizations;
- the growing reluctance of younger workers to work in certain sectors of the economy, and their preference for variety and independence rather than conventional career patterns as employees of one organization;
- the prevalence, particularly in many EU countries, of job-protection measures and an associated mindset which help to keep people in obsolete or less marketable skills and holds back their retraining in more valuable ones;
- restrictive immigration policies, which may have been intended to protect the jobs of domestic workers but also have the effect of stifling the flow of talent across borders.

Some of these are worth considering further, particularly the challenges of the education gaps.

THE IMPORTANCE OF LEARNING AND SKILLS DEVELOPMENT

Accelerating demands for new skills and capabilities combined with worldwide skills shortages have made learning and skills development a strategic necessity for all organizations. In an increasingly talent-dependent global economy, talent-powered organizations emphasize learning and skills development to create the prepared, adaptable workforces necessary for strategic success.

IS EDUCATION CREATING THE SKILLS WE NEED?

The world is becoming more educated as availability of basic education spreads. For example, upper secondary-level education (beyond the compulsory level of education) typically starting at ages 15 to 16 is now close to 80 per cent across the 25 EU countries. Across all OECD countries, the proportion of the population now attaining tertiary-level education is around one third for 25–34 year olds versus 17 per cent for those in the age group 55–64, according to the OECD. In countries like the United Kingdom and the United States, around 40 per cent or more of the population today now reaches tertiary-level education. Continuing vocational training varies widely, and adult learning is becoming a significant issue, as we shall see.

This percentage is of course very variable around the world. Numbers of tertiary-educated students are still highest in the United States, with over 14 million, although a significant and increasing proportion now come from overseas, especially Asia. India now has more than 6 million students, followed by Japan at almost 4 million, and China currently also at around 4 million, although increasing fast. Russia has a relatively small student population of 2.6 million. The world looks to these ranks of students – or graduates – to supply management talent, engineers, scientists, doctors, lawyers, technologists and others that businesses are so hungry for.

But what sort of education and qualifications are these students coming out with? Are they gaining the skills that businesses need? In the developed world, there appears to be a growing trend of failure by secondary and tertiary education to produce the right basic skills. In the United Kingdom, employers have complained of low-quality science qualifications, and the disappearance of physics, mathematics and language students, while media and cultural studies become ever more fashionable. The Confederation of British Industry (CBI) has deplored poor literacy and numeracy skills among college graduates as well as school leavers, and a lack of basic communications, decision-making and leadership skills.

The Corporate Executive Board (a Washington-based research and education organization) recently surveyed 4,000 hiring managers in over 30 US companies. They complained that the average quality of candidates had declined by 10 per cent since 2004, and that the average time to fill a vacancy had increased from 37 days to 51 days (*Economist*, 2006a). A recent employers' survey showed school leavers to be seriously deficient in applied skills – 'those skills that enable new entrants to use the basic knowledge acquired in school to perform in the workplace'. In written communications, the survey found 81 per cent of high-school graduates, 47 per cent of two-year college graduates and 28 per cent of four-year college graduates to be deficient. In leadership, it found deficiencies ranging from 24 per cent to 73 per cent. In professionalism/work ethic, the deficiency ranged from 19 per cent to 70 per cent (Casner-Lotto and Barrington, 2006).

These statistics are worrying. But it cannot be that younger people in the developed world have inexplicably become less able than previous generations. It has much more to do with the education they pursue. The nature of graduate qualifications has changed quite significantly over the years in the United States and Europe, and this has exacerbated the declining populations of young people we described earlier:

- Although the number of UK graduates increased by 30 per cent between 1996 and 2004, the percentage of students studying physical sciences and architecture declined by 0.8 per cent and 0.48 per cent respectively. Comparatively, the biggest increases were found in the social, economic and political sciences (5.42 per cent) and studies allied to medicine, principally nursing (4.4 per cent) (UK Higher Education Statistics Agency).
- In the United Kingdom, there were more media studies undergraduates (21,655) in 2004 than biology (17,380), maths (17,925), chemistry (11,070), physics (9,350), philosophy (7,630) or finance (6,750) graduates (UK Higher Education Statistics Agency).
- In 2003, the United States graduated more than twice as many performing arts students as those studying maths and the physical sciences combined: 77,181 compared with 11,171 and 17,983 respectively (US National Center for Education Statistics).
- Approximately 15,000 UK students took A-level further mathematics in each year during the late 1980s. In 2004 the number was 7,270 (figures from UK Higher Education Statistics Agency).
- The number of graduates from German colleges with degrees in computer science is expected to drop from 17,000 in 2006 to some 14,000 in 2010 (Heise Online, 2006).
- In France, the number of registered students taking bachelor-level science degrees dropped from 46,000 in 1995 to 29,000 in 2002, a fall of 37 per cent.

These concerns are being raised with increasing frequency, but it is not clear how this trend will be reversed – especially since the

National Commission on Mathematics and Science Teaching for the 21st Century found that two-thirds of mathematics and science teachers in the United States would be retiring between 2000 and 2010. However, perhaps all is not lost. In the 29 years that the Harris Poll has been tracking the prestige of different professions, teaching is the only occupation to have seen a rise in prestige. In the last quarter century, the percentage of adults who see teachers as having 'very great' prestige has risen from 29 to 52 per cent (Harris Interactive, 2006).

Meanwhile, the slack is getting picked up in the developing nations around the world. The number of tertiary graduates in 2003 in the field of science, mathematics and computing has more than doubled since 1998 in the Czech Republic, Latvia, Lithuania, Malta, Poland and Slovakia (Eurostat, 2003).

In Asia there have been some huge changes in education. Korea has transformed itself in the last 50 years to one of the most modern economies in the world, and in large part this is the result of investments by government, often working together with industry, in expanding the education sector, particularly higher education. Today, 97 per cent of Korean 25–34 year olds have a high-school education – the highest rate in the principal industrialized economies of the world. Key characteristics of a successful education system, well demonstrated in Korea, include business working as a training provider and investment in lifelong learning and reskilling.

In India there are now around 200,000 new computer science graduates a year, mostly from the six Indian institutes of technology. Last year China graduated more than 820,000 engineers, of whom 30 per cent can compete internationally (Heise Online, 2006). Around one-third of students in China study engineering, compared with 20 per cent in Germany, and around 4 per cent in India (IHT, 2006). In China, the total number of qualified scientists and engineers working in R&D is expected to exceed the total in Europe by 2010, and the country has committed itself to significant increases in spending on education from a relatively low 2.55 per cent of GDP in 1998 to 4 per cent by 2010 (Government of China, 2006). In 2003, 25 per cent of all college-educated workers in science and engineering occupations in the United States were foreign-born.

LEVELS OF INVESTMENT IN EDUCATION – AN ISSUE OF NATIONAL COMPETITIVENESS

The reality is that all countries are competing in the global talent market, and it is vital for each country's competitiveness that it continue to produce a significant proportion of its population with the skills and experience the global economy needs. But some countries are spending a significantly higher proportion of their GDP than others on education.

Figure 1.8 illustrates the point in differences in the developed economies of the world.

As noted, the developed economies of the world appear to be falling behind increasingly in producing the skills needed, and there is already evidence that Europe is failing to keep up with the demand for skills driven by the knowledge economy. For example, it is estimated that in 2005 Europe had a shortfall in advanced network technology skills (security and new network developments such as internet-protocol telephony, security and wireless networking) of around 160,000 people, and that this will rise to 500,000 in 2008. This represents a skill gap of 8.1 per cent of total demand in 2005, rising to 15.8 per cent in 2008 (IDC, 2005).

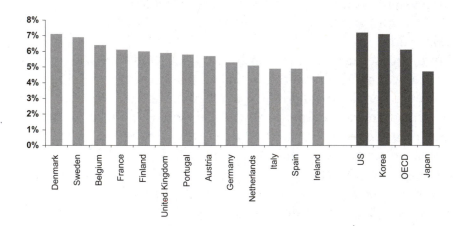

Figure 1.8 National education spending
Expenditure on educational institutions as a percentage of GDP, public and private, 2002
Source: Ederer (2006).

The Lisbon Council for Economic Competitiveness and Social Renewal (an influential think tank) carried out a study in conjunction with Zeppelin University in Friederichshafen on understanding human capital across Europe (Ederer, 2006). It focused on how countries are investing in and building their human capital, principally through education and training. The key conclusion was that 'some countries are courting disaster by allowing their human capital to stagnate', and the report urged policy makers in Europe to invest more in the individual citizen. At the top of the Human Capital Index list in Europe were the Nordic countries, followed by the United Kingdom and the Netherlands. Propping up the bottom were Italy, Spain and Portugal, with Germany not far away. The Lisbon Council believes that countries towards the bottom end of this index risk economic stagnation.

Although it is easy to focus on the education of children, the reality is that around 70 per cent of the workforce that we shall have in 2020 is already out of school and college. Therefore there is a critical need for governments and corporations to concentrate on adult learning and development. Right now, their willingness to invest varies enormously. In Europe, the Nordic countries and the Netherlands fare best, with almost twice the level of comparable investment of countries like Italy, Germany and Spain, according to the European Union. We shall discuss this issue further in Chapter 4.

MIGRATION OF SKILLS AND JOBS

Relative weakness in building home-grown talent can be compensated for by the immigration of talent. Today people are mobile, and in particular, young people from Asia are moving to take advantage of learning opportunities or jobs.

Australia has been one of the world's greediest nations for skilled workers from abroad. For over three decades, successive governments policies have systematically encouraged large-scale, explicitly skill-selective immigration. Without such policies, it has been estimated that Australia's current population would be about 12 million instead of 20 million (Kippen and McDonald, 2000). At the 2001 population census, about 23 per cent of the resident population were foreign-born. Since 1996 there has been a shift towards importing skilled workers on a temporary basis, and a proliferation of separate visa categories. This has had the effect of raising the proportion of immigrants in skilled categories from 29 per cent in 1995–96 to 62 per cent in 2003–04, and improving the labour market performance of migrants to Australia – in sharp contrast to the experiences of Canada and the United States, where the labour market situation of immigrants has deteriorated in recent times (Hugo, 2006).

To an extent, India represents the obverse of Australia, since for the past 20 years it has been one of the world's most important sources of skilled migration. There are currently estimated to be more than 20 million Indians living abroad, generating about US$160 billion in annual income, and accounting for US$400 billion in output. Until recently, this has been perceived as a classic 'brain drain', not entirely mitigated by the earnings sent back to India by emigrants – accounting for nearly 2 per cent of India's GDP during the 1990s. Since the millennium, it has gradually become clear that through diaspora networks, skill and technology transfer, cross-border investment flows and the operations of multinational companies, India itself has reaped benefits not only economically but also educationally.

What goes around comes around, it seems. And in 2006, the pendulum is shifting to the point where Australia is increasingly concerned about its brain drain, while India is enjoying some of the benefits of return migration, and the assimilation of skilled workers from abroad.

There has also been a strong trend in recent years to move jobs to other countries to access their talent. This is starkly demonstrated by the growth of offshoring of jobs in the IT industry from the United States and Europe to India in particular, which has around 80 per cent of this market today. While estimates of the impact of offshoring vary widely, the United States and the United Kingdom are most exposed, and this trend may impact as many as 40–50 per cent of new jobs in this sector, as shown by the research findings in Table 1.1.

Table 1.1 The impact of offshoring on European and US industry jobs
Sources: Forrester Research, Gartner Group, Global Insight, Estimation Oddo Securities.

Offshoring: impact on IT jobs	Existing jobs (2003–2005)	Job creation capped by offshoring (2006–2010)
US	Between −2 and −4% p.a.	Between 25% and 50% of jobs
UK	Between −2 and −4% p.a.	Between 25% and 40% of jobs
Continental Europe	−1% p.a.	Between 10% and 25% of jobs

Offshoring in this context is being driven not only by labour arbitrage opportunities, but also access to talent and the quality of skills and work performed.

THE CHALLENGE OF ENGAGEMENT

Changes in attitudes about work and life priorities, the rise of knowledge work and workers, and changing patterns of work have made engaging employees simultaneously more important and more difficult. Talent-powered organizations understand that engagement is the powerful force that enables them to multiply their talent. As business becomes ever more dependent on talent, truly talent-powered organizations engage employees to achieve superior performance.

ATTITUDINAL SHIFTS TO WORK AND LIFE: GENERATION X, GENERATION Y AND THE NET GENERATION

Many demographers and social commentators have drawn attention to the shift in attitudes across the generations, and the apparent lack of willingness and interest in the current generations to commit to work in the ways that previous generations did. Understanding these shifts is vitally important in understanding how to manage and attract the different generations.

Although we talk about generations, the different cohorts of people being born in different decades do not fit neatly into actual generations, but rather into social groupings with particular characteristics. The descriptors and characteristics most often used in the past were most applicable to the West, and most closely aligned with the Anglophone world. Attitudes shift as people grow older – the idealized worldview of the young inexorably shifts to the more pragmatic, world-weary view of maturity. Practicalities such as raising families force economic considerations to the fore, so that job security becomes more important, as does work–life balance – although recent surveys on this topic show that some attitudes to issues such as work–life balance apply across the generations.

Attitudes also vary across regions of the world. Although the internet and common access to global media have created some homogeneity in the political and social outlook of younger generations, a stronger work ethic and focus has been detected among young people in the developing economies of the world. Having had less opportunity until recently to build their own wealth and enjoy its trappings, they seem to have a greater hunger. And they are the first generation of their people to see these opportunities opening up, just as the baby boomers were the first generation to see new opportunities in the post-war developed world.

A recent Gallup poll of young Chinese showed that the first priority for more than two-thirds of respondents was to 'work hard and get rich'. Young people in the West would often prefer to skip the first bit. The mantra across the United States and Europe today is work–life balance, in contrast with the developing world's work-hard-and-succeed mantra. But this is also a reflection of contrasting attitudes between older and younger workforces. The Corporate Research Council in its 2006 series on *Competitive Employment Value Propositions* highlighted some of these variances. In China, for example, no potential employees mentioned work–life balance among their desires. In all the cities surveyed, compensation came at the top every time. In the United Kingdom, Australia and New Zealand, by contrast, work–life balance figured highly.

As Thomas Friedman observed in *The World is Flat* (2005), 'young Chinese, Indians, and Poles are not racing us to the bottom. They are racing us to the top.' They are not content with where they are and they want to compete with, not just support, enterprises from around the world.

The first significant shifts in attitudes and beliefs came with the baby boomers – the celebrated post-war generation born between the 1940s and 1960s. They were part of a population boom as the world came out of general economic depression. They were also seen as a reactive generation, wanting to change much of what previous generations had created. That done, they mostly settled into predictable patterns of work and employment, and they worked hard to accumulate. They are now rapidly approaching retirement.

The baby boomers were followed by what became known as Generation X – those who were born between the end of the 1960s and the end of the 1970s. This generation was smaller, and generally viewed as being more cynical; to an extent, they seemed to feel overshadowed by the baby-boom generation. But Generation X also grew up during a period of significant social change. This generation attracts different names in different parts of the world: in the West, it is also known as the Nineties generation, whereas in Russia and Eastern Europe, it is often known as the Glasnost-Perestroika generation. In the developing world, this generation had to adapt to huge and rapid social and economic changes, including the emergence of women into the workforce. There was a historic view that this generation did not want to work hard, but again as they have aged, the pressures on them of making money, general social conformity, and work–life balance mean they are relatively stable in the workforce, although not always content.

The most recent generation was born from the beginning of the 1980s. It is now entering the workforce in strength, and producing the greatest worry over recruitment and retention. It is often reffered to as Generation Y, but has other names or subgroups that people study around the world. They are the offspring of baby boomers and are the largest generational group ever, although evenly distributed across the world. They are also defined by their use and appetite for technology and the internet, and hence the more familiar title 'Net generation' or N-Geners', as defined by Don Tapscott in his seminal book *Growing Up Digital* (1997).

In understanding the various generational differences there are broad circumstances that have shaped the thinking and attitudes of the different age groups in the workforce today. Warren Bennis and Bob Thomas (co-author of this book) in their book *Geeks and Geezers* (2002) looked at these and observed the following.

Workers now aged 70 or more ('geezers') are more likely than younger generations to have:

- been brought up in stable families with one (usually male) bread-winner;
- undergone stricter and more formal methods of teaching;
- strong loyalties to their birthplace, community, country, family and employers;
- changed jobs and working practices infrequently if at all;
- lived and worked in hierarchical environments, with clear decision-making structures, which put a premium on predictability and security.

By contrast, workers under 35 ('geeks') are more likely to have:

- experienced greater variety and instability in family relationships;
- experienced less rule-bound methods of teaching (although these may have returned in many countries for the youngest generation of workers, in response to media and political pressures);
- no strong loyalties to any particular environment;
- changed jobs and careers more often (typically they expect to work for seven to eight employers, compared with at most three or four for the older generation);
- changed not only working practices but entire lifestyles rapidly and frequently in response to changes in technology;
- developed little respect for hierarchy or security, and to have come to expect and demand the maximum opportunity for personal fulfilment.

In the generation now entering the workforce we are seeing some very different signs on how they want to work, and the huge influence that technology and modern media are having on their lives. This is also the generation that makes up most of the new workforces of the developing world – in China, Brazil, India and Vietnam they represent over a third of the total available workforce, more than double the proportion of the baby boomers.

Although this generation lacks certain key skills demanded by business, its members are imbued with expertise in the new forms of media and technology, which they improve year by year to capture the new entertainment and lifestyle opportunities provided. In addition, they have typically grown up in relative security and affluence, giving them a sense of being able to accomplish almost anything, according to Pattie Giordani in her article '"Y" recruiting' (2005). They have grown up totally at ease with technology and with high expectations of its performance and potential. In the United States, it is estimated that over 90 per cent of people aged 15–17 are computer users, and in other countries the young have greater broadband penetration. Given the globalized nature of the workforce today they are also the most racially diverse and egalitarian group to come into the workforce.

Most important, the Net Generation has used digital media to create new and personal forms of entertainment, collaboration and connection. Their parents, the boomers, may have been the first to enjoy 'youth culture', but they had to take what they were given from radio, television, movies and music companies. The Net Generation have been given interactive, inter-exchangeable media, giving them unprecedented opportunities to customize and invent not only their

"For Father's Day, I'm giving my dad an hour of free tech support."

Figure 1.9   The Net Generation
First published in *The New Yorker*, 19 June 2006.

choice of entertainment but their entire personal space and identity. As Don Tapscott observed, when members of this generation enter the labour force, they are culturally resistant to any form of centralized control and to any working demands that rob them of their 'right' to personalize their environment. He defined their norms as:

- freedom – choice, mobility, integrate home and social lives with worklives;
- customization – workplace, processes information access;
- scrutinizers – demanding more, authentication, trust and transparency;
- integrity – alignment of values, consistency;
- collaboration – interacting through media, sharing knowledge and experience;
- entertainment – at work and in learning; fun experiences;
- speed – rapid communication, information flows;
- innovation – challenging norms, use of technology.

Understanding and making use of these characteristics offers exciting new possibilities in how we access and engage this new generation of talent. They are adaptable and quick to grasp new ideas, having become so familiar with sharing and collaborating. We may just have to go out into the world of the internet and find them, and they will provide their brainpower – often just for the fun of it. We shall come back to that in Chapter 3.

Somewhere between the geeks and the geezers are the workers of 35 to 70. Many of them lead lives of anxiety, juggling work, family and relationship demands without enjoying either the security valued by the previous generation or the fulfilment sought by the next. These people, particularly middle managers, are becoming less loyal to their employers, and expect to move jobs more rapidly to meet their expectations (or cope with those of their circle). Accenture's surveys of middle managers have consistently shown that this is a group of unsettled people. No fewer than two-thirds of today's middle managers would consider changing their jobs, and half of these people are actually doing something about it.

The day-to-day management of multigenerational teams is tough enough, let alone retraining and reskilling them all, and making each member more motivated and productive. But these are challenges facing more and more organizations. They will not succeed without rewards and performance management systems, that make separate personal sense to each one of their people, while simultaneously generating a sense of common cause in line with the organization's strategic priorities. Understanding the generational differences is crucial to understanding engagement and motivational issues, career direction and aspiration, leadership role models and expectations, and work styles. These will be reviewed later when we consider discovering and recruiting talent in Chapter 3, skills development in Chapter 4, and the challenge of engagement in Chapter 5.

THE CHANGING NATURE OF WORK: KNOWLEDGE WORKERS

The nature of work has been changing for some time now, as the developed world has shifted away from reliance on manual work towards an economy based primarily on knowledge work. Even in the developing economies, talent shortages and competition are mostly associated with knowledge workers. Earlier on we noted the growth in the intangible value of enterprises – a phenomenon directly related to the rise in knowledge work.

What are knowledge workers and how well do we understand them? The term was coined as early as 1959 by Peter Drucker, to describe people who add value to their organization through their ability to process existing information to create new information which could be exploited to define and solve problems. As examples, he cited lawyers, doctors, diplomats, law makers, marketing experts, managers and bankers, which might reflect a certain bias towards people with specific professional skills.

Many commentators have identified particular characteristics of knowledge workers, including problem-solving and learning ability, individuality and a need for autonomy, and the ability to absorb new information or see existing information in a new light. They have a strong sense of their own worth, and they want to demonstrate it and have it recognized.

Economists have also studied this phenomenon, and even within knowledge-based work, have noted that the nature of the skill requirements has been changing. In an article in 2006 in the *Journal of Labor Economics* published by the University of Chicago, Alexandra Spitz-Oener demonstrated that 'occupations require more complex skills today than in 1979 and that the changes in skills requirements are most pronounced in rapidly computerising occupations'. No wonder it is getting more difficult to find the right skills and we worry about shortcomings in education.

Drucker's ideas have been taken on by others, and most recently developed by Thomas Davenport, whose 2005 book *Thinking For a Living* took a close look at knowledge workers, whose expertise and experience lies behind the success of many of the world's leading companies. 'Knowledge workers,' says Davenport, 'are going to be the primary force determining which economies are successful and which aren't. They are the key source of growth in most organizations.'

Lest you doubt the importance of knowledge workers, consider these recent findings. According to *American Demographics*' analysis of the US Bureau of Labor Statistics 10-year projection report published in December 2001, 56 per cent of the American workforce belonged to a major occupational group that gathered, processed or used some type of information to conduct their work. And according to the European Commission, the combination of people working in market services and non-market services (public services and non-profit) across the EU25 is now 67 per cent, or 130 million people out of a total of 195 million (Eurostat report 2005 – data 2004). Figure 1.10 shows the shift

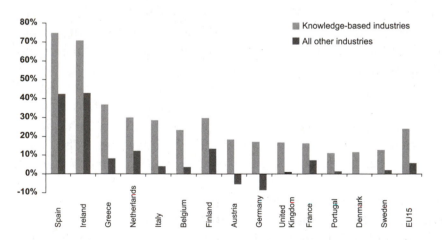

Figure 1.10 New jobs in knowledge-based industries versus all other industries, 1995–2005 (EU15 excluding Luxembourg)
Source: ESRC (2005).

in new jobs from 1995 to 2005 in the 15 EU countries, with a very strong bias towards knowledge-based industries.

The shift to knowledge work places a higher premium on education and training, and on people's ability to learn new skills, notably their ability to work with the almost ubiquitous computers and technology. Along with that comes a need for general skills, including problem-solving ability, team-working, adaptability and informational skills, as well as specific technical or content skills such as science and engineering, languages and commercial knowledge.

Managing knowledge workers is bound to be difficult, and very different from the approaches to improve the efficiency of manual workers that began with F W Taylor in the early 1900s and his principles of scientific management. Talent is not a commodity, nor is one unit of talent a perfect substitute for another. Knowledge workers' value lies somewhere in the recesses of their brain – so how can you extract and evaluate that? Their job is to think, but how can you tell when they are thinking? You certainly can't tell *what* they are thinking. Even in a national company, your knowledge workers are probably widely spread, and in a global company, they may well be in a different time zone. So how can you keep tabs on them?

It sounds impossible, which may be why many organizations seem to adopt the HSPALTA policy. This is Thomas Davenport's acronym for Hire Smart People And Leave Them Alone. But this is not enough. We need to improve output productivity, innovation, collaboration and other facets of knowledge work to drive real value and improvement in business performance. As Davenport observed, 'everybody else has already been squeezed, so now it's the knowledge worker's turn' (2005).

Knowledge workers have been newly empowered by technology and globalization. As Friedman described in *The World Is Flat* (2005), the world has been 'flattened' by a combination of geopolitical change, breakthroughs in information technology and new ways of working. He writes of a 'triple convergence – of new players, on a new playing field developing new processes and habits for horizontal collaboration' that has rendered irrelevant most of the old command-and-control work structures. We are now starting to see ways to improve the performance and productivity of these types of workers, but as we shall see later, one of the biggest challenges is in engaging them and motivating them to give of their best.

CHANGING PATTERNS OF WORK

Changing attitudes are being reflected in changing patterns of work, and for example, can be observed in declining average job tenure. According to Peter Cappelli (1999), George W Taylor Professor of Management at the Wharton School, average job tenure in the United States began to decline significantly in the mid-1990s, especially for managerial employees. Declines in long-tenure jobs explain much of the overall decline. The number of people in jobs for 10 years or more declined slightly from the late 1970s through to 1993, and then fell sharply through the end of the 1990s to the lowest levels in two decades. Increased career mobility is evident among workers at every career stage. Young workers now make 10 per cent more job changes in their early careers than previous generations of young workers did. Meanwhile, fewer men in the later stages of their careers (ages 58 to 63) have been with the same employer for 10 years or more than in the past – only 29 per cent in 1989, compared with 47 per cent in 1969 (Parker, 2006).

Conversely, there are fewer and fewer employers actually making that offer to them. More and more jobs, particularly first jobs, are offered on fixed-term contracts or in the expectation that their occupiers will move on.

These figures mask the growth of self-employment – increasingly a deliberate choice for workers who trust in their ability to sell their skills and do not wish to commit themselves to any particular employer or work environment. In fact, as Daniel Pink revealed in his provocative book *Free Agent Nation* (2002), over 25 million Americans are now self-employed. There are more 'free agents' than the combined total of all employees of federal, state, county and local governments – 'Free Agent Nation is larger than the entire public sector.' In addition to self-employment, more and more people are joining or forming small businesses which can offer the same variety of working assignments as self-employment and the same opportunity to change direction. According to Pink, fewer than one in 10 Americans works for a Fortune 500 company. Entrepreneurialism is rampant: Census Bureau figures indicate that 70 per cent of businesses in the United States have no paid employees.

There is much evidence to show that the self-employed work longer hours than their peers in organizations. The self-employed have no paid holidays and no sick leave. Every day of leisure, illness or pure idleness comes out of their own pockets. Small wonder that average weekly hours worked by self-employed people are higher. On average, men (in the United Kingdom and United States) who are self-employed work between 54 and 56 hours a week compared with employees who work around 44 hours (Parker, 2006). In Canada, the self-employed worked 41.4 hours per week in 2005 compared with 35.6 hours for employees, on average. Thirty-five per cent of self-employed persons worked over 50 hours compared with only 5 per cent of employees (Statistics Canada, 2006).

Many of the same things apply to those who work in small companies. There is little or no fat in such companies – if their workers slack they not only hit themselves in the wallet, they let down their colleagues. Again, figures suggest that hours worked by those in small companies are higher than those worked in bigger ones.

- In Belgium there is a significant difference in the number of hours worked depending on the size of the company. According to the European Social Survey (2002) analysis of Belgian employee data, the actual number of hours worked decreased in inverse proportion to the company size. An average of 44 hours a week are worked in companies with fewer than 10 employees, 38 hours in companies with 100–500 employees and just over 40 hours for those with 500 or more (EIRO, 2006a).
- Similar findings are present in Germany: 40.5 hours were worked a week in companies with 10–49 employees, 40 hours for those with 50–199 employees, 38 hours for those with 200–999 employees and 37 hours in organizations with 1000+ employees (EIRO, 2006b).
- This phenomenon was also apparent in Japan. Work hours totalled 42 for companies employing less than 30 people, 40 hours for those employing 100–999, and 38 hours for those employing 1,000-plus (Japan Institute of Labour, 1995).

Employers in large organizations can take advantage of these changing work patterns and preferences, but they require more flexible ways of contracting for work and engaging this pool of talent. We shall examine some of these points in the next couple of chapters.

MANAGING TALENT THROUGHOUT THE ORGANIZATION

Given the strategic importance of talent and the ability to create and develop it, nurturing and developing talent has to become everyone's responsibility in every organization. In talent-powered organizations, organizational capabilities in defining, discovering, developing, and deploying talent allow everyone in the organization to identify and nurture talent in ways that enhance performance. In a talent-driven economy, talent-powered organizations understand that while top leadership and HR involvement are essential, a talent mindset and capabilities must be embedded and sustained throughout the organization.

TALENT vs LABOUR vs HUMAN CAPITAL

These changes in the type and content of work are why the word 'talent' has come to be used so much now in business, as opposed to the general term of 'labour'. The traditional use of the word 'talent' usually refers to a special gift, particularly in relation to arts, sports or intellectual pursuits. In business it has come to encapsulate all the various attributes of people today. Essentially, talent means the total of all the experience, knowledge, skills, and behaviours that a person has and brings to work.

Talent therefore is used as an all-encompassing term to describe the human resources that organizations want to acquire, retain and develop in order to meet their business goals. Described in this way for each person, it can be developed and augmented, or reduced and left undeveloped, and that is the challenge for every organization today. The support people receive from relationships and their environment at work, organization and process, technology, information, and from factors outside work, including family, friends, health and recreation, are all factors that influence how effectively talent is engaged, developed and directed.

That is why talent means something different from labour. In classical economic theory 'labour' is one of the three necessary factors of production, alongside capital and land (which includes foodstuffs, raw materials and other extracted products of land). Labour is anonymous and impersonal, and it is ascribed properties which are required to make sense of the relationships in classical economics. In particular, labour is subject to the law of diminishing returns. As we shall see, talent is not. It can be multiplied constantly to create value.

We also use the term 'human capital' to convey a greater sense of the value attached to the employees of an organization, and a wider sense of economic contribution than is implied by the term 'labour'. We see the terms 'human capital' and 'talent' as broadly interchangeable, although human capital tends to get used when we think about the strategic, economic and financial aspects of talent, particularly how human capital contribution could be permanently increased by investments in human development, such as in learning, working environments and support systems. But 'human capital' has fallen out of favour in some quarters, because it seems to treat human beings as an impersonal resource.

In general, we prefer the term 'talent', particularly when we want to capture the qualities that set it apart as a factor of production: uniqueness combined with ubiquity; diversity combined with dynamism; its ability to multiply and create ever-increasing sources of new value.

One important aspect of talent is its mobility. As Bill Gates once observed, the key assets of Microsoft go up and down in the elevators and in and out of the doors of the company every day. Today, they are less and less likely to even come in and out of the doors.

NEW WORK ARRANGEMENTS

One of the exciting phenomena of the modern workplace is that it is no longer a single physical workplace. You can work the way you want: from home, on the move, invisibly. You can wear what you like, eat and sleep when you like, invent your own work patterns.

We are seeing much greater flexibility in how people contract their skills and time to employers – and these are challenging the old disciplines of the workplace and chains of command. The problem is that traditional organizations often lag far behind the changes in the way people want to work.

We have yet to catch up fully with these changes, to adapt to them and to take advantage of them. But start-up companies are showing the way: some have thriving multi-million-dollar businesses with almost no full time co-located employees. By contrast, many large organizations are still struggling to make matrixed or networked structures work, and many remain stuck in organizational hierarchies that reflect old command-and-control thinking, but do little to facilitate collaboration, networking and innovation across business areas and functions. Imagine how the new Net Generation feels about such environments.

Major changes have happened since William Whyte, an editor at *Fortune* magazine, wrote *The Organization Man* over 50 years ago, a book that defined the nature of corporate life for a generation. It described an America whose people had 'led in the public worship of individualism' before turning into a nation of employees who 'take the vows of organization life'. The company that used to be most closely identified with this way of life was IBM. For many years it was characterized by its managers who wore only dark blue suits, white shirts and dark ties, symbols of their lifetime allegiance to Big Blue. But as *The Economist* reported in an article on 'The new organization' in January 2006, today 50 per cent of IBM's 320,000 employees have worked for the company for under five years, 40 per cent of them are 'mobile' and do not report daily to an IBM site, and about 30 per cent are women. It has also changed from being chiefly a seller of computer products to becoming a broad-based services supplier. Many organizations have undergone similar changes.

The changes at companies like IBM are broadly reflected in the shifts in working patterns across the working population. Flexible and part-time working, independent contracting, virtual or teleworking have opened up new options and flexibility for employees as well as new sources of talent, particularly people with caring responsibilities and older workers, while meeting the preferences of younger workers for new career patterns.

These are some recent findings on new ways of working:

- The number of virtual workers in the United States – full-time employees who work remotely or contractors who never leave their home offices – increased by 800 per cent from 2001 to 2006 (this increase masks a decline in 'home workers' in the agricultural sector) (Nemertes Research, cited in *Small Business Review*, 17 August 2006).
- Currently, there are an estimated 18 million teleworkers in the United States, compared with 10 million in 1996, according to the US Bureau of Statistics. That number rises to 22.2 million if you

count every American worker who spent at least one day a week working from home or another out-of-office location in 2005 – an increase of 30 per cent from 2004 (*Forbes*, 2006).

■ Part-time work accounts for around 11 per cent of employees across the European Union, averaging just under 20 working hours per week: the number of people working on limited duration contracts has increased from less than 12 per cent in 1996 to 14 per cent in 2005 (Eurostat data, 2005).

There is also some evidence of the preference of the new generations of workers for working alone, sometimes on a subcontract basis, but also in small groups or 'micro-enterprises' of fewer than 10 people. Not only are micro-enterprises by far the most numerous in terms of numbers of organizations, but today they also employ the most people as a segment by organization size. In 15 EU countries, micro-enterprises employ 54 million people whereas large enterprises (more than 250 employees) employ 41 million (KPMG/EIM, 2003).

We shall explore the implications of these findings in Chapters 2 and 3 as we look at new ways of sourcing and recruiting talent.

SUMMARY

Whatever its business or activity, your organization's survival depends on the ability to define discover, develop and deploy talent of every kind. This is the new competitive paradigm, and the challenge is different from anything your organization has faced before. It demands a new mindset – inspired by new leadership, informed by new strategy, supported by new capabilities. We are entering a new Age of Talent, and we must move beyond the oft-quoted platitudes of 'people are our most important assets' to meaning it and doing something about it.

Very few organizations have the right resources in place to meet the new talent challenge. Their methods and basic approach to talent issues, supporting infrastructure, and management focus are inadequate for the task. Their metrics, both internal and external, fail to recognize the new nature of value in the business, let alone provide guidance to good investments to increase it. The specialist department usually assigned to talent issues – Human Resources – often lacks the skills and capabilities, and in many cases the confidence and credibility, to manage all these issues and treat them strategically. Now, as top executives become more and more aware of these issues and failings, there is a new focus of attention on talent management practices, capabilities, and measurement.

In the ensuing chapters we shall show how and why:

- your organization's leaders must create the right mindset and culture to **multiply the value of talent** in every part of your organization, together with a new approach and a new model to sustain it;
- you must **embrace diversity** in many different ways to gain competitive advantage from the proliferation and complexity of talent markets;
- you must **invest in learning and skills development**, but in a much more focused way;
- you need to work hard to **build engagement** in all your talent to add much greater value to your organization;
- you must **share the responsibility for talent multiplication throughout the organization**, so that it supports all your strategic goals.

2

A Strategic Approach to Talent

Our task is not to foresee the future, but to make it happen.
Antoine de Saint Exupéry, 1900–44

In this chapter we set out a framework to achieve the necessary strategic understanding of the talent issues and their importance in relation to the organization's business strategy. The framework reviews all the human capital elements of the business required to meet the goals and objectives set out in the business strategy, and pulls them together in the form of a unifying **human capital strategy**. Not only will this help you meet the specific talent demands derived from your business strategy; it will also point you towards the dynamic, transformational possibilities of multiplying talent to augment your organization's value and competitiveness.

To achieve this, all your talent related processes and capabilities need to be aligned and integrated so that they are working towards the same end. This is the essence of **talent multiplication** – the key differentiator for a fully talent-powered organization. It begins with properly defining talent needs based on a clear understanding of the business strategy, integrating all the possible options and sources to discover talent, and then developing and deploying talent in the right way at the right time.

In this chapter we shall also explore the positioning of Human Resources (HR) as the key function most involved in talent issues, and its role in the necessary evolution of talent management into talent multiplication. We shall discuss the specific direction for HR, including its structure, capabilities and responsibilities, further in Chapter 6.

But first we need to stress the importance of visible leadership on talent issues. Senior management must genuinely view talent as being strategic, and they must routinely and consistently understand and communicate the importance of talent to the organization. This is the first crucial element in establishing talent multiplication as the fuel for a talent-powered organization, by putting in place a talent mindset throughout the organization.

THE EXECUTIVE PERSPECTIVE

Talent issues are clearly on the core agenda of top executives, and concern them more and more. They are experiencing many of the management challenges of the new economic world we have described, and discovering how talent really is the source of competitive advantage and sustainability. Most top executives today are spending more and more time on talent-related issues. A 2006 survey by the Economist Intelligence Unit and Development Dimensions International showed that on average CEOs thought they were spending around 20 per cent of their time on people issues, and many reckoned it was a lot more.

This is substantiated through various surveys of the key issues that keep top executives awake at night. A *Business Week* survey in 2006 (Minton, 2006) across a wide range of executives in Europe showed the high importance now being attached to human capital within organizations as the most important issue in maintaining long-term high performance. The results of the survey are shown in Figure 2.1.

Accenture also carries out a survey called the High Performance Workforce Study approximately every 18 months to measure workforce management trends among executives in large corporations in the United States, Europe and Australia. The latest survey (Accenture, 2007) of more than 250 senior executives found that only 14 per cent of respondents described their organization's workforce skills as industry-leading. Furthermore, just 20 per cent of respondents said

Figure 2.1 Factors most important to maintaining high performance in the long term (number of respondents mentioning each factor as 'most important')
Source: Minton (2006).

that most of their employees understood their company's strategy and what was needed to be successful in their industry.

Respondents also reported that even functions they considered critical – sales, customer service, finance and strategic planning (cited as critical by 62 per cent, 43 per cent, 23 per cent and 23 per cent respectively) – were not performing as strongly as they should. In fact, among those who rated these functions as among their three most important, just a quarter (25 per cent) assigned the highest rating to the performance of their sales function, and under a third provided the same rating to their customer service, finance and strategic planning functions (25 per cent, 19 per cent and 33 per cent respectively).

When we compare the ratings of the workforce initiatives that top executives regard as most important with how well they think their organization is doing, we can see why they do not believe that their workforces are sufficiently competitive. This is shown clearly in Figure 2.2.

These findings, which have been consistent over the last several years, are alarming. They show that, despite the importance that top managers now attach to human capital and workforce perfor-

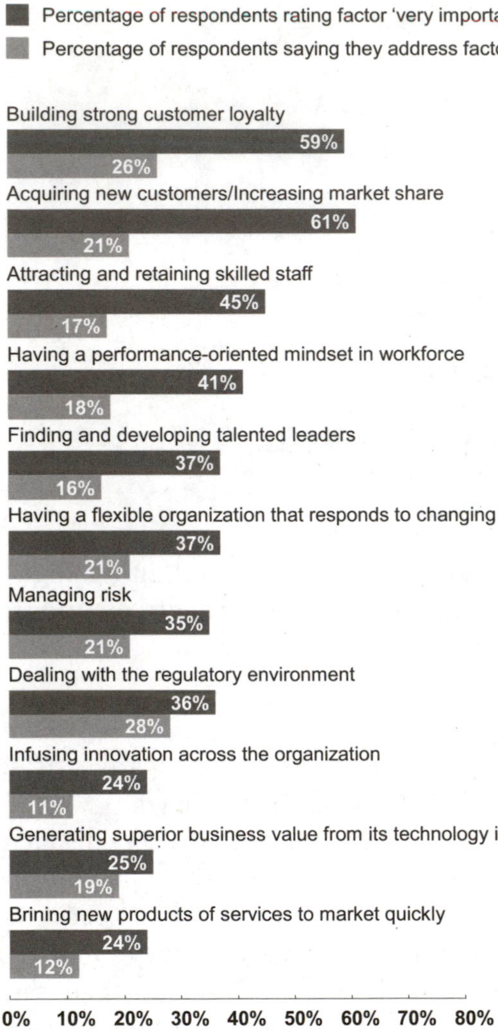

■ Percentage of respondents rating factor 'very important'
■ Percentage of respondents saying they address factor 'very well'

Building strong customer loyalty
59%
26%

Acquiring new customers/Increasing market share
61%
21%

Attracting and retaining skilled staff
45%
17%

Having a performance-oriented mindset in workforce
41%
18%

Finding and developing talented leaders
37%
16%

Having a flexible organization that responds to changing market conditions
37%
21%

Managing risk
35%
21%

Dealing with the regulatory environment
36%
28%

Infusing innovation across the organization
24%
11%

Generating superior business value from its technology investments
25%
19%

Brining new products of services to market quickly
24%
12%

0%   10%   20%   30%   40%   50%   60%   70%   80%

Figure 2.2   Key factors in achieving high performance: importance versus performance
Source: Accenture (2007).

mance, executives do not feel that their organizations are responding adequately.

It is good news that talent issues are at the top of the agenda for business leaders. This should create a sense of urgency and focus, which is the first critical part of having a corporate talent mindset, but we obviously have some way to go in addressing the issues. At least they should finally put to rest concerns from HR about not 'having a seat at the table'. If they are not at the table now, then they are probably in the wrong job.

HIGH PERFORMANCE – THE KEY DRIVERS

Over the past three and a half years, Accenture has been researching why high-performance businesses outcompete their peers over changes in markets, technologies and leadership teams. The research involved detailed examination of more than 500 companies, and it began with some sobering statistics: only 62 of the Fortune 500 companies of 1992 still ranked in the top 500 in 2005; the average life span of an S&P 500 company is less than 15 years; and fewer than 10 per cent of companies outperform their peer group for more than 10 years.

So how do the high performers get ahead and stay ahead? The principal conclusions from the research, and our own experience in working with many organizations around the world, are that there are three building blocks of high performance, as shown in Figure 2.3.

Market focus and position are about understanding the markets you are in, sensing the need for change ahead of the competition, and recognizing the value of market leadership, but not just pursuing scale for scale's sake. As has been frequently demonstrated, the costs of complexity are usually underestimated,

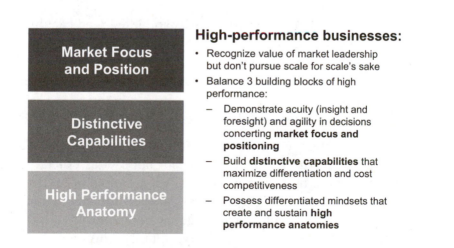

High-performance businesses:

- Recognize value of market leadership but don't pursue scale for scale's sake
- Balance 3 building blocks of high performance:
  - Demonstrate acuity (insight and foresight) and agility in decisions concerting **market focus and positioning**
  - Build **distinctive capabilities** that maximize differentiation and cost competitiveness
  - Possess differentiated mindsets that create and sustain **high performance anatomies**

Figure 2.3   Characteristics of high-performance businesses

and alignment and engagement are much more difficult than anticipated when organizations try to scale too quickly or pursue mergers and acquisitions too aggressively.

Distinctive capabilities are very important in the context of talent. They are much more than simple functional mastery, and are at the heart of what defines the organization's competitiveness and makes it different from its peers. They are typically informed by a clear and distinctive view of customer value and innovation, and are so focused as to promote differentiation and cost-effectiveness simultaneously.

It is not difficult to identify the distinctive capabilities of high-performing businesses – they usually highlight it in their marketing and emphasize what makes them different or better. Think of Dell and its ability to meet customer demand by assembling to order and dealing direct, or Wal-Mart and its supply-chain excellence, or BMW and its engineering excellence, or Samsung and its product development and marketing. The talent and specific competencies required for these distinctive capabilities of the organization must be the centre of attention for a human capital strategy, and we shall return to this shortly.

Finally, what we have termed the **high performance anatomy** encompasses elements that also become central to building a human capital strategy. We have defined performance anatomy as a set of mindsets that permeate an organization and are observable in actions and decisions. These include:

■ leadership – having market-making talent and ability to drive through execution;
■ people development – a talent mindset and integrated capabilities that multiply talent;
■ technology – viewing IT as a strategic asset;
■ performance – measuring all the critical areas and having a selective scorecard;
■ agility and innovation – ability to renew continuously.

Almost all these areas must be part of thinking strategically about talent. We have already touched on a talent mindset as crucial right from the outset for a high-performance talent-powered organization. In such organizations, talent generates high performance, which in turn attracts new talent and creates the means to reward it. Talent drives improvements in productivity, quality, innovation and customer satisfaction, which in turn feed into bottom-line results.

HOW TO MULTIPLY TALENT

So how do organizations deliver that promise to themselves? They multiply talent by combining and recombining knowledge, skills and competencies throughout the organization to generate superior levels of effort, imagination, creativity, learning, adaptability and performance from the entire workforce. The essence of the truly talent-powered organization is that it has a distinctive capability. In today's world given all the changes we summarized before, having such an ability to unlock talent's full potential will give a long-term sustainable competitive advantage.

A virtuous cycle of talent multiplication (shown in Figures 2.4) is set in motion by strong leadership, clearly articulated strategies, and a fervent belief in the strategic value of talent that permeates an organization's mindsets and culture. When four key talent management capabilities – defining talent needs, discovering talent sources, developing talent potential and deploying talent strategically – are aligned with

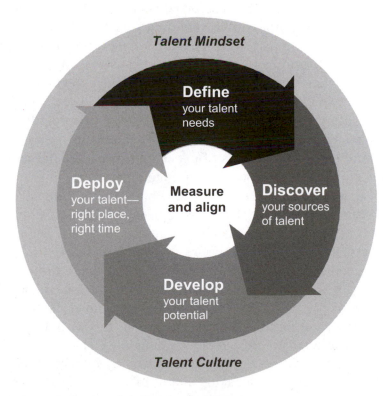

Figure 2.4   Talent multiplication model

each other and with business strategy and are highly integrated into business operations, organizations can stimulate the virtuous cycle of talent multiplication and increase the knowledge, skills, competencies and engagement of the workforce to fuel outstanding performance. Measurement is central, as is the understanding of investment needs at all parts of the talent multiplication cycle, and how these drive value and generate extraordinary business results.

We shall explore each of the elements of the talent multiplication model in turn. But first we must discuss the importance of establishing a comprehensive human capital strategy that shapes what talent the organization defines as strategic, how the organization will discover the needed talent, what training and development is required to build the critical skills, and how best to deploy to where it is most needed and best suited.

ESTABLISHING A HUMAN CAPITAL STRATEGY

If you were to go about constructing a building, you would begin with not just an architectural blueprint, but a clear understanding and articulation of the purpose of the building – its presentation, its functions, its positioning and so on, and you would think about these for the long term, not just the immediate construction. You would certainly do that before engaging all the various experts and tradespeople you would need to execute your building vision. Every decision on form and function of the building directly affects the materials and processes used to construct it, and at the same time, you would listen to the views of experts on materials and construction which might make you alter your building vision.

The same applies with talent, yet how often do we think about it in these terms? How can we decide what talent we need to support our distinctive capabilities and sustain our business strategy, and how can we set up all the different processes and systems we need to manage that talent effectively, without starting with a vision and strategic plan?

In Chapter 1, we indicated how much human capital contributes to the value of present-day companies, and also how elusive it is to measure that contribution. We need to go a bit further in understanding the key elements of the so-called intangible elements of value, so much of which is driven directly or indirectly by human capital.

Consider the challenge facing many of today's fastest growing companies – entities like Google, Infosys, Amgen and indeed

Accenture. A big part of the enterprise value of these businesses – whose principal assets are intangible – is represented by assumed growth in future cash flows. They must get talent management and all elements of their human capital right if they are to have any hope of delivering on the promise of future growth. They therefore rely on the effective management of people, relationships, intellectual resources and proprietary organizational processes. Wall Street analysts recognize this, but they lack the tools to effectively communicate their expectations or systematically measure whether a firm has the ability to fulfil them. But it's not just a problem for Wall Street: most executives struggle to articulate what their intangible assets are and how they should be valued.

Generally Accepted Accounting Principles (GAAP) were designed in the 1930s and do an excellent job of monitoring companies' performance by the standards of the 1930s. They report after the event on historic performance and on movements in values of traditional fixed assets. They account inadequately, or sometimes not at all, for such major drivers of shareholder value as brand, intellectual capital and proprietary networks. Worse still, they treat most investments in intangible assets as expenses which decrease earnings per share. The major part of money sunk into the development of intangible assets has to be expensed immediately, instead of being written off over years. This sends the worst possible message about the development of human capital. Spending money on a piece of machinery is treated as a productive investment, whereas spending money on training is treated as a cost.

Our task here is not to solve the problem of accounting principles, but it is important that senior leaders in knowledge-based companies become much more comfortable in distinguishing among the assets through which their firms create value – and developing useful ways to differentiate the returns they get from those assets. AssetEconomics Inc, a research consultancy which has advised governments and regulatory agencies on such matters, has put forward a comprehensive framework for integrating accounting categories and asset types (see Table 2.1). Aside from conceptual clarification, the AssetEconomics approach is valuable for the attention it draws to human, organizational and relational assets – sources of value whose significance has grown dramatically in concert with advances in technology, knowledge work, and globalization as we have discussed. This framework is

Table 2.1 AssetEconomics approach to sources of value
Source: Ballow *et al* (2004).

Resource recognizability	Resource Form				
	Traditional accounting resources		Intellectual capital resources		
	Monetary	Physical	Relational	Organizational	Human
Tangible resources	• Cash • Investments • Receivables/debtors • Payables/creditors	• Property • Plant • Equipment • Inventory – Finished goods – WIP – Parts/raw materials	• Customer contracts • Formal alliances, JVs, supply agreements	• Software systems • Formalized processes • Codified knowledge • Patents • Brands • Mastheads	• Management contracts • ESOP programs • LTI programs
Intangible resources	• Credit ratings • Undrawn facilities • Borrowing capacity (relative to like companies, based on character) • Borrowing covenant slack • Receivable certainty • Quality of earnings • Balance sheet strength	• Plant flexibility • Plant modernity • Infrastructure surrounding plants • Stranded assets? • Tradability of assets? • Access rights • Balance sheet strength • Inventory (good and usable, obsolete, redundant)	• Customer loyalty – Behavioural – Attitudinal • Quality of supply contracts • Right to tender, right to complete, right to design • Strength of stakeholder support (including opinion leaders) • Networks • Regulatory imposts	• Structural appropriateness • Informal processes • Organizational reputation • Brand meaning (strength, stature) • Productivity of R&D process • Quality of corporate governance • Know how, show how • Tacit knowledge	• Top management quality • Top management experience • Ability to execute on strategy • Bench depth • Problem-solving ability • Employee loyalty – Behavioural – Attitudinal • Personnel reputation

▓ Tracked by traditional accounting systems
░ Not tracked by traditional accounting systems

Note: Contents of each box are not all-inclusive but merely meant to show examples.

helpful in focusing attention on the talent-related aspects of value, and tees up our thinking on human capital strategy.

The essential links between business strategy and human capital strategy are shown in Figure 2.5. Understanding the organization's distinctive competencies is essential, and the business strategy should be articulated in terms of those competencies, the business strategy and distinctive competencies. As we develop the human capital strategy this should in turn inform what the HR function needs to do to enable HR processes in support of the requirements for talent across the organization.

Components of human capital strategy that particularly need to be thought through include **leadership, critical skills, organization** and **culture**. These elements are interdependent but also distinct in the thinking they require. Business leaders themselves repeatedly cite leadership as a critical competency, crucial for fulfilling business strategy – and they express little satisfaction with their own efforts to address it. High-performance businesses clearly differentiate themselves through the quality and depth of leadership, and they are better at building leaders. Jack Welch has said frequently that leadership was the distinctive competence he prioritized at GE, and evidence of his success is seen in the number of top corporate leaders who came

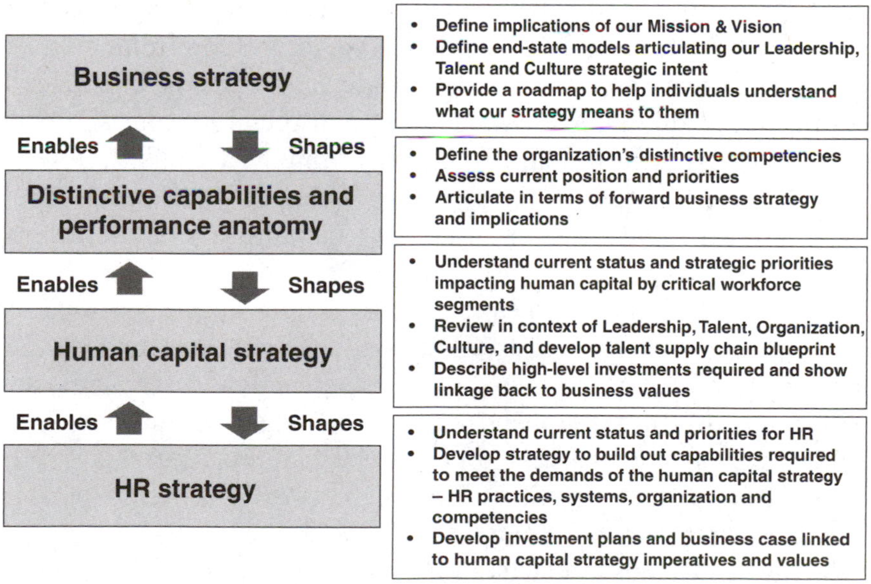

Figure 2.5   Strategy components and linkages

from GE. BP is another exemplar, with its passion for learning and the leadership development programmes that start deep down in the organization – its so-called 'turtle programme', which provides the opportunity for young future leaders to work alongside today's corporate leaders.

Consider also the challenges of finding leadership talent in the emerging economies, which we highlighted in Chapter 1. If the business strategy calls for expansion in China, then getting the leadership there becomes a key strategic issue to be addressed as part of a human capital strategy.

The importance of **critical skills** is clear. As we have noted, the focus at this level is not about every kind of talent, but rather the key positions, critical workforces and distinctive competencies that we need to understand in order to review our talent supply chain and options for sourcing. More of that later.

Organization is about assembling and structuring our talent in the best combinations to generate high performance. There is much talk today about networked and connected organizations that facilitate the flow of knowledge and connection of talent, and we shall explore some aspects of that in Chapter 4 on skills and learning. Governance and operating models are also much under study as organizations strive to find that balance between thinking globally and acting locally. It is interesting to note how much the management of people, and therefore the role of HR, is coming to the forefront of these exchanges. Consistently managing people is an essential characteristic of being a truly global organization, and therefore comes directly into our thinking in the human capital strategy. We shall return to some of these thoughts in Chapter 6 on embedding and sustaining a talent mindset and talent-multiplying capabilities in the talent-powered organization.

As to **culture**, the definition we use is one developed by Rich Hagburg: 'the shared set of assumptions, beliefs, values, understandings and meanings that guide a group's perceptions, judgments, and behaviours'. It affects the way people work together and how decisions get made, and is reflected in policies and procedures. It is reinforced through the evolution of social networks as well as formal structures, and it manifests itself both tacitly, through assumptions, and visibly, through artefacts and values. Changing it is a complex and time-consuming task.

Understanding the key cultural dimensions of your organization is an essential start – what characterizes it, where is it weak and where is it strong? Does it need to be uniform and consistent across all parts of the organization, or should it flex to reflect different business dimensions while retaining a common core? Does it need to change fundamentally?

In the context of the talent-powered organization, we shall be focusing in this book on the cultural attributes that relate to how people are managed and developed within the organization, and how they share knowledge and collaborate. In turn these will influence how engaged people are, and how they behave with others inside and outside the organization. We have talked of a talent mindset, and for that to permeate the organization, it must be intrinsic to the culture.

It starts with the espoused values, is reflected in the behaviours and actions of the top leadership team, is reinforced through communications and cultural symbols, is enacted through processes, and lived by every level of the organization. Lack of alignment at any point results in weakening of the culture and potential disengagement of the workforce. When practice starts to diverge from the espoused values, integrity is lost. We need look no further than Enron to see where failure can lead. Its espoused values were respect, integrity, community, excellence, innovation. What it practised was something very different.

All these aspects of your organization's culture should be assessed and evaluated as part of understanding this crucial dimension of human capital strategy. There are various tools and diagnostics available to provide objective understanding of the important elements of culture, such as Accenture's Culture Value Analysis (CVA), which provides a qualitative and quantitative snapshot of an organization's perception of its culture and the key elements that drive high performance. The CVA evaluates culture strengths and weaknesses given a particular strategic intent – thereby identifying gaps between what an organization needs to be and what it is. The analysis also:

- allows senior management to gain an objective and realistic understanding of the organization they lead;
- gives people who are further down in the organization a chance to have a voice;
- provides an understanding of subgroups within the organization, and hence points of synergy, fragmentation or conflict;

Figure 2.6　Closing the gap

■　establishes whether espoused values are consistent with practices, and you can honestly say you are walking the talk.

So as you work through a human capital strategy for your organization, you will need to think about each of these elements of leadership, talent, organization and culture within each primary business segment, geography and critical capability area identified. As with any strategy, there needs to be an objective assessment of current status – diagnosis of capabilities, critical workforce strengths and weaknesses, leadership talent and bench strength, cultural resonance and alignment, and organizational structure and effectiveness. You will need to assess what needs to change, where investment is required, and the case for those investments in improving business performance.

Finally, as we understand all the implications of the human capital strategy, it will become apparent that there may be implications back on the business strategy itself. As we have observed, organizations today are already struggling with shortfalls of talent and capability, and this is affecting their ability to execute their business strategies as they would like. We must therefore also consider the degree to which all these issues should shape the thinking of the business strategy.

DEFINING TALENT NEEDS

In creating a human capital strategy, the first task therefore is to understand the business strategy and define the talent needed to deliver that strategy, starting with a clear understanding of the talent on hand today. At Accenture, for example, we looked at our strategy for the next five to seven years and realized that we needed to hire many more people. When we set this against current attrition rates, we realized this meant that over the next few years we would be recruiting almost as many people again as we then had on the payroll. We wanted to continue expanding geographically, especially in Asia, and had to work out where and how we would get the people. Business issues and a human capital strategy were inextricably linked.

In much the same way, Harley-Davidson, the famous motorcycle maker, has been expanding out of its existing core markets of North America and Europe, into Asia and China in particular. Harold Scott, HR vice-president, talks about the challenges demanded by this business strategy – it entails not just having capability in China, but ensuring consistency of practice and people management across a new global business (Henley Media Group, 2007). Gruppo BBVA, the Spanish financial services giant, has set a strategy to support its goal of being among the world's top 10 financial services companies by 2010. Juan Ignacio Apoita, the chief manager of HR, is in no doubt about what he has to think about: 'We need to have the right people in the group to implement our business strategy,' and they have to think globally and not be too Spain-centric (Henley Media Group, 2007).

The second task is for the business strategy and leaders' vision to identify clearly the distinctive capabilities and how they need to be developed. This entails at least some basic segmentation: distinguishing between talent (present and potential) that is truly critical to strategic objectives and the development of the business's distinctive capabilities, and talent that is not.

For many organizations this should be fairly clear. For example, providers of public and consumer services will usually tell you that customer service is a critical capability. At Wynn Resorts, owner of the prestigious Wynn Las Vegas hotel, Arte Nathan (until recently the head of HR) clearly understands there is a 'direct relationship between employee satisfaction, guest satisfaction and profitability', so he concentrated on satisfying employees, the better to execute the company's business strategy (Henley Media Group, 2007). AT&T's Karen Jennings, the senior executive formerly responsible for HR and communications, is intimately engaged at the top levels in executing AT&T's acquisitions strategy and keeping AT&T as the world's most admired telecoms company. Developing the capabilities that drive successful acquisitions is therefore a distinctive competence and crucial to their business strategy (Henley Media Group, 2007).

Every organization needs more than one kind of critical talent, and will accordingly need to respond to the particular issues in acquiring different types of talent and the multiple strategic investments in talent needed. There are several options for classifying the different clusters of critical talent needed to execute strategic goals. One approach, advanced in McKinsey's so-called 'war for talent' and subsequently embraced widely in the business press, is to find and develop 'A' players (Chambers *et al*, 1998). Many companies have well-developed processes for identifying high-performing 'stars' and 'HiPos', high-potential employees, and then investing in attracting, developing and retaining that talent. However, you cannot multiply your organization's talent only by making disproportionate investments in the top 10 per cent of your workforce. A more holistic view of talent and a more comprehensive strategy are necessary.

To get the greatest return from human capital investments, your organization must know where it has leverage – which workforces and areas of business have the greatest strategic impact and are critical in maintaining your distinctive capabilities? High-performing organizations segment their workforces based on the strategic importance of particular workforces, skillsets and positions. They identify 'A positions' (Huselid *et al*, 2005), together with what we call mission-critical job families – the work most strategically important to the organization. They also develop deep understanding of the skills, capabilities and resources required for high performance in those roles.

We believe that a critical workforce now includes the HR staff who are or should be the principal enablers of creating and sustaining the distinctive competencies of a talent-powered organization. They are not often thought about in these terms, but organizations with good talent-management capabilities also tend to attract the best HR talent – so the best are likely to get better and those that do not or cannot respond will get weaker.

DISCOVERING TALENT SOURCES

Once you have identified the critical talent needs to support the business strategy, the next challenge is to consider where that talent might come from. One reality must by now be evident – we have to be very open to sourcing talent very widely, and greater diversity in the workforce and the ways in which people work will be the new norms. Our workforces in the coming years are going to be increasingly:

- diverse across every dimension – age, gender, ethnicity, personal circumstances, location, motivations;
- demanding in their expectations;
- global, virtual, mobile;
- different in the way they provide their services.

So how do we source such talent, and what implications will it have on the design of working practices, processes and jobs? Best practices in sourcing come from the disciplines of supply chain management, and high-performance organizations are starting to apply these techniques to the world of talent sourcing. Given the dynamic changes in the present age of talent, this must be one of the most important parts of any business strategy.

In thinking about talent we must use an approach which should be familiar from managing supply chains. This means asking questions such as: What talent have I got (inventory)? What sources of supply are available to me (supply sourcing)? Should I push inventory on my suppliers (contingent sources of talent)? Where should my people be located (warehousing)? Can I source from lower-cost locations? What attrition rate am I incurring (loss and shrinkage)? And do I understand future demand for skills (supply/demand balancing)? We shall return later to some of these areas, but in the context of strategy we need to think about strategic sourcing of talent, and this will need to include:

- A comprehensive understanding of current and future workforce demographics and their implications for talent supplies.
- A strategic approach to sourcing talent that reflects an organization's competitive strategy, present and future global workforce needs, and available talent pools to meet staffing needs.
- Talent supply chains which rapidly adapt sourcing channels and targeted talent pools to accommodate new strategic objectives and changing business conditions.
- Talent supply chains agile enough to allow the organization to manage changes in talent needs or supplies, adapt over time to changes in markets or business environment, and align the interests of all participating parties.

▪ Constant monitoring and adjustment of talent supply chains to ensure the continuous supply of talent needed to achieve business objectives.

▪ The right technology and analytics, so that predictive models can be constructed to produce forecasts of talent needs and improve talent-sourcing decisions.

As we have seen, in today's economic world a talent strategy cannot be static. Once you establish a global talent supply chain, however successful, you must keep it under continuous review to keep track of new sources of talent and new means to acquire it, which could at any time render your talent sourcing assumptions obsolete.

Valero Energy: an early talent supply chain

Texas-based oil refining giant Valero Energy boasts one of the first talent supply chains created by a global organization. The talent supply chain has dramatically reduced time to fill (from 120 days to 40 days) and cost per hire (from US$12,000 to US$2,300) during a time of phenomenal growth which turned the once small company with 2,000 employees into a US$75 billion global employer of 22,000 in just six years (Frauenheim, 2006).

This remarkable achievement is even more impressive when one considers the fact that when Valero hired Dan Hilbert in 2002 to manage employment services, the company's recruiting operations were entirely paper-based. From day one, Hilbert set out to build a world-class staffing capability to meet the needs of the rapidly growing and increasingly international company. It regularly faces difficult sourcing problems: for example, the start-up of a new refining complex. Valero needs to source talent from a variety of talent pools across the globe, from internal employees to outsourced contractors. As Hilbert explains, 'Project managers might be in the United States, combined with outsourced engineers from Canada, plus programmers in India and manufacturing workers in China.'

Hilbert designed a 'labour supply chain' system to monitor closely talent needs, sources and acquisitions: 'We wanted to have the right people, in the right amount, in the right place, at the right time, with the right skills' (Schneider, 2006). Projected talent needs are determined through analyses of past experience. The performance of various components in the chain – that is, current talent suppliers such as online job boards – is continuously monitored to assess the cost, speed, quality and dependability of talent acquisitions through those sources. Moreover, by analysing aggregate data on the sources of talent and subsequent job performance, fit with organization, culture and retention, Valero can determine the best talent suppliers.

The efficiency and effectiveness gains from this talent supply chain capability have been enormous.

The most significant results, however, are strategic. The 'global labour supply chain on demand' enables Valero to forecast demand for talent three years out – at the division and title level. These projections, together with talent supply and supplier data, allow Valero to make strategic decisions about whether to hire new employees, enlist contractors, or outsource the work. 'For the first time, talent pipelines can now be developed years in advance to meet specific future talent needs', Hilbert says. 'It's pretty revolutionary stuff' (Schneider, 2006).

Let us now explore some of the specific issues we have to consider in making talent-sourcing decisions.

Evaluating talent sourcing options – 'rightsourcing'

As we described in Chapter 1, talent can now be discovered just about anywhere in the world. At the same time, we have many different ways of accessing that talent. The traditional model of full-time employment with perhaps some supplementary part-time or contingent labour is no longer the only option. There is now an entire spectrum of strategies for accessing raw brainpower, many of which do not involve bringing people onsite, or even having them as employees. Hence, strategic sourcing entails an examination of all the possible options for accessing talent, and finding the best method, or the best mix of methods, for acquiring the specific talent and competencies needed to meet the demands defined through the human capital strategy of your organization. It requires much more creative thought than in the past.

This is what we mean by 'rightsourcing'. This concept has moved far beyond the opportunistic use of outsourcing for short-term gains in cost or capacity. Rightsourcing demands making a whole series of choices concurrently, assessing their rewards and penalties concurrently, and making the choices which, taken together, offer the best possible support for the organization's strategy.

Therefore rightsourcing means asking simultaneously: Where should we employ this talent – in our current locations or in new ones? Should we employ it ourselves or acquire it from outside suppliers or partners? Do we need it in one place or can we access it from multiple locations, through technology? Do we need it permanently on call or just at predictable intervals? Are there talent pools that are more or less attractive to us? Does the source of talent we have identified require changes to processes or tasks to access it effectively? Could we change the need for talent by changing the business requirement in some way?

These last couple of questions are very important. With the wide range of possibilities now open to us to connect and engage talent with our organization, we have to think through the design of working processes and the jobs themselves. This is requiring new levels of innovation in order to allow us to connect with these new pools of talent. There are many ways to do this, such as:

- Jobs or tasks can be redesigned to reduce the level of skills proficiency required – **downskilling**.
- Jobs can be moved or relocated to access different talent pools – **nearshoring and offshoring**.
- Jobs can be given over to another organization better equipped to find the right talent – **outsourcing or partnering**.
- Technology can reduce the need for some jobs completely and provide many opportunities to change job and skill requirements – **automation**.
- Jobs can be structured to be carried out virtually to allow people to do the work from anywhere – **restructuring**.

There are many examples that illustrate these, and we shall go through a number as we consider the many different ways to source talent today. Let us consider the extreme end of talent sourcing first – the phenomena of 'open sourcing' and 'crowd sourcing'.

Sourcing free brainpower via the internet

Open sourcing has gathered pace in recent years, and its best known manifestation is as an open collaboration amongst people to create complex software. The Linux operating system and the Firefox browser are the classic examples. Controls need to exist, and they work largely through peer reviews and peer control. Crowd sourcing (a term apparently attributable to contributors to *Wired* magazine in June 2006) takes this a stage further, as it relies on people simply volunteering knowledge or information, but with no controls or means to verify beyond that available to the originator of the request. For the purposes of this discussion we can effectively group them together as a new and creative means of accessing talent and brainpower.

They essentially rely on the principle that a growing number of people – especially in the Net Generation – value the creation and sharing of knowledge for its own sake, without the promise of financial or other reward. The motives of such people are myriad: some are altruistic, some are vain, some are following new models of creating value by building networks.

The best-known and widely used product of this movement is Wikipedia, the free online encyclopedia. At the time of writing (February 2007) the English edition had over 1.6 million articles, which made it the largest encyclopedia ever created. In a single month (December 2005) 17,000 users made five contributions or more to the English edition (source – Wikipedia's own entry on Wikipedia). The term 'wiki' is increasingly the term now used to encompass all technologies that support these forms of knowledge-sharing and collaboration. There are numerous forms of online forums and collaboration seemingly limited only by the imagination of the people who want to participate.

There are many examples of how organizations are starting to use these new sources of talent. Wikipedia's own entry on crowd sourcing lists a whole range, many of which have been reported elsewhere. Here are some examples:

- **Procter & Gamble** employs more than 9,000 scientists and researchers in corporate R&D, and still has many problems they cannot solve. They now post these on a website called InnoCentive, offering large cash rewards to more than 90,000 'solvers' who make up this network of backyard scientists. P&G also works with NineSigma, YourEncore and Yet2.
- **Amazon Mechanical Turk** coordinates the use of human intelligence to perform tasks that computers are unable to do. For example, it was used to compile content for a book published just 30 days after the project was started.
- **iStockphoto** is a website with over 22,000 amateur photographers who upload and distribute stock photographs. It now has a library

of more than a million stock photographs, mostly supplied by amateur photographers for a small fee if their image is used. Not surprisingly, it has captured a great deal of the market for stock images from expensive professional picture agencies.

▪ **Cambrian House** applies a crowd sourcing model to identify and develop profitable software ideas. Using a simple voting model, it attempts to find sticky software ideas that can be developed using a combination of internal and crowd sourced skills and effort.

▪ A **Swarm of Angels** is a project to use a swarm of subscribers (Angels) to help fund, make, contribute to and distribute a £1 million feature film using the internet and all-digital technologies. It aims to recruit earlier development community members with the right expertise into paid project members, film crew and production staff.

▪ **The Goldcorp Challenge** is an example of how a traditional company in the mining industry used a crowd source to identify likely veins of gold on its Red Lake Property by posting geological survey data on the internet and setting up a competition with a half a million dollar prize to anyone who could help it find the gold. It effectively got the mine surveyed, with over 1,400 entries from geologists, mining engineers and enthusiastic amateurs, for the cost of the prize money.

Personal web logs or 'blogs' are essentially the modern version of writing to corporations or newspapers, and some organizations take advantage of this form of individual expression quite overtly to gather feedback for themselves. For example, the Walt Disney Corporation can read detailed reports on every one of its resort operations from visitors who simply want to share their experience with others. So can any other major resort operator, but it seems there is a particularly large number of online Disney forums, and Disney customers are highly communicative – even reporting on the thrill factor of individual rides. This is a level of analysis never previously available to the resort industry, and it comes direct from the customer.

In all its forms, sourcing brainpower across the internet can put an immense variety of talent at your company's disposal. It requires some real creativity and imagination, as well as thinking about work in very different ways. It is of course a different form of talent, not directly connected to your organization (although the same tech-niques can be used to access internal 'brainpower'), and the obvious cautions apply. But given that the number of internet users has more than doubled since the year 2000 and that in 2006 the internet was available to over 1 billion people worldwide, every organization must consider how to use this resource in the future. According to the China Internet Network Information Centre in January 2007, China alone now has 137 million internet users (up 24 per cent from last year), and the annual growth rate of Chinese web pages is now over 80 per cent.

Virtual workers, teleworkers, home workers

From these new forms of talent sourcing, where the talent may be unknown to its user and certainly not contracted, we move on to virtual workforces. In Chapter 1, we noted some shifts in working patterns, such as the number of virtual workers in the United States rising eightfold since 2001. These workers are usually a form of contingent labour working on time- or materials-related contracts, but with growing demands for more work–life balance, there has also been a significant increase in fully contracted employees working virtually or from home.

Because technology allows us to access talent anywhere, anytime, it has allowed people to choose where they work from. This has made available under-used resources such as people with depen-dants at home. Virtual workers, teleworkers or home workers all have the great advantage of being able to work flexibly. Working hours are much less constrained, and mothers of young children have suddenly become able to make profitable use of those hours at the end of the day when the children are asleep. This sort of flexibil-ity can allow organizations to hold on to talent that might otherwise have left them.

Self-employed people are the largest contingent of the workforce working from home, but they are also an accessible source of talent. The young adults entering the workforce now, Generation Y, which we explored in Chapter 1, are perceived to favour self-employment as it gives them greater freedom and the power to shape their own jobs. However, personal economics usually get in the way as they start out. In the United States, according to the Bureau of Labor Statistics, only

1.9 per cent of workers under 25 are self-employed, compared with 5.3 per cent for those between 25 and 34. The over-35s account for 52 per cent of all self-employed people (2004 figures).

Virtual, home workers or self-employed people can save major overhead costs in accommodation, insurance and support infrastructure. Organizations in turn can save money by allowing the existing workforce to work virtually, or by a policy of hiring more of a virtual workforce. But these workers also bring great challenges of routine management and control, let alone alignment and engagement. It is much harder to instruct people, let alone inspire them, if they are not physically within reach. Working processes are significantly impacted, and virtual and contingent workforces put a heavy premium on effective use of IT, and even more on really good communications and management skills.

Virtual workforces work best when the nature of their job and their output allows them simultaneously to work in their chosen style and achieve their employer's chosen objectives. In those circumstances, alignment and engagement of the workforce become less of a problem and may even become self-reinforcing.

One well-reported example of an organization that made a specific strategic choice to access a talent market virtually is the US discount air carrier JetBlue. JetBlue has established a network of reservation agents who work out of their homes all over the United States. CEO David Neeleman's strategy was based on the assumption that happy workers would provide the best service, and so it has proved with his virtual workforce of home workers. Although JetBlue might have saved some money offshoring those jobs, the company gets good service from the home-based agents and turnover levels are very low (4 per cent in 2003) (Whelan, 2004). However, recently JetBlue has attracted media criticism over scheduling errors attributed to management failures – which demonstrates the importance of a continuous review of talent strategy to ensure that it delivers business objectives.

Location, location, location

Of course most organizations will continue the traditional mode of employing people to come to a place of work, and many forms of work still require it. As we noted in Chapter 1, questions of physical location have become much more complex because of the talent issues. To a great extent, as the estate agents or realtors like to say, it is all about location, location, location.

When it comes to employing an onsite workforce, one of the most visible signs of the new global war for talent is the feeding frenzy which develops at the discovery of new local talent markets. Talent hunters move even more quickly than tourists move to a new, virgin, tropical beach, and with the same effect. All of a sudden there is no room anywhere, there is no accommodation or service anywhere, and the price of everything shoots up. Once-attractive talent locations can very quickly become overheated and played out.

Cities such as Bangalore, Hyderabad, Dublin, Shanghai, Manila and Prague became fashionable as 'first-tier offshore cities' by offering abundant highly skilled, highly motivated labour at significantly lower wages than traditional locations (Hansen, 2006). But although emerging economies are still supplying new streams of talent in this way, the original first-tier locations have become much more difficult as places to locate operations. Wage rates are rising rapidly, accommodation is limited, and there are often problems with transport and infrastructure. It is especially important to understand these issues in considering where and how to locate operations in the developing economies of the world.

Table 2.2 shows the labour costs for IT and general back-office processes that might be sourced from lower-cost locations in developing countries. Business process outsourcing (BPO) has included not only true back-office-type functions such as finance and accounting and HR processes, but also customer-facing activities including call centres and customer support functions. The data come from leading service providers in Tier 1, 2 and 3 cities in 20 key sourcing destinations in Europe, the Middle East and Africa (EMEA), Asia and the Pacific (APAC) and the Americas. The average salaries are the mean of salaries at three experience levels – entry level, team leader and project manager. The data show that the most significant salary growth from 2005 to 2010 is expected in India, followed by Vietnam, China, Russia and Costa Rica. The squeeze on talent, particularly in IT services, has created different rates of wage inflation in different cities.

In May 2006 the journal *Workforce Management* reported on average projected 2006 base salary increases for technical workers at technology companies around the world. Its survey showed Indian

Table 2.2 Labour costs for IT and BPO
Source: neoIT (2006).

Region	Country	Salary average ($/pa) – 2005	Index 2005 (% of US)	CAGR 2005–10	Salary average ($/pa) – 2010	Forecast Index 2010 (% of US)
APAC	India	8,485	12	8.7	12,877	15
APAC	Vietnam	5,503	8	7.3	7,827	9
APAC	China	8,455	12	7.2	11,970	14
EMEA	Russia	17,882	26	7.2	25,316	30
Americas	Costa Rica	18,641	27	7.2	26,390	32
APAC	Philippines	10,736	15	6.8	14,918	18
EMEA	Czech Republic	19,125	27	6.5	26,203	31
EMEA	Hungary	22,760	33	5.8	30,172	36
Americas	Brazil	14,087	20	5.4	18,324	22
EMEA	Poland	26,380	38	5.3	34,152	41
EMEA	Romania	13,708	20	4.8	17,329	21
Americas	Mexico	19,427	28	4.8	24,559	29
APAC	Malaysia	18,564	27	4.4	23,024	28
EMEA	Slovakia	14,786	21	4.2	18,163	22
EMEA	South Africa	31,957	46	4.0	38,881	47
APAC	Thailand	9,651	14	3.9	11,686	14
Americas	Canada	37,589	54	3.9	45,513	55
Americas	United States	69,936	100	3.6	83,464	100
APAC	Singapore	36,700	52	3.3	43,169	52
EMEA	Ireland	48,178	69	3.2	56,396	68
EMEA	Israel	32,599	47	3.1	37,975	45

salaries rising at more than 11 per cent over the year. The Philippines was next at 9.2 per cent, with China and Russia both at 6.3 per cent.

Across general professional wage categories, countries in Europe come out on top. The Nordic countries, Switzerland and Germany are highest, followed by Japan, then the United Kingdom and the United States, which is lower than Europe and Japan in general, particularly at the moment given the relative weakness of the dollar. Some European countries such as Germany also have their average hourly labour cost raised by the relatively fewer hours worked – Germany, for example, stands at a yearly average of 1,700 hours compared with India at 2,300 hours.

Strategic sourcing in this context requires organizations to look ahead and ensure that they are not locked in to one location, but have the flexibility to move or open new offices when existing locations get too hot. There are still major advantages to using the talent in new and emerging locations, but in order to exploit them any organization needs:

- sufficient scale and visibility in a local talent market to influence local conditions rather than simply take what the market gives;
- flexibility and mobility to avoid getting trapped in an overheated location;
- the ability to spot talent in apparently unlikely places;
- high awareness of local laws and regulations, customs and cultures, constantly updated.

In any new talent location, familiar practices cannot be taken for granted: for example, in many parts of Europe drug tests and criminal background checks are not lawful. You also need to know how people like to work. In Poland, for example, workers, especially the young, have a very strong preference for working for themselves or for small companies. To use the best Polish talent in Poland, you may have to sign contracts with myriad small companies or self-employed people rather than employ directly.

Even with that kind of knowledge and awareness, your organization may not have the support systems necessary to sustain talent discovery and management, particularly recruitment and training. It may not be a big enough employer to exercise any influence in the local labour market. You may easily recruit and train local people only to lose them to a bigger local player.

Your organization may well decide that it does not have the capabilities to overcome such local challenges. You might well decide to find a partner with established local presence to supply the talent you need in a favourable location, by outsourcing, subcontracting or partnering. But that decision brings challenges of its own. If you do not know a place well enough to hire and develop your own talent there, what guarantee is there that you will find the right local partner to do it for you?

Essentially, you will need to be as rigorous in assessing the talent discovery and management processes of a partner as you would be in assessing your own. Will the potential partner show the precision and detail you need in delivering the specific mix of talent you want? This partner will be representing your organization in the chosen location, but will it reflect your values and preserve your brand or reputation? Will it pursue your strategic goals, and align and engage the local talent it recruits on your behalf? You must look for evidence on all these points – and learn from the good or bad experience of others.

DEVELOPING TALENT'S POTENTIAL

We have explored the **define** and **discover** elements of the talent multiplication model in some depth, although we shall have much to say about recruitment and the discovery of talent in the next chapter. We turn now to the remaining elements of the model, develop and deploy, but only in outline in this chapter, because they will be explored more fully in Chapter 4.

A capability for developing talent involves ensuring that employees continually acquire new skills and capabilities and prepare to take on new responsibilities. It establishes a central link between the development of employees' talents and the accomplishment of the organization's purpose and strategy. In that way, employee development is both ongoing and strategic. Although this capability embraces specific education or training initiatives, the talent-powered organization achieves much essential development simply as part of its daily work, through work roles and special assignments, and through relationships at work, particularly with line managers. It trains and develops all managers to attract, retain, motivate, nurture and grow talent. It rewards them when they achieve this, and sanctions them when they do not. They ensure that all managers develop the individual talents for which they are responsible and adopt this as their key priority.

DEPLOYING TALENT STRATEGICALLY

Organizations with capabilities in deploying talent adopt methods which match and align internal and external talent to where it is most needed and, best suited, and which allow it to meet both current needs and future challenges or opportunities. They create the best possible match between their employees' talents and aspirations and the needs of the business, day to day and in the longer term. They show imagination in giving their people opportunities to move within the organization, discovering new capabilities within themselves and gaining insights from previously unfamiliar parts of its business.

Talent-powered organizations are also adept at combining and recombining talent within the organization, enabling the sharing of knowledge and best practices, and encouraging continuous renewal and improvement of current practice within the organization.

Finally, they create expectations of high performance from all the people they employ, make them aware of how they can use their talents to greatest effect, give them the will and opportunities to do so, and provide them with continuous, constructive feedback on their performance.

UPS offers a good example of a talent-powered organization that creates value by multiplying talent (see box).

Case study – UPS

UPS, the global delivery company, has created a distinctive capability in multiplying talent as a foundation of its high performance. It has a system of highly integrated capabilities in defining, discovering, developing and deploying talent.

- **Defining Talent: The 'Winning Team' Imperative.** UPS's competitive strategy is to deliver value to customers through its ability to facilitate global commerce by synchronizing flows of goods, information and funds. This strategic focus requires efficient and reliable operations, excellent customer service, creative systems and technology applications, and a highly adaptable organization. Core competencies that are required of every employee include commitment to service, initiative, good judgement and loyalty. The company has also identified the 100,000 part-time workers who staff its hubs and the thousands of drivers who are its face to customers as mission-critical workforces. To build a winning team, UPS continually defines talent needs in terms of its strategic goals, including its commitment to preserving and building upon its strong culture (Soupata, 2005).

- **Discovering talent: Creating 'UPSers'.** At UPS, most people start their careers as part-time package handlers, drivers or clerical employees. Very often college students will work for UPS during their holidays and take up full-time positions with the company on graduation. This 'feeder system' of part-time recruits creates a huge internal pool of young talent to fill full-time and management positions. (Thomas *et al*, 2006a).

  UPS also believes strongly in promoting from within and actively discourages hiring managers from outside the organization. More than two thirds of its full-time management employees were promoted from non-management positions.

UPS leaders believe that managers who rise through the ranks are more committed and aligned to the UPS culture and business. Employees are hired for careers, not jobs. 'It really is a building process,' says John Saunders, vice president for human resources. 'We don't view it as, "We hired you to do this particular job." We view it as "This is going to be a 30-year process."' UPS hires people when they are young and attempts to keep them 'UPSers' throughout their careers. (Thomas *et al*, 2006a; Thomas *et al*, 2006b).

▪ **Developing talent: Build the person, build the business.** Building a workforce from the ground up requires significant investments in employee development. UPS invests heavily in its talent to ensure capability and commitment throughout the organization and through the various stages of employees' careers spending US$380 million a year on training and education (Hollis, 2004). UPS holds formal review sessions at which training opportunities, lateral assignments and other learning and growth options are discussed. Managers are routinely assigned to new projects within unfamiliar functional areas to develop their skills or deepen their knowledge of the company's operations. Investments in training, the strategic use of developmental assignments, and an emphasis on learning through relationships (eg mentoring and peer consultation) allow UPS to build its people as they build the business.

▪ **Deploying talent: Embrace change.** At UPS, job assignments have the double ambition of increasing employees' skills and expertise and creating business opportunities. UPS routinely assigns managers to new projects or positions within unfamiliar functional areas to develop their skills, deepen their knowledge, and broaden their understanding of the company's businesses. UPS also takes employees out of their regular departments and temporarily assigns them to problem-solving teams in order to stimulate new ideas and new solutions, share best practices and innovations, and encourage greater communication and collaboration throughout the organization. In addition, UPS often deploys star performers to start strategic initiatives that become significant new lines of business. The UPSers deployed to the initiative are able to expand their own skills and experience while making meaningful contributions to the business.

UPS's distinctive organizational capabilities in defining, discovering, developing and deploying talent enable the company to multiply talent, producing sustained high performance and a distinctive competitive advantage.

Source: Thomas *et al* (2006).

THE HR FUNCTION IN THE SPOTLIGHT

We have consistently made the point that in a talent-powered organization, the discovery, development and deployment of talent is the focus of the whole organization, bolstered by a pervasive talent mindset. However, we have so far said little about HR as the specific function that is most central in enabling these capabilities.

HR has long argued that it should become more strategic, is now positioning itself at the high end as a 'business partner', sees itself often as the champion of the employee, and certainly should be the enabler of finding and managing talent. But as a function it has suffered from under-investment compared with the other business and corporate functions. HR is not part of the so-called 'order to cash' cycle that defines the operating functions of a business, and it was too often left out in the large-scale investments in ERP systems and process re-engineering that characterized much of the focus of business change in the 1990s.

HR skills and focus for too long remained in the old paradigm of personnel administration and control, and the function was not outward looking or sufficiently business competent or focused. Policies and processes have not been harmonized or simplified, and have built up in inefficient and ineffective layers as organizations have grown through acquisitions and other changes. HR capabilities and governance are often fragmented across the organization and much of the time is spent on administration activities. Some of the critical talent development activities, such as training and learning, are also too often scattered around the organization and not managed as a critical investment and business capability. Change may also be constrained by the different business unit leaders who HR often have been reporting to and who like to keep things as they are.

The comic strip Dilbert brilliantly caricatured this form of HR in the character of Catbert, the evil HR director with his consistently incoherent application of policy and control. As recently as August 2005, one of the most popular articles among senior business leaders was Keith H Hammonds' account in *Fast Company* of 'Why we hate HR'. The article described well the frustrations many people have felt in the past with HR, but it also highlighted its importance to the organization, and what was needed from it. HR is a vital strategic function, but all too often it has not been up to the job. It now needs to change and respond, and with a significant sense of urgency:

> The human resources trade long ago proved itself at best a necessary evil – and at worst, a dark bureaucratic force that blindly enforces nonsensical rules, resists creativity, and impedes constructive change. HR is the corporate function with the greatest potential – the key driver, in theory, of business performance – and also the one that most consistently under-delivers.

(Hammonds, 2005)

We therefore agree with Dave Ulrich, the well-known academic and commentator on HR matters who recently observed:

> Some write about why they 'hate' HR, because essentially it does not respond to the opportunities of today's business challenges. It is probably more useful to figure out how to adapt HR so that it can adapt to and thrive in the business context facing most companies. Thinking about how HR can and should respond to these business challenges, evokes a number of new demands on HR.

HR AND TALENT MANAGEMENT: AN UNFINISHED EVOLUTION

HR is not talent management alone, nor is talent management only HR. HR is an enabler of many of the processes, but talent management is much more pervasive and requires engagement of the whole organization and the notion of the talent mindset.

But we are on a journey only partly completed, and new ideas, new approaches and new challenges are emerging all the time. Today, even agreeing on what talent management should be defined as or encompass seems to be a challenge. An article entitled 'Talent management: a critical review' published in the journal *Human Resource Management Review* (Lewis and Heckman, 2006) revealed many different definitions and areas of focus by analysts. At least most of them agreed that talent management is not just about HR.

It is interesting to observe the parallels of the development of talent management and the HR function with quality management and IT. The discipline of quality management began as businesses strove to meet the quality demands of government procurement in two world wars and mass consumer markets in peacetime. The initial response for many businesses was to set up a quality control function – special units or people with specialist responsibility for quality inspection and control. This tended to isolate quality issues in a silo, and antagonize operational staff and managers. As a separate concern, quality was always in competition with quantity, rather than enabling it. Auto companies, for example, would set aside great expanses of factory space to stockpile cars with quality defects so as not to shut down the assembly line.

Fortunately, companies moved beyond this stage of control and gave operational units management responsibility for quality, through systems such as Six Sigma and Total Quality Management. By making quality an integral part of the production process, rather than an antagonistic control function, many companies were able to achieve significant improvements in both productivity and consumer satisfaction. But they were still failing to integrate quality into their strategic objectives or make it part of the everyday mindset of their businesses. That is why the most successful companies moved beyond the stage of managing quality in individual units. Instead they made quality multiply throughout their businesses – making quality issues pervasive and a personal responsibility for everyone from strategic leaders to line managers and, indeed, all their workforce.

A very similar evolution took place in business data and systems technology. During the 1960s and 1970s many businesses became aware that they suffered from a mass of data from separate sources which was never collated, organized or made available for management. The initial applications of computers gave a powerful means of collecting and controlling data – hence data control departments. This offered businesses order and method, but it left operational managers dependent on the data control unit for essential or valuable management information. The personal computer revolution encouraged businesses to move to the next stage, and allowed operational units to access and manipulate data for themselves. So companies learnt to multiply information and knowledge – to inform and improve both long-range strategy and everyday operations. The function became more widely known as information management or information technology.

But information and knowledge were still difficult to access and share, and the various data management processes were not all integrated. IT was still not being seen as strategic in most organizations until late in the 1990s. This perception was changed by the internet explosion and dotcom boom: now IT is clearly seen as a strategic asset, and is an integral component of broader business strategy, and pervasive through all processes and parts of an organization. It is also interesting to observe how the IT function has also become much more business-oriented. There are many examples of people coming in to the IT organization from other business areas, and people moving from IT to other parts of the business as well. IT has, in most organizations, become 'mainstream' in a way that HR too often has yet to become.

By analogy with quality and data, we may distinguish three separate approaches in the evolution of talent management, as illustrated in Figure 2.7.

With **personnel control**, organizations are simply trying to achieve the basic people administration activities. They make little attempt to create comprehensive or integrated people development processes, but tend to focus on activities such as the administration of pay and benefits, the recording of attendance at formal learning and the control of recruitment processes. They have little understanding of what talent and competencies are needed and where there are gaps. People are treated as headcount, and the focus is on administrative

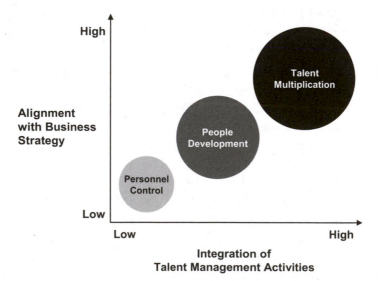

Figure 2.7 The evolution of talent management models

efficiency. Just as with quality and IT in the past, all the emphasis is on the control of inputs, and there is little understanding of the linkage between inputs and outputs and business goals.

In the **people development** approach, HR is focusing more on the development of people. Some form of performance management is in place, more or less supported by compensation and rewards and penalties, learning is better focused on improving performance, and most parts of the organization probably have some form of objective-setting process. But these processes are not truly integrated and are not executed consistently, and therefore the connections are not fully understood or recognized by line managers or clear to employees. There is no real understanding of the mix of competencies and skills in the organization, and talent is not being looked at collectively or strategically. Although some people metrics are in place, they are not sufficiently connected to business outcomes, and fail to show how to drive up value by investing in people. Here too is an analogy with quality and IT in the past.

With **talent multiplication** talent is viewed as a strategic asset and an integral component of business strategy. This approach, as we have already explored, begins with a pervasive talent mindset and culture driven by top leadership, top-down understanding of a human capital strategy required to support the business strategy, and understanding of the value linkages. Key talent needs are defined at a competency level, and this underpins the close integration between all the talent discovery, development and deployment processes. Employee value propositions are tailored and targeted with a clear understanding of the needs of the different segments of the work-force. HR supports consistent processes across the organization, but is also able to support a range of working arrangements and total reward programmes. Outcome and value measures associated with workforce performance are understood, while direct investments in talent and associated key performance indicators are tracked across the organization.

Most organizations today appear to us to be employing some version of the people development model of talent management, and rather too many are still taking a personnel control approach. To move toward talent multiplication, organizations must:

■ improve the degree of alignment between talent management activities and the business strategy (travel north along the Y axis in Figure 2.7);

■ achieve integration of all talent management activities (travel east along the X axis);

■ move from adding value by managing talent efficiently and effectively to creating extraordinary value for the organization by multiplying talent (create a bigger bubble of value);

■ shift responsibility for talent management from the HR function alone and get the entire organization involved in multiplying talent (make more people responsible for growing the bubble).

Evolving talent management capabilities to achieve talent multiplication must now be a critical strategic goal for any enterprise. It requires drawing on a wide range of capabilities new to the world of people management, such as supply chain management, to innovate in the area of talent discovery and supply demand balancing, marketing, to innovate in the area of communications, and branding, to attract potential talent. Given the range of challenges in finding and managing talent described in Chapter 1, we believe that the definition of talent management now needs to be all embracing to cover all the activities of discovering, developing and deploying talent. This is then clearly not the responsibility of the HR function alone, but needs to engage all of the organization leaders and managers, and other functional areas that support some of the processes involved.

SUMMARY

This chapter has argued that talent has become the single most essential factor in executing your chosen business strategy. Talent is a fundamentally new factor of production for any business – altogether more volatile, dynamic and transformational than those described in conventional economics.

A human capital strategy is essential to support your organization's strategic goals. Only with such a strategy can you:

■ anticipate and meet the talent demands of your chosen goals;

■ map how talent impacts on your whole organization;

∎ use the dynamic possibilities of talent to create new intangible value for your organization;

∎ create a 'virtuous cycle' of talent multiplication to power your organization to high performance.

We have presented a basic framework for talent multiplication. We have outlined the need to build new capabilities in defining, discovering, developing and deploying talent. The following chapters will now go on to discuss how to:

∎ discover talent from many sources and make diversity your biggest asset (Chapter 3);

∎ meet the skills crisis, developing and deploying skills throughout your organization, and make learning and development a key capability (Chapter 4);

∎ understand engagement and how best to assess it and maximize its strategic impact, making engagement the magic additive to your business performance (Chapter 5).

3

The Discovery of Talent

The wave of the future is not the conquest of the world by a single dogmatic creed but the liberation of the diverse energies of free nations and free men.

John F Kennedy, 1917–63

We have established the crucial importance of talent as part of business strategy, and we have identified the need to think broadly about talent sourcing strategies. Now comes the crunch question: how can you actually discover the individual talent you need and attract it to your organization? This question has become vastly more complex because of the need to source talent from increasingly diverse and unfamiliar talent pools.

Not long ago, companies could generally afford to limit their search for people to places or methods that were familiar to them. But now the familiar places are shrinking as sources of talent. And increasingly the most sought-after people – particularly those with special skills – are turning their backs on familiar methods of working and relationships with conventional employers.

A few decades ago you might have concentrated your search for some kinds of expertise on certain business schools, or leading international companies, or global IT hotspots and other specialist clusters. Today the rapid growth and spread of talent, knowledge and technology make it not just harder but also distinctly foolish to narrow your choices. You might easily be searching for some kinds of talent in, say, Bangalore or San Francisco, when the best sources are now in Zhengzhou or Rio de Janeiro. Indeed, thanks to the internet, the talent you need may even be in cyberspace. Then you have to figure out how to reach the right people and persuade them to work with your organization.

The global talent market has made workforce diversity inevitable. Successful companies are those that do not wait to be forced into it but actually embrace it as a source of advantage. Diversity should become your biggest asset.

In this chapter we shall focus on the key processes of discovery, from identification and attraction to recruitment and onboarding, and explore how to:

- identify the specific competencies you are looking for;
- ensure that all your recruitment channels and processes are geared to seeking out the specific talent you need;
- establish and sustain a distinctive employer 'brand' that can appeal to different segments of the talent market;
- promote word of mouth in establishing your reputation as an employer;
- make every part of the recruitment process attractive and effective for applicants;
- match the promises made in the recruitment process to the reality of working for your company, from the first day on.

This last point is especially important because it is going to take us to key messages of later chapters, especially on engagement and on sustaining the right talent culture in your company.

Talent is precious to your company – and to everyone else's. It is also precious to itself: people are becoming much more aware of their value, and in the markets with significant talent shortages, they are being made aware of that every day. That is why you must now put so much effort into your recruitment processes, and why that effort can be particularly rewarding. Best practice in recruiting is a form of learning which can quickly be transferred to all parts of your organization. Even more precious is what you discover, through successful recruitment, about what attracts talent to your company – and what repels it.

This learning does not end at recruitment – on the contrary you must use it to retain and motivate your workforce and enlarge its capabilities. Otherwise talent withers or walks away from you. What you learn from discovering talent is just as vital for developing it and deploying it. Best-practice talent-powered companies recognize that they are in a never-ending process of continuing to attract their existing talent, ensuring the promises made to them on recruitment and the brand values they have projected are fulfilled. It is a mindset which imagines that you have to re-recruit your workforce almost every day.

IDENTIFYING YOUR TALENT NEEDS

In the previous chapters we explored how economic change has created the new phenomenon of the 'knowledge worker'. This phenomenon has transformed the concept of 'labour', as an anonymous commodity with readily interchangeable units, into 'talent', a new kind of productive resource, far more varied in its attributes, one which is easy to combine but far more difficult to replace.

Yet the very qualities that make knowledge workers such a vital strategic resource make them very much harder to incorporate into a conventional supply chain model. If you are serious about meeting your needs for these essential people, you need to look beyond simple headcount. You need to create a clear picture of the specific combinations of knowledge, skills and attitudes now available to you in your present supply of talent, and match that against the specific combinations you need, now and in the future, to execute your chosen strategy.

To give a simple analogy: consider the task of soccer managers when they plan their squads of players. They need a combination of knowledge, skills and attitudes. From all the players they need knowledge of the rules of soccer, positional awareness, standard techniques and tactics, and their team's basic strategy and approach. Within the squad, the managers will need a blend of specialist skills – goalkeeping, defending, midfielders, strikers. They want some players who can play on the left of the pitch, some who can play on the right, and some who can play equally well anywhere. They want some expert tacklers, some expert passers, some expert dribblers, and a range of free-kick specialists. They also need certain standards of basic behaviour from the entire squad (arriving on time for matches and training, avoiding drink and drugs), and a range of other behaviours which may be appropriate for particular situations (some unselfish runners and passers, some solo artists).

The best soccer managers carry this detailed picture constantly of the blend of talents they need in their squad. They give themselves the ability to re-mix their talent blend to meet the needs of particular matches. They see where gaps are, and plan how to meet them (by developing existing players, or buying or borrowing new ones). They manage both to plan strategically for the future (anticipating retirement, injury, player departures) and take advantage of sudden opportunities (a desirable player storming out of a rival club). In all of these ways the best soccer managers – perhaps instinctively – are understanding their talent at a more detailed skill or competency level.

Managers in more conventional businesses also have to be able to understand their talent needs at the level of specific and general competencies that are necessary to fulfil the tasks and jobs required. They have to be able to model those competencies to map out where the requirements are as they look ahead, and where the gaps are today and in the near future. Competency modelling has proven to be a challenging area, but one where success ultimately is a prerequisite for high performance in every stage of the talent cycle. Fortunately success is becoming more reachable as new tools and techniques prove their worth.

COMPETENCY MODELLING AND ASSESSMENT

Competencies are the set of skills, knowledge and behaviours needed for an individual to carry out his or her role effectively. *Skills* are what the individual is able to do, developed from learning and experience. *Knowledge* is what he or she knows or needs to know to apply these skills and carry out the role or task, and *behaviour* – or attitude – is how the individual needs to act to be most effective. Behaviour incorporates both emotional and social components, and therefore includes characteristics such as self-awareness and confidence, and willingness to collaborate. Business performance is achieved by building the right set of competencies in the workforce, and aligning and deploying these most effectively to the particular job functions.

Understanding of competencies required should form the basis for linkage across all the talent management and development processes, from recruitment, through learning and development, to performance management, as shown in Figure 3.1. But it has proved hard in many

Figure 3.1 Competency processes

organizations to develop, implement and maintain, and has too often produced little of value to support decision making.

This area is now producing some evidence of best practice. Competency frameworks are most useful when they offer a pragmatic view of the most critical and distinctive competencies on which the organization depends, and when they are maintainable.

The process of competency management brings together several elements that result in a maintainable competency model. The first area is the competency framework which sets the standards for us to map our talent needs. The key elements of the competency framework are the competency categories we are seeking to track. These should focus on the critical competencies and common competencies required for different work groups, and aim for the right balance between being pragmatic (in other words, not too many of them) and giving sufficient insight on what is needed. Competency categories need to be demonstrable, measurable and observable. The principal competency categories usually divide into three main areas:

▮ core competencies – common skillsets and traits that reflect the organizational values and culture, and skill needs across the workforce;

▮ functional and technical competencies – the skills and knowledge required to perform the job or tasks;

▮ professional competencies – the behavioural aspects of competency such as personal and interpersonal skills and leadership characteristics.

The Lisbon Council's examination of skills of the future in Europe (Ederer, 2006) led us to consider a workforce skills framework to illustrate the range of skills and competencies needed in workforces today. This is shown in Figure 3.2.

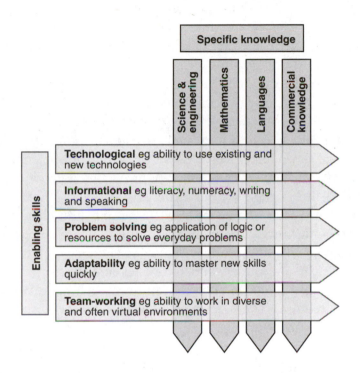

Figure 3.2   The knowledge-based economy demands a mix of both enabling skills and specific knowledge
Sources: OECD (2006b), Accenture (2007). (Note: this draws on some elements of the ongoing discussion surrounding the OECD's PIAAC programme.)

As individuals progress through the organization their roles may shift from execution and team support to managing and leading teams. Professional competencies such as leadership become more important as they progress upwards, while functional and technical competencies become less important. The importance of this will become clear in the next chapter, when we explore skills development and the common failure to develop professional competencies, particularly leadership, in the middle ranks of management.

There are many competency models and scales now available for particular competency areas, such as sales and computer programming, which can be used as a starting point for tracking your needs for functional and technical competencies. In the United Kingdom, for example, the Sector Skills Councils which cover a wide range of job areas have been developing such models for some time. The professional skill areas are more likely to need tailoring to the particular needs of your organization.

Next, you need to establish standards that provide a measurable scale of proficiency for each competency category. You can then set basic standards of proficiency for the critical competencies you need for particular jobs and positions, and use these to guide your talent discovery and development processes. Measuring proficiency levels has also proved difficult, and organizations employ a variety of techniques to do this. Generally, our experience suggests that no more than five-point scales should be used in setting proficiency levels, while in some instances, for example around the core competencies, bi-polar scales (IS/IS NOT proficient) may be enough.

You need clear and understandable scales and descriptors for the different levels of competency you require in each area. When you define each required competency, use observable-action words to begin the definition, such as 'identifies/utilizes/integrates/develops/ applies', not words that you cannot observe in action, such as 'knows' or 'leverages'. Identify the objective of the competency, and end the definition with an outcome. Use broad definitions that are action-oriented, so that they can be used across the organization, not just one job. One example would be '*Follows through with customer problems to ensure needs are being met.*' Such a definition will capture the general concept of a competency, not the specific tasks associated with it (which you can establish when you set the proficiency levels). Needless to say, your proficiency levels should build on each other, so that people with a given level of proficiency are assumed to have attained the next level below it.

We have gone into this detail to show that your definitions of competencies are critical to making them usable and maintainable in identifying your specific talent needs. Your individual workers need to understand them, so that they can maintain them for themselves through initial skill surveys or ongoing upkeep. Indeed, your definitions need to be usable in all the talent processes.

"The weird thing is we can't find anyone qualified to replace him."

Figure 3.3 The indispensable
First published in *The New Yorker*, 16 July 2001

ASSESSING COMPETENCIES AND PROFICIENCY LEVELS

If you have defined your required competency categories and proficiency scales well, individuals should be able to rate themselves with reasonable accuracy. Your organization should then need no more than a fairly summarized level of data which supervisors can check off to ensure that their people have the right proficiency levels.

There are also some interesting technologies somewhat akin to search tools that can automate some of the process of competency modelling and surveying. An example is a tool by the French company TriviumSoft. It offers a clever and distinctive way to assess and map the competencies in an organization's people using available information, such as their basic qualifications and CVs or skills maps. It then traces, in the form of a tree, the basic competencies that are common to all the workforce (the trunk of the tree), competencies that belong to certain sections (the branches), and those that are unique to individuals (the leaves). Figure 3.4 shows this for a real workforce, with the second tree-map indicating skills that are going to be lost through retirements in the next five years. Each block represents a specific competency, with the shades indicating depth. This gives a graphic and powerful view of which competencies need to be developed or recruited to rebuild the lost capabilities.

Within Accenture, we have developed a competency management framework that has helped us identify our own current and future talent needs. It combines common competencies required in all workforces, for example some of the professional competencies, together with specific competencies required for technical and functional skills for each workforce area. Self-assessments, skills surveys, CVs and peer and manager reviews are all used to keep competency models with proficiency levels for individuals up to date. We use this inventory in every part of our business, distinguishing the core skills we need in every member of our workforce from specialized technical, functional, managerial, industry-specific and other role-related skills. This inventory gives us a basis to plan, source and select talent, develop and retain talent, reward and manage talent, and plan its deployment throughout the organization.

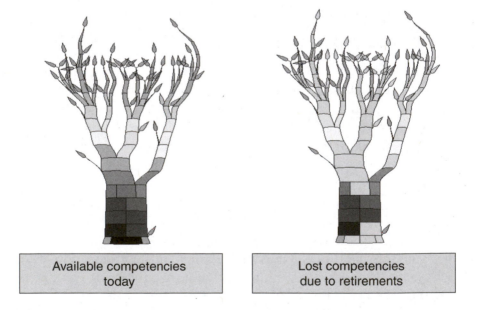

| Available competencies today | Lost competencies due to retirements |

Figure 3.4   A TriviumSoft picture of workforce competencies
Source: TriviumSoft.

RECRUITMENT: WILL YOU DISCOVER TALENT OR DRIVE IT AWAY?

We have looked at the challenges of identifying your detailed needs for talent and mastering the complications of seeking talent in new locations or new methods of access. It is time now to look at recruitment – the means by which you attract the right talent for your company, or the wrong talent, or no talent at all. To get the right result from your recruitment effort, you have to align every part of it with your overall talent strategy. Provided that you maintain that alignment, it might be right for you to outsource some or even all of your recruitment processes, or find a partner, particularly in unfamiliar locations.

Recruitment is a key strategic task for your company. An Accenture survey of 150 HR managers, carried out in 2003, showed that they rated recruitment in their top three of 13 processes. No surprise really, for if the recruitment process fails to discover the talent you need, your company will wither, as your current talent falls off the tree and is not replaced by new growth.

Recruitment, as we have said, begins with assessing in detail what specific combinations of knowledge, skills and behaviours you need to find by bringing new people to your company. This enables you to be much more specific and targeted in identifying recruitment needs, and using that information to identify the talent markets and segments to go after.

All your recruitment processes need to be aligned to that task, to make your company appeal to the specific people you need. Those processes have to create a positive experience of your company for all applicants. And all your recruitment channels, formal and informal, must deliver the same message about your organization and the employee value propositions you are positioning. Much is now being learnt in this area from the practices and experience of marketing. Concepts of brand, customer segmentation and marketing channels are all being applied to the process of talent discovery and recruitment.

WHAT APPEALS TO TALENT MARKETS TODAY

To begin with, it helps to have an understanding of what appeals to your market of potential recruits, and how they perceive you. The appeal of organizations to potential recruits begins at a general industry level. Some industries are seen by people today as very appealing and some are not. There are market workforce surveys of employees that give a good indication of how your particular industry is perceived. Accenture carries out regular surveys of graduates in order to understand what they are looking for. For the most recent survey in 2005 which covered five major countries and over 1,600 responses, graduates were asked a series of questions about what industries they found most and least attractive. The responses are shown in Table 3.1.

There are some surprises in there for certain industry sectors, which urgently need to discover what it is that makes them seem unattractive. In some cases concern centres on environmental issues and social responsibility. In other cases it may be because the industry is seen as dull or unappealing to the new generation of graduates and school leavers. Insurance appears to be suffering from this perception, which may or may not be fair, but which has been recognized, at least in the United Kingdom, as an industry-wide issue. The Chartered Institute of Insurers in the United Kingdom is setting up programmes to change the image. Perhaps given that insurance is really about assessing risk, comparing it to high-stakes poker would appeal to more people.

We have already touched on some of the things that Generation Y looks for – early responsibility and ability to shape their own jobs, investment in their training and diversity of experience, and even things like casual dress environments and informality. These are things that organizations in any industry could provide.

Apart from your particular sector's appeal, people judge your organization against more general attributes of work they are looking for. A number of surveys can give you insight into this. One example is a recent Gallup survey in the UK that covered more than 500 people from a range of backgrounds. It found that workers care most of all about finding their job fulfilling or a good match for their skills. This was mentioned by 18 per cent of respondents, closely followed by having opportunities to interact with the public or to help people, mentioned by 15 per cent. Various aspects of job flexibility were also

Table 3.1 Most and least attractive industries

Most attractive industries

	No 1	No 2	No 3
United States	Health and life sciences	Government	Electronics/high tech
United Kingdom	Media and entertainment	Health and life sciences	Government
Spain	Media and entertainment	Banking/financial services	Health and life sciences
France	Banking/financial services	Health and life sciences	Communications
Germany	Media and entertainment	Health and life sciences	Communications

Least attractive industries

	No 1	No 2	No 3
United States	Metal and mining	Retail	Chemicals
United Kingdom	Metal and mining	Retail	Aerospace and defence
Spain	Metal and mining	Government	Insurance
France	Metal and mining	Chemicals	Government
Germany	Metal and mining	Aerospace and defence	Capital markets

significant, for example in the way respondents were able to do their jobs (mentioned by 13 per cent), having flexible hours or a favourable work schedule (12 per cent), or being able to perform a variety of duties while at work (5 per cent). Many organizations recognize the importance of these attributes today, and it is not difficult to adopt them and use them as part of a selling message to prospective recruits.

Your brand as an employer

To extend the cross-over from marketing, it is quite common now to think in terms of an employer brand. An employer brand, just like the company brand, should represent the sum of your parts and describe what makes your organization unique, what you stand for, your cultural 'personality'. It therefore communicates your employer brand promise and what potential employees should expect if they were to join you.

Although it is very important to recognize what is attractive to potential recruits in general terms, the specific brand that your organization projects, no matter how clever the marketing is, must be authentic and reflect the realities of your organization. If you end up attracting people on a brand promise that you cannot deliver, then you are wasting their time and yours. In addition you will certainly upset your existing employees who will see it for what it is. So if you recognize a real mismatch between your organization's realities and the characteristics that attract potential talent, then you should look very closely at how to change those realities.

Your company has a brand image as an employer as much as it has to customers. Nike, Coca-Cola, Microsoft and Goldman Sachs (for example) all have strong brand images that will set expectations to potential employees about those organizations, and their employer branding should align with that. There is an important connection between how organizations generally market themselves, their services and their products, which will also set the scene for employer branding, and potentially vice versa. The messages need to be consistent. If you trade on your reputation for selling family-related products you must be a (reasonably) family-friendly employer. You cannot afford for your customers to hear that you make lone mothers work long hours for a pittance with no child care.

The employer brand should then be built on understanding the characteristics of people who are likely to succeed in your organization, and expressing the brand in a way that attracts more of those people. So you must accentuate qualities which everyone working for you would accept as part of the basic character of your company, and which foster their personal success: they might be things like swift recognition for outstanding performance, or particular care with working conditions, or high-quality relationships at work.

One brand value that has now become very important is the ability to demonstrate a sense of corporate responsibility. Barely mentioned 20 years ago, this is now a key factor in attracting and retaining talent. Quite simply, people want to feel that they are doing some good in the world through their work – or at least doing no harm and they are more often looking for some meaning in the jobs they are performing. Many organizations today are offering their people direct opportunities to do good works.

Organizations whose activities attract controversy – including energy, chemical and tobacco companies – are making increasing efforts to re-identify themselves as people who make the world a better place, and provide opportunities for their employees to help them in that quest. BP's environmental awareness efforts are an example.

Case study: BP

With a series of acquisitions in the 1990s, British Petroleum shifted its strategy and focus from oil to energy. The company was renamed BP in 2001, with the old initials reflecting its new identity as a global energy company with interests 'Beyond Petroleum'.

> No other giant oil company comes close to BP's alternative-energy efforts – except perhaps Royal Dutch Petroleum based in the Netherlands, which includes various companies under the Shell name....BP and Royal Dutch are making strategic bets that renewable-energy technology will advance, grow cost-efficient, and move from niche markets to the mainstream sooner rather than later. The two companies 'actually have taken forward-thinking positions on these issues,' says Eric Orts, a professor of legal studies and management at the University of Pennsylvania's Wharton School.... The game plan for companies like BP and Royal Dutch is to be ready when that changeover occurs, likely in the coming decades, and be positioned to reap a financial windfall.
>
> (Wee, 2002)

Indeed, in 2005 BP launched BP Alternative Energy, a new business dedicated to the development and wholesale marketing and trading of low-carbon power (DataMonitor, 2006).

In today's very competitive talent market, as much effort needs to be spent on building and promoting what you represent as an employer as on establishing your brand as a supplier.

The power of word of mouth

The next challenge is to ensure that your employer brand is projected consistently and with sincerity. In today's connected world it is all too easy for any lack of consistency in your brand promise and reality to be exposed ruthlessly and rapidly. Online forums such as Vault.com now serve as a 'global grapevine', giving an instant message about your company to potential employees with the authority of those who have actually worked for you.

Here is a sample entry from Vault.com (company name suppressed and employee name changed):

> For the first several years it was not too bad a place to work, even though the place was highly chaotic and a substantial number of employees were dysfunctional. They hired a production manager named Kurt. The guy was good at managing inventory, but the problem was he treated people like inventory also. He managed by fear and intimidation, he had absolutely no people skills. He once told me in a meeting, 'I fought in the war for you!' I thought he was crazy. Anyway, complaints about Kurt (there were many) went unheeded by top management. They did not even want to hear about them. Their quality policy? I was once told by my supervisor 'You're in charge of quality.' This company was a textbook case for bad management. One could write a book about it.

Through Vault.com and similar sites, potential recruits worldwide can read this sort of entry about your company as an employer. However, that is not the only lesson from this extract. Notice the power of the bad line manager to destroy the company's reputation and drive present and future talent away from it. Notice the generational gap in attitudes between the war veteran Kurt and his younger workers, a point we shall touch on later. Notice also how this company throws a new and important responsibility on its employee without preparation or support or even notice. We have all been warned.

TAILORING THE EMPLOYEE VALUE PROPOSITION: THE WORKFORCE OF ONE

We have talked so far in general terms, implying a single employer brand and value proposition. But we know that every worker you employ or use has a separate and personal mix of hopes and fears, which will make his or her alignment with your organization strong or weak. The increasingly diverse talent we have to attract from the much broader range of talent pools makes this ever more important to recognize. Tolstoy once suggested that happy families resemble each other but every unhappy family is unhappy in its own way. In the workforce context, Tolstoy was wrong. Every worker is happy or unhappy in his or her own way.

This means that modern organizations have to move beyond presenting a single employee value proposition (EVP) to all their employees. Instead, your organization must seek, as far as possible, to customize the value proposition to the needs and hopes of each sought-after employee, within the overall framework of consistent messages about your brand. This idea we characterize as the 'workforce of one', and it bears a close resemblance to the concept in modern marketing of mass customization (Cantrell, 2006). Just as global organizations seek to make each of their customers create a personal relationship with their global brand, so employers must seek to induce each employee to form a personal link with them as an employer of repute.

Effectively, organizations need a menu-driven approach, which as far as possible allows individuals to pick the personal gains and working relationships they seek from their work – and to change them at different stages of their lives. That will mean offering your people the chance to balance their desires for money, personal time, job satisfaction, status, progression, social life and general self-worth. It is certainly a challenging idea to implement, but one that will be increasingly necessary in order to hold on to people and make any organization appealing to a demanding generation of workers.

Companies should segment their talent in order to offer different experiences and values to specific groups of employees or potential employees. Once an organization has identified distinct employee segments with shared needs and preferences, it is possible to manage them with differentiated talent management practices. Treating the workforce as a collection of distinct groups of employees who share certain characteristics – age or generation, geography, work role, career values, etc – allows organizations to vary reward, development and learning practices accordingly. So, for example, in attracting older workers to stay or join the organization, part-time working or job sharing, benefits with more of a bias towards health insurance and support, or job support that is focused on their capabilities, will all be important in creating a compelling EVP for them. These characteristics will be different from those that might excite young workers in their first job.

Yahoo! created a compelling EVP to help the company attract, engage and retain talented employees. Yahoo! wanted its initial EVP to speak to all of the different kinds of people who were attracted to working at the company and all the different reasons they were engaged in their work there. Yahoo! brought the lessons and principles from product branding to the employee realm, to build an EVP and internal brand that communicates the meaning, promise, and overall employee experience that is unique to Yahoo! Libby Sartain, chief people officer, worked with the chief marketing officer, Cammie Dunaway, to come up with 'life engine' as the internal and external brand: 'The simple phrase was meant to convey empowerment and direction' (Stanford, 2006).

For Yahoo! customers, 'life engine' would suggest all the ways in which the Yahoo! search engine served as a 'guide' or 'compass'. To employees, the 'life engine' EVP conveyed a sense of aspiration as well. It gave employees and potential recruits the sense that Yahoo! was something bigger than themselves, while being at the same time uniquely personal for each employee. Employees are encouraged to define for themselves how Yahoo! is their life engine. For instance, with the rollout of the EVP, each employee received a customizable license plate frame that read: 'Yahoo!: My _____ Engine'. Employees filled in the blank with their own EVP. For example, Sartain's said: 'Yahoo! My FUNPLACE2WORK Engine'.

The Yahoo! EVP engaged employees by infusing their day-to-day work activities with greater meaning, by connecting them to something bigger than themselves, and by enabling them to identify with Yahoo! on a personal level.

Your organization should build into its recruiting strategy the fundamental idea that people will be valued if they become part of it

– and not only the recruits but the circle of family, friends, community and culture to which they belong and which help to define them.

Harrah's Entertainment is a good example of this all-embracing culture. Harrah's code of commitment – something every new employee learns at orientation – is a verbal and written promise the company makes to its customers, employees and communities. It demonstrates that Harrah's wants to treat the employees well and give them a great place to work, treat customers well, and be a responsible corporate citizen. The code is not just a set of values espoused by senior leadership: Harrah's employees actually live by it, and it is widely acknowledged to have been the first in the industry. Jerry Boone, Harrah's vice president of human resources, claims that 'at Harrah's, our word is our bond' and 'responsible gaming is something that Harrah's pioneered'. Indeed, Harrah's has been a good corporate citizen by giving back to the community and being honest with the community, regulators, and employees (Thomas, 2005b).

Many organizations such as the Campbell Soup Company are now contemplating how to tailor human capital management practices to different age brackets. Nancy Reardon, Campbell's chief human resources officer, explains:

> We've long segmented potential employees by generation-based preferences to help with our recruiting efforts. For example, if a person is graduating from college and looking for the best job, we know people of this age may value an ethical employer with a warm, team-oriented work environment over an employer with the best financial remuneration. We'll target them accordingly. Now we're taking this notion beyond recruiting and exploring how to build work environments that appeal to each generation. Our goal is to make our employee value proposition more customizable.'

To further this goal, the company has been working with the Institute for the Future on further defining generation-based differences, and has started to experiment with programmes such as offering reduced work hours, telecommuting, and other flexible work arrangements for those nearing retirement age (Cantrell and Foster, 2005).

RECRUITMENT CHANNELS

Having decided your brand strengths as an employer and the mix of rewards you are going to offer to potential talent, you need to communicate these things effectively through all available channels.

Your first step should be to use internal recruitment channels, such as intranet communications, newsletters and word of mouth. It is obviously cheaper to hire internally, and the individual will be a known quantity, adapted to the company culture and processes, and therefore also able to become productive quickly. Most important, internal recruiting allows you to develop people and give them additional opportunities within your organization. Job mobility does not have to mean moving jobs between organizations.

For external recruits, the first channel you must look at is your website. The web has become a prime source of job applications for modern organizations, second only to employee referrals in importance as a source for new talent (24.7 per cent vs 27.1 per cent: see Table 3.2). Almost every applicant will go to the website to get more information on your organization and a feel for it. If you want to attract talent, you need a compelling website, offering a clear and immediate appeal to potential applicants from all the segments you seek to access. It needs to be easy to use and responsive – as quick and convenient as buying online. Of course its content should be matched and reinforced in all the other recruiting channels you use, including agencies, public job websites, advertising, direct recruitment and not least, word of mouth and personal contacts. Websites today must be exciting and compelling – if you are trying to attract tech-savvy people, then having a mundane website is simply going to put them off.

There is a range of public recruitment websites and specialist sites that focus on particular types of jobs and industries. They are all channels to which you need to connect in order to open up access from as many sources as possible. Public websites are evolving to provide more direct guidance to applicants on what skills they need to be successful in a job. For example, the German Ministry of Employment has looked at setting up their website to include the ability for people to search for applicable jobs based on their skills – effectively a job-matching service. Beyond that it could identify where the skill gaps are for people who were interested in particular jobs or areas of work, and recommend training courses for them to take to close those gaps.

Whatever recruitment processes you use, it is essential that they all deliver the same message about your basic brand as an employer.

Table 3.2 Traditional sources for hiring employees
Source: Crispin and Mehler (2006).

Sources	2005	2004	2003	2002	2001
Employee referrals	27.1%	31.7%	28.5%	26.6%	23.3%
Internet	24.7%	29.6%	31.8%	27.0%	20.5%
College	8.0%	5.6%	2.4%	Not surveyed	Not surveyed
Direct Sourcing	7.4%	6%	2.6%	Not surveyed	Not surveyed
Print	4.6%	5.5%	3.8%	4.8%	Not surveyed
Career fairs	5.2%	3.2%	2.8%	3.2%	Not surveyed
Third-party agencies	5.2%	3.2%	1.2%	Not surveyed	Not surveyed
Walk-in	4.2%	Not surveyed	Not surveyed	Not surveyed	Not surveyed
Temp-to-hire	3.2%	Not surveyed	Not surveyed	Not surveyed	Not surveyed
All other	5.5%	15.2%	26.9%	38.4%	56.2%
Just don't know	5.0%				
Total	100	100	100	100	100

There is some scope for using specialist channels to deliver a more tailored EVP to particular segments of talent, especially at a personal level when you are approaching a specific individual. But these efforts should not be at odds with your employer brand. If you need to recruit through a fundamentally different EVP from your core values as an employer, there is something wrong, either with the values themselves or with the talent strategy you have adopted to execute them.

THE RECRUITMENT PROCESS

You need to ensure that your entire recruitment process is as fast and effective as you can make it – from the moment a requisition is raised for a new recruit, through to selection, induction, training and placement. With the shortages in talent, new skills being demanded by organizations, and the increasingly diverse talent sources being accessed, the whole process has become more complex and involved. In hot talent markets such as the ones in IT services in India that we looked at earlier, we have been looking at as many as 30 or 40 CVs on average for each job position we fill. Processes to work through this effectively have therefore become paramount. The golden rule is to think how applicants to your company would feel about the treatment you give them at each stage of recruitment.

Best practice today uses the defined competency models for the positions being sought as a means of screening potential employees. This provides much greater assurance that the right talent will be found efficiently: it saves effort both for you and for applicants. Within Accenture, we use the competency models to assess candidates from their CVs, and refine the views of proficiency through structured interviews. Professional competencies will be assessed through other structured techniques such as team exercises to provide insight into leadership and team-working competencies of candidates, which go together with reviews of their leadership history.

A word of caution is due at this point about psychometric tests. Many companies are still using the same kinds of respondent tests that were developed in the 1970s and 1980s, and people usually have some ability to see through them and give the right answers. Applicants for a position in sales, for example, are unlikely to tick the box saying, 'I do not like meeting new people.' If you rely on psychometric testing you need to verify its results empirically: did it really help you find the right profile of talent?

After screening, it is extremely important to give all applicants a good experience of your recruitment process, particularly in your speed of response to them and the quality of your communications. The people who represent you at any recruitment event should give a good impression of you – but how often do companies send their best people? Many do the exact opposite. They send the people they think they can spare from supposedly more important tasks.

By the same token, many companies do not spare their best people for actual recruitment interviews. They often delegate this to HR people, sometimes with specialist help from psychologists. The future line manager for the position concerned often fails to show up, or fails to make any significant contribution. This too is a very poor signal to future recruits. You should recognize that a recruitment interview is a two-way process – it is not just about you assessing new talent but also about them assessing you.

Marriott executives will tell you that in a service industry, nothing is more important than hiring the right people. As a result, hiring by gut instinct is frowned upon at Marriott. Hirers at Marriott use a quantitative, predictive model that combines assessment of job skills with an evaluation of candidates' mindsets and values – attributes that Marriott considers to be more important than skills or experience. 'We can teach people the job, but you can't teach people to be friendly, for example, if they aren't that way already,' says COO Bill Shaw. Executive vice president of human resources Brendan Keegan agrees, 'Marriott drives and supports its culture by hiring people who already live by its values' (Thomas, 2006).

Your recruitment process is a very important factor in creating good or bad word of mouth about your company, which again can be magnified and disseminated by the global grapevine. Applicants to your organization influence other potential applicants – a poor experience for one applicant may put off thousands of other people you do not know. Here are two negative samples, from a forum in www.pinoyexchange.com on call-centre recruitment:

> My friend actually had to wait up to 3 am for final interview. I hope this interviewer can be more considerate, knowing most of them were there from 9 in the morning. During the online test... lot of system crash and some of the applicant had to come back and re-take the exam.

> I got there around 11 am and was finally interviewed around 5 pm and then final interview at 6 pm. They were so disorganized (and obviously undermanned) and could not give the applicants a timeline of when we would get our turn. I only stayed that long because I drove so far to get to that darn place. After the final interview (with a girl who wouldn't even look at me the whole time, she was typing on her laptop) I wasn't even told what to expect next. They just shook my hand and showed me out. I waited along with some other applicants at the reception – there were only a couple of us left. We had to knock on one of the HR room doors just for someone to tell us what to do! I don't even feel bad that I didn't get the job, i would hate to work in such a hell hole!

Such word of mouth could lose the companies concerned thousands of applicants. The damage could be magnified in that such forums tend to be studied by the most ambitious, discriminating and of course internet-savvy talent.

Keep your promises

It is even more important to match the promises made to successful applicants in your recruitment process with their actual experience when they start work for you. The first day at work is a major talking-point for people among their family and friends. Many of the 'hot' new locations for talent are places with extended family or communal networks, where new recruits to your organization are a major source of information about it.

But new employees can sometimes have a wasted first few days or even weeks. They may wait hours to meet their line managers – perhaps they never do, if the line manager has decided to go on leave or on an out-of-office assignment. Clear objectives for their roles might not be immediately available; there might be no space, or telephone, or computer termina ready for them. Their pay and personnel administration might not be in place. The impression that treatment gives to new employees – and everyone who talks to them or reads their comments online – can be fatal and irreversible.

Bright Horizons Family Solutions, the world's leading provider of employer-sponsored childcare, is well aware of the importance to new employees of their first experience of joining the company. Indeed, this is used to engender a culture of respect as a key to building engagement. Dan Henry, senior vice president of human resources, explains that Bright Horizons provides what it calls 'world class welcomes' whenever a new employee joins the organization. They welcome new recruits the family into the Bright Horizons 'family' with gift boxes and flowers delivered to the home, announcements with photos wherever possible, and welcomes at quarterly staff meetings. In this way, the company demonstrates that it respects and values employees and their families (Henry, 2006). Note too how this initiative aligns the brand as an employer with the brand values to consumers.

Outsourcing recruitment

The recruitment process has become so important and so much more complex that many organizations have turned to recruitment outsourcers, especially in new and unfamiliar locations. It is possible to outsource the entire recruitment process, from finding applicants to making the successful ones ready to work, and this may create opportunities to build an integrated recruitment process. Alternatively, your organization can outsource individual components of the process, particularly interviewing and filtering applicants. Some outsourcing companies have built up notable expertise in screening out the talent you do not want: much of this can now be done automatically by sophisticated technology which matches the specific knowledge and skills you demand with applicants' CVs.

Whatever decisions you make on your recruitment process, you need to make an informed and holistic judgement on the results. You need to know whether the outsourcers are delivering to your organization the talent it needs to fulfil its objectives. That is infinitely more important than making short-term savings – particularly since technology is constantly reducing the cost of recruiting people. There is no point in saving recruitment costs and then recruiting the wrong people, who actually drive down value in your organization. If you do decide to outsource any part of your recruitment process, you must give the outsourcer a clear idea of the talent you are looking for, and base your relationship on the outsourcer's ability to supply that talent as quickly as possible.

In this connection, you might like to study the many online forums which rate recruitment agencies – often as scathingly as those who rate actual employers.

Retrieve information

Whoever does your recruitment, you should remember that at every stage of each process and through every channel you are going to receive valuable information about different talent markets and your strength in them as an employer. You need to retrieve every nugget of this information and use it to update your global talent supply-chain and sourcing policies, and indeed your entire human capital strategy. Again, your competency model will enable you to do this in sufficient detail to relate information to your specific talent needs.

Particularly through your internal recruitment processes, and their success or failure, you may derive insights into the learning and development needs of your people and their engagement levels. Above all, your recruitment results will tell you whether or not you are becoming a more diverse organization or simply replacing like with like.

SUMMARY

Talent-powered organizations embrace diversity in many different ways to gain competitive advantage from the proliferation and complexity of talent markets. They recognize new sources of talent and new working options for the best talent, and leverage these new opportunities to enhance their organizational capabilities and performance. Talent-powered organizations build capabilities in defining their talent needs, discovering talent from many sources, and appealing to diverse talent because they understand that diversity – in their talent and in their methods for discovering talent – is a critical source of competitive advantage.

Discovering and recruiting talent is becoming a lot harder, and the impact of more diverse sources and types of talent through new recruitment channels is putting renewed attention on the processes and capabilities involved. As you plan to source talent, you need to be aware of all the rewards and risks of using new talent locations and new methods of access to talent.

When you have identified the sources and type of talent you need, you need to send people a double message: first, about your general 'brand' and appeal as an employer and second, about the specific expectations that individuals can meet by joining your organization. You need to maintain those double messages consistently in every recruitment channel you use – especially your own website – and at every stage of your recruitment process. You must seek to extinguish everything that might contradict those messages to a potential recruit. Finally, and most important of all, you must keep the promises you make to new recruits as soon as they start working for you – and thereafter throughout their careers.

4

From Talent Development to Deployment

> If money is your hope for independence, you will never have it. The only real security that a man will have in this world is a reserve of knowledge, experience, and ability.
>
> Henry Ford, 1863–1947

In the first chapter we described the increasing talent shortages caused by a range of demographic factors and competitive pressures. We also highlighted current concerns around education, particularly in the developed world, which further squeeze the supply of talent entering the workforce. All these factors have greatly increased the challenge of having the talent ready, able and willing to work towards your business goals.

Your prime response must be to work hard to retain the skills and resources you have and develop them further. In Chapter 3 we talked about employee value propositions (EVP), and few propositions are more valued by employees than seeing their organization invest in them and help them to build their skills and competencies. In this chapter we turn our attention to talent development and deployment as key organizational capabilities of talent-powered organizations that support talent multiplication and competitiveness.

We shall first take a look at the changing nature of skills required by modern businesses, to provide a context for examining approaches to training and learning. We shall spend some time considering what makes a high-performance learning organization, and then review the approaches and techniques that are helping to accelerate new skills uptake and knowledge retention. Finally we shall discuss strategies for deploying talent, focusing on the two interdependent aspects of managing the distribution of work and developing workforce capabilities.

NEW DEMAND FOR NEW SKILLS

The rise of the celebrated knowledge worker is a reflection of changing skills requirements in the workforce. As businesses continually apply new techniques, new processes and new growth models, and work in new locations, their need for upskilling becomes constant and continuous.

It is hard to get any real quantitative view of the likely future need for skills retraining or upskilling, but the American Society for Training and Development has estimated that no fewer than 75 per cent of existing American workforces will need retraining over the next 10 years. This estimate could even prove to be optimistic as globalization and the advancement of technology are such forces for change, and the competitive edge of organizations and indeed even of countries is now more and more dependent on the skills of their workforces.

The knowledge economy constantly redefines the skills it demands from current workforces. In particular it requires ever-greater competencies associated with information technology, to a point where it has become a basic currency of knowledge workers – perhaps we have to think about a technology quotient in people alongside the idea of an emotional quotient. Problem-solving skills, ability to innovate, dealing with change, team-working and people management skills are other important primary skills for every modern organization. As noted in Chapter 1, other skill sets in short supply are engineering, technology and IT systems development capabilities, and leadership skills at all levels. Moreover, most businesses have a constant need to upskill sales and customer services.

In recent studies on adult competencies and learning (such as OECD 2006b, on which these comments draw), the OECD has observed that

the facility to learn new skills is itself becoming a critical competence. This is undoubtedly true, and it can be extrapolated to the
organization itself. A talent-powered organization is also a learning
organization: it has mastered how to invest in learning and development, and knowledge management capabilities, and use them to
accelerate skills building and thereby improve competitiveness in all
its critical workforces.

But the harsh truth is that few organizations today are achieving high
performance in learning and skills development of their workforces.
There are significant gaps between the expectations of top leaders and
what is really happening in their organization's training and learning
functions. These have been the consistent findings of Accenture's High
Performance Workforce Studies over the last several years. The study in
2006 (Accenture, 2007) again found that few respondents described the
performance of their top three functions as high:

Among executives citing this function as one of their three most important...	Per cent rating the function's performance as high
Sales	25
Customer Service	25
Finance	19
Strategic Planning	33

These low assessments by top executives of the performance of these
key functions can be attributed to their equally low assessments of
their training and learning functions. First, they do not see a sufficiently clear connection between business needs, and HR and training
initiatives – only 36 per cent of respondents said their companies
tailor their HR and training support to each function's needs and
contributions to the organization. Second, many companies do not
measure the business impact of HR and training efforts, or they use
metrics that do not necessarily translate into business results. Nearly
40 per cent said they had no formal measures to gauge the impact of
their HR and training efforts on the performance of their top three
workforces, while 39 per cent said they had such measures but only
for some HR and training initiatives. Finally the survey also showed
low confidence by top executives in their organization's capture and
sharing of knowledge: nearly half the respondents described this as a
challenge or a severe challenge.

These findings emerged despite evidence that organizations are spending more on training. According to the research group Bersin & Associates (2007), spending on training in North America increased in 2006 by 7 per cent to reach 'record levels'. The average corporation spent just short of US$1,300 per person, although there were wide industry variations, from healthcare at US$400 per employee to more than US$2,000 per employee in professional services. Evidently current practice falls short of best practice, and it is clearly worth exploring further the nature of a high-performance learning organization as a critical facet of a talent-powered organization.

DEVELOPING TALENT: CREATING A HIGH-PERFORMANCE LEARNING ORGANIZATION

A learning organization is one that values, enables and measures learning as a critical part of the way it does business and what defines it. It begins with the notion of a talent mindset that we described earlier. From the top down, people have to see learning as important, part of their job, and part of the culture and fabric of the organization. Such organizations systematically share best practice, learning and knowledge, and they focus responsibility for learning and development across the organization at a senior level. Moreover, they innovate through continuous capability development, to replace established routines by something more effective.

In a more expansive way Peter Senge, who developed the idea of learning organizations, described them as 'organizations where people continually expand their capacity to create the results they truly desire, where new and expansive patterns of thinking are nurtured, where collective aspiration is set free, and where people are continually learning to see the whole together' (Senge, 1990: 3).

We would also argue that to be a great learning organization, you also have to be a teaching organization. An organization that talks about stewardship or development of people must emphasize everyone's role in teaching and developing others as a core value. Noel Tichy, University of Michigan Business School, the respected commentator on leadership, observed, 'We have looked at winning companies – those that consistently outperform competitors and reward shareholders and found they have moved beyond being learning organizations to being teaching organizations' (2004).

Learning is not just what happens in training courses and programmes, but something that happens continually. Long-standing experience, confirmed by countless studies, shows that most of what people know and retain is from what they learn on the job through actual experience: the more they experience, the better they become. A learning organization must be one where experience is passed on and shared, and where people coach and teach each other naturally as part of their everyday routine, and one that invests seriously to improve formal learning experiences and the management of knowledge across the enterprise.

We discussed earlier how talent-powered organizations are now making more focused investments in workforce performance. In human resources, in learning and development, and in knowledge management, leading organizations are targeting the specific workforces and processes that are most critical to business performance and form part of their distinctive capabilities. A recent study by Accenture in conjunction with Babson College, Boston, on 20 US organizations selected from the top 100 performing companies as assessed by *BusinessWeek* (Accenture, 2006), conducted in-depth interviews with their top learning executives and drew the same conclusion. Of the executives surveyed, all but one reported a greater corporate-level focus on mission-critical workforces or jobs.

Why do the best companies work to achieve that focus? We spoke with the chief learning officer (CLO) of an insurance company which is currently analysing its business unit strategies to determine which units and people are the most important contributors to the execution of strategy. The CLO noted:

> What led the businesses to move toward more focused investments is that budgets just couldn't cover all the learning needs within a business. So impact on strategy is being used as an allocation mechanism. Where should our limited resources be applied? In the past, we have spent a lot of money on a lot of people; today our budgets are smaller. As a result, we need to spend more on some workforces and less on others. We pay people differently, so educating them differently makes sense too.

The priority is not only to target investments appropriately, but also to make sure that the learning and development programmes are closely tailored to the specific competency gaps and needs of the critical workforce areas.

In fact, high-performance learning organizations run learning like a business. They focus on value optimization in learning delivery, as well as rigour in planning and measuring learning. They therefore ask hard questions about who needs what types of learning investments. The CLO of a large US bank told us:

> We used to have something for everybody, but now we've reduced widespread access to 'high-touch' and expensive classroom training. We now have more than 800 online courses available, and we will soon have a self-assessment tool to help people guide their own learning plans. The cost of instructor-led training is enormous, and you have to pick your greatest skill gaps and your most important populations, to leverage the return, and the business impact, from instructor-led training.

These observations are from high-performing companies, yet investments in training and learning have so often proved a soft target for cost reduction programmes, and are cut without any understanding of the impact. Unfortunately, as we noted earlier, our accounting standards and processes are not helping since they oblige us to treat these critical investments in the development of human capital as expense items. But organizations have also generally done a very poor job in equating investments in skills development to business outcomes. It is hard for an organization to claim to be a true learning organization if its leaders do not understand the relationship between their spending on learning and development and its outcome, and therefore oscillate continually between raising spending and cutting it.

Our research shows the impact of being a high-performance learning organization on business results: see Figure 4.1.

Good learning organizations also most often brand their learning function to help communicate its importance and value, and the commitment they are making to their employees. The most visible branding is through learning academies, or corporate universities as they are sometimes called, at organizations like Halliburton, and McDonald's well-known Hamburger U. Dedicated facilities for training are the most obvious example of corporate branded learning, but organizations can also create such branding from learning approaches using technology and e-learning.

- A high performing learning organization (HPLO) was defined against 7 criteria
- 23 out of the survey sample of 285 were regarded as HPLOs
- HPLO companies returned better revenue and profit growth compared with their competitors and industry peers:
  - Productivity (as measured by sales/employee) was 27% greater
  - Revenue growth was 40% greater
  - Net income growth was 50% greater

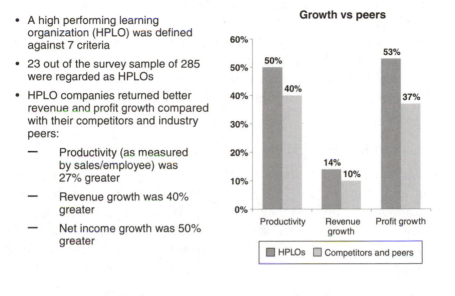

Figure 4.1 Results from high-performance learning organizations
Source: Accenture (2005).

LEARNING FASTER, LEARNING BETTER: SEVEN KEY PRINCIPLES

Accenture has made many studies of learning (particularly a major 2004 survey of learning executives, *The Rise of the High Performance Learning Organization*), as well as supporting organizations of all kinds in learning. Our research and practical experience alike have led us to summarize high-performance learning in seven key principles:

- **learning with purpose**: close alignment of learning initiatives with the organization's strategic goals;
- **learning with impact**: measuring the business contribution of the learning function;
- **learning with outreach**: movement of learning outside the 'four walls' of the organization to reach and influence suppliers, customers and other partners in the organization's value chain;
- **learning with leverage**: focusing on developing competency in the places where it is most critical to the organization's success;
- **learning with integration**: ensuring that learning is integrated with other talent management processes and functions, including

knowledge management, performance support and reward systems;

- **learning with variety**: using a blend of learning methods to greatest effect, including classroom teaching as well as synchronous and asynchronous electronic learning;
- **learning with maturity**: mature design and delivery of leadership courses.

Learning with purpose: alignment of learning with strategic goals

High-performance learning organizations link their learning initiatives and content to strategy objectives. They offer learning programmes to address key strategic priorities such as top-line growth and revenue generation, improving productivity, customer service and customer satisfaction, attracting and retaining talent employees, reducing costs and improving quality, and/or global expansion into new markets.

A good example of aligning learning with strategic goals is at Becton Dickinson and Company (BD), a medical technology company. Learning at BD is totally integrated into the fabric of BD. Ed Betof, head of BD University – the learning function at Becton – sees the university as stronger than just 'alignment' with business strategy. 'The university is used not only as a learning and development lever, but it's one of the company's strongest resources to be used for communication and cultural assimilation,' explains Betof.

Becton-Dickinson's success is its 'leaders as teachers' initiative. More than 90 per cent of the company's internally delivered programming is taught by BD professionals and executives, including the chairman, president and CEO. Approximately 570 of these 'faculty' members in the 25,000-strong company have been certified to teach one or more programmes. The executive participation has built strong awareness not just of BD University but also of the business as a whole, and the company's leaders see the university as a key to cultural assimilation and integration of the company's different segments. The initiative builds a huge network of people who are now much more aware of other people and functions of the company.

Halliburton, a global service provider to the oil and gas industry, has established the Halliburton University as a learning and development organization. Its director Joanne Kincer explains, 'Aligning training and development to the business isn't rocket science. It's just a matter of figuring out what the business drivers are and focusing on the same metrics that the revenue-generating parts of the business measure.' Kincer and her team aggressively pursue those drivers in a way that helps shape strategy, not just support it. They met with major stakeholders in each of the company's main divisions, and from those discussions emerged a validated list of the fixed priorities that were common among those divisions. Halliburton University then aligned its programmes to those priorities. Kincer also works to maintain alignment by assigning people from the learning organization to each of Halliburton's main divisions, as well as to the support functions and the company's geographic regions. 'The result,' Kincer notes, 'has been a change in how we perceive and measure the business impact of what we do.'

Learning with impact: measuring the business impact of learning

High-performance learning organizations seek to measure and communicate the business impact of learning. They are sophisticated when it comes to measuring business impact in ways that are meaningful to the business. They measure business impact in terms of: improved satisfaction and retention of customers, improved satisfaction and retention of employees, improved product and service quality, improved safety, and ability to enter new markets. They are also more likely to have their future funding and growth tied to their ability to measure success.

Avaya, a leading communications systems, applications and services company, has also established an in-house university as a centre of learning. Avaya has moved well beyond defining its learning value as 'amount of training delivered'. Dan Gorski, director of Avaya's global learning, explains, 'We now have broad acceptance throughout Avaya University – and throughout Avaya itself – that value will be defined as "results enabled through effective training".' Avaya develops solid business cases, identifies the anticipated return on investment and then selectively measures investment versus value delivered.

In addition, Avaya leadership has implemented a principle called 'Business Interlock', a formal business function with services, interactions, metrics and application capabilities that link learning outcomes to business objectives. By institutionalizing the Business Interlock concept, Avaya has directly linked learning content development and delivery to the new product development process, enabling predictable and timely delivery of learning events to sales, support and service, and channel partner workforces globally. A product launch readiness scorecard integrates training capability with product management and channels. Thanks to this formal Business Interlock structure, Avaya University has delivered significant cost savings. More important, it has enabled and successfully supported the corporate business strategy of accelerated new product introduction.

General Mills, a leading consumer products company, uses a balance of effective metrics to measure the success of the learning it delivers to its employees. Measurement is seen as the means of understanding the impact and effectiveness of the learning effort, and not primarily to prove the 'worth' of learning. Kevin Wilde, VP and CLO, explains:

> All members of my team are charged with monitoring the follow-through and impact of their programs. Proving value means linking what employees do with strategy, and then establishing credibility through strong relationships. Measurement is the pro's way of doing the job well. Through relationships, one can build credibility with senior leaders and link what he/she is doing to the strategy.

This is how Wilde has been getting his training organization to 'speak the language of the business'.

Learning with outreach: moving learning outside the organization

High-performance learning organizations understand that there is a growing importance of offering learning programmes across a company's value chain. No fewer than 81 per cent of the organizations in Accenture's 2004 learning survey offered either customer or channel partner education programmes. The resources most frequently shared between the external and internal programmes were technology infrastructure (learning management system), course content and instructors for delivery of instructor-led courses. Organizations shared such resources to increase customer satisfaction and build loyalty – and by extension, to increase revenue and shareholder value, but also to create an enduring point of competitive differentiation in the marketplace. Organizations also sought partnering arrangements with business schools, for-profit universities, for-profit online universities, online traditional universities and traditional training companies.

Nielsen University is the learning arm of Nielsen Media Research (the leading provider of television audience measurement and related services). The university offers training on its software applications to a variety of Nielsen customers (television networks and affiliates, independent stations, syndicators, cable networks, agencies and advertisers). The customers need to be able to use Nielsen's software applications efficiently in order to get the full value of the service. Nielsen University offers a combination of tutorials, synchronous online classes and classroom offerings, allowing clients to choose the method of training that best suits their learning preferences. Convenient scheduling suits the requirements of busy clients. Customers can register through Nielsen University for training programmes and individual learning activities on how to use various Nielsen software applications and services. The university provides Nielsen Media Research clients with a way to maintain their level of proficiency with Nielsen's software products. Not only does this learning programme increase customer satisfaction, it also helps decrease the number of calls that clients make to Nielsen's client support helpline.

Hitachi Data Systems (HDS) Academy developed a new channel partner education programme to deepen relationships with the company's vendors. Nick Howe, VP of HDS Academy explains, 'channel partners are also selling products from Hitachi's competitors. Therefore, the relationship these partners have with our educational program is a fundamental part of their entire relationship with HDS.' The company has been proactive in surveying its partners to develop a business case to transform its channel partner education programmes.

Toyota University has developed innovative ways to help Toyota dealers achieve optimum performance. Its School of Professional Development offers targeted learning to more than 110,000 dealer associates, not only through classroom and e-learning, but also through coaching. According to the school's leader Bob Zeinstra, 'This year we will do about 2,900 days of in-dealership coaching, where one of our coaches will go into a dealership in order to bring new content to them or to reinforce some content they have previously learned in class.' Coaching is now a vital part of our mix of learning. Zeinstra and his team continue to explore how e-learning, delivered to dealers on the foundation of instructor-led courses and coaching, can be even more effective.

Unipart (the automotive components company) has also been a leader in developing learning programmes across its supply chain. Suppliers and customers have been involved in courses and learning events in the company's in-house Unipart University. Its well-known programme 'Ten(d) to zero' was developed to help the company compete successfully in the future by working across the supply chain to meet the needs of its customers better than anyone else. The programme changed attitudes among all parties to develop supplier partnerships based on mutual trust and on a common toolkit to drive down cost in the supply chain. The programme thus helps the company 'tend toward zero' in terms of the non-value-added activities along the supply chain. According to John M Neill, group chief executive, Unipart University is an essential means to help Unipart become the world's best 'lean enterprise. It has become the platform which we can see the direction for the future. There's a good commercial argument for it; it's a route to competitive advantage and it enhances shareholder value by preventing our people's skills from becoming obsolete.'

Learning with leverage: developing competency where it is most critical

A key part of making the right learning investments and aligning those with the business is to focus on the particular strategic workforces whose performance is most directly linked to overall company performance. High-performance learning organizations focus their performance improvement efforts on employees or groups that add most directly to the organization's bottom line.

The Tennessee Valley Authority (TVA) is a renowned US government agency. Its workforce ranges from the agency's own law enforcement personnel to its custodians. Lane Fitzgerald, manager of solutions support for TVA's learning organizations, notes:

> If you look at the critical path for what TVA produces, the most important job families can be classified in four major buckets: our trades and labor employee population, our engineers, our clerical administration people and our management. Each one of those has its own profession-specific learning team, which guides the needs assessment and the curriculum design for its job classification.

Learning with integration: integrating learning with the rest of talent management

A growing number of successful learning organizations are incorporating learning with knowledge management and performance support. By doing so they are able to capture and deliver relevant knowledge and experience to the workforce at the point of need. The integration of learning and knowledge management also serves another important purpose: to help organizations cope with the potential loss of critical knowledge and experience as the workforce ages. Finally, the integration of learning, knowledge management and performance support creates applications called 'workspace solutions'. These applications offer role-based and performance-specific support to workers, integrating knowledge, content and learning into a single desktop.

Defense Acquisition University (DAU) is the learning organization for the US Department of Defense and its acquisition, technology and logistics workforce. It has overseen a wide range of initiatives to provide easy-to-access information and performance support tools to its workforce. Its president, Frank Anders, comments:

> A central issue for enterprise learning organizations is how to capture and deliver relevant knowledge and experience to the workforce at the point of need, and you can't do that with a classroom-type structure alone. It is crucial to build an environment that encourages and rewards knowledge sharing.

Knowledge sharing figures prominently now in what DAU calls its technological 'road map' for e-learning success.

British Telecom (BT) has been particularly innovative in the area of workspace solutions. BT initiated a project called 'knowledge management for customer contact advisors'. This solution allows BT advisors to be no more than 'two clicks' from accurate data and supporting knowledge about anything a customer might ask, providing the right people with the right information at the right time for them to do their jobs. BT initially rolled out the solution to more than 6,500 call centre representatives in less than five months, providing significant service improvements and cost savings. The new workspace solution has driven millions of dollars of incremental benefit over the last three years, primarily due to reduced time to handle key processes. BT has now expanded the original solution to other workforces within the company.

Learning with variety: using a blend of learning methods to greatest effect

High-performance learning organizations make greater impact on business by increasing the variety of learning delivery through technology. They explore the use of leading-edge technologies: knowledge management applications, performance simulation, performance support tools, advanced classroom interaction technologies, and handheld and wireless devices.

Randstad North America, provider of office, industrial, technical, creative and professional staffing services in the United States and Canada, looks to have the right blend of technology that is aligned to business strategy, not the latest technology for its own sake. CLO Vince Eugenio notes that:

> Our intent is always to begin with how to increase organizational capability, then match the most appropriate technology to the need. For us, a technology must effectively support the performance goals and intended business impact of the initiative, or it must reduce delivery costs or reduce time in class.

Randstad considers a learning management system, e-learning, a corporate intranet site and teleconferences as part of the mix.

The US Federal Reserve Bank System uses technology to meet specific training needs of its employees, who come into the organization with a range of skills and experience. Sue Gerker, director of the Federal Reserve Bank of St Louis's Center for Online Learning, comments, 'Rather than sending everyone through the same curriculum, which can be inefficient and costly, blending training, performance support and knowledge repositories is something that drives course development.' One of the centre's more recent offerings, covering the Community Reinvestment Act, combines a one-week online course with a one-week class. The online course is a combination of interactive self-study, video tapes, virtual presentations, and synchronous and asynchronous online discussions. The course designers used a variety of media to fit the needs. Gerker elaborates, 'What we've tried to do is use technology to help us build and deliver our content in a way so that it's scalable for a variety of needs.'

Learning with maturity: mature design and delivery of leadership courses

High-performance learning organizations have effective leadership development. They not only develop capable learning executives but also design successful leadership courses and offer them to the entire organization. The most effective leadership development programmes are focused on improving critical leadership skills and competencies, as well as creating greater alignment. They can even help to achieve a productive shift in the entire company culture.

Johnson & Johnson (the consumer products company) has established a School of Leadership within the Johnson & Johnson eUniversity, which is dedicated exclusively to leadership development. The school is structured to support the critical developmental points of leadership change and growth. New managers receive a tailored curriculum, and then other tailored offerings are made available as a person moves up to take on more challenging positions. The school combines technology-delivered learning for the fundamentals with interactive experiences and coaching as the leadership challenges become intensified.

At the National Defense University, the centre for joint professional military education in the United States, leadership is one of the core competencies at the heart of its mission. Elizabeth McDaniel, Dean of Faculty and Academic Programs for the Information Resources Management College of National Defense University, explains:

> We have become increasingly explicit about our responsibility to incorporate leadership development in everything we do. Specific course content always changes and even grows obsolete over time. But what remains constant is the need to teach our students how to learn, how to find information, how to make executive decisions, how to be good problem solvers and how to communicate well.

At General Motors the learning organization has moved from offering general executive development courses to one specifically designed for GM leaders, and taught by GM leaders. The result is that the very top leaders of the company are personally focused on designing and delivering the topic that is their area of responsibility. They talk about personal challenges they have faced in their leadership roles, and allow the other executives attending to learn from those real-life experiences. According to Donnee Ramelli, President of General Motors University, one outcome of the programme is that:

> It changes the level of dedication or passion around the business topic. From the participants' standpoint, they get to see their very top executives – people they generally don't interact with every day – and they see these leaders get personal and passionate about how to change the business.

GM has created a global base for these training classes, and generated a dynamic relationship between the leaders and the executive attendees. More importantly, it has also created a network among the participants and a collaborative working environment from different business units and geographies.

One way of learning with maturity is to run 'train the trainer' sessions. This is a familiar idea, yet many companies continue to invite experienced practitioners to run a training course or pass on their wisdom, without giving them any teaching skills. But knowing something is no guarantee of being able to teach it to others. Business schools rarely teach effective people management, and this skill is not easy to pick up on the job. It requires specific training, and the establishment of forums and networks that encourage less formal sharing of knowledge.

At SAP North America, HR has switched its attention from junior employees to line managers. Lisa Lord, director of organizational development, explains why:

> HR business partners used to spend a lot of time supporting employees, but we realized that this was a common mistake. Doing so only atrophies and weakens the ability of managers to do what they should do best – manage their people. We now conceive of HR as a coach to the coaches, or line managers.

HR business partners at SAP North America now reckon to spend more than half their time coaching line managers.

MEASURING LEARNING EFFECTIVENESS

We have mentioned measurement as an important characteristic of high-performance learning organizations. Most organizations do a poor job of measuring the impact and outcomes of learning. They take the easy route and measure typical input measures such as

Figure 4.2 Untraining

course attendance, hours of training, and satisfaction with training programmes. Investment in learning is about improving skills and competencies in order to improve performance, so we need to focus much more on outcome measures and measures of learning effectiveness.

Some well-established models are now in common use to assess the degree to which skills have been enhanced as a result of learning interventions. They tend to focus on absorption of learning to produce sustainable performance improvement. The Kirkpatrick Model, first presented in 1975 by Donald Kirkpatrick, is still widely regarded as a standard. It measures learning on four levels:

- **Level 1: Reaction of students** – what they thought and felt about the training.
- **Level 2: Learning** – the resulting increase in knowledge or capability.
- **Level 3: Transfer** – extent to which skills are transferred to the job.
- **Level 4: Impact** – the effects on the business or environment resulting from the trainee's performance.

Each level understandably becomes more complex to assess, but you must try to reach Level 4 to make a full and meaningful evaluation of learning in your organization.

Another model, with some similarities, is the Conscious Competence learning matrix. This measures the success of a learning or training programme as a progression through four stages:

- **Unconscious incompetence.** Students are unaware that they lack a relevant skill.
- **Conscious incompetence.** Students become aware of their need for the skill and commit themselves to learn and practise it.
- **Conscious competence.** Students have learnt to use the skill reliably if they think about it. They can demonstrate it to others but not teach it.
- **Unconscious competence.** Students become so practised in the skill that they can perform it automatically. They can teach it to others – although later it may with repetition become so automatic that they can no longer explain it. (This points to the need to check routines constantly against new standards.)

These are useful constructs in focusing attention on the ultimate purpose of developing learning in combination with on-the-job experience, but they do not contribute very much to measuring the value of learning.

We think of learning measurement in three distinct categories, with examples as shown below.

Learning efficiency:

- Use of a common enterprise-wide learning management system (LMS).
- Accuracy and cost-effectiveness of learning administration and record keeping.
- Improved measurement of learning compliance and completion.
- Cost of learning development and delivery.
- Cycle time of course design and delivery.
- Efficient and coordinated learning vendor management providing full visibility to learning costs.

Learning effectiveness:

- Improved access to learning at reduced cost.
- Improved time to competency.
- Better alignment of learning delivery to learning objectives and business priorities.
- Higher levels of knowledge retention over time.
- Higher employee retention and satisfaction.
- Increased level of involvement of senior business leaders.

Business impact:
- Improved sales performance.
- Improved customer satisfaction and retention.
- Improved leadership surveys and leadership capacity.
- Improved levels of corporate compliance.
- Other key performance measures targeted from the learning initiatives.

These three categories make it easier to find ways of measuring learning effectiveness and impact on performance. Measures could be applied at individual and team or organizational levels. Even leadership development (which often generates very significant expenditure on individuals) should logically be measured first and foremost against how it has improved leadership performance. Improving leadership survey responses would be a good place to start examining how much individual leaders have benefited from leadership training. Retention and employee satisfaction rates would be another – for if the leadership training investment has not caused recipients to lead people better, it will have missed one of its major purposes.

LEARNING TECHNIQUES AND APPROACHES

Research and experience have shown that different modes of learning produce different learning outcomes. Figure 4.3 summarizes research carried out by the National Training Laboratories and replicated in numerous other studies. Note that the findings are independent of the technology (if any) used to deploy the learning.

'Teaching organizations' soon discover that teaching others is the most effective means of retaining knowledge. We have all experienced this. Having to teach others is a clear test of your own confidence and knowledge, and as often as not requires some quick refreshers yourself on the topics to be taught. The effectiveness of learning by doing confirms our earlier emphasis on learning on the job.

The role of coaches

Because teaching others and on-the-job learning are so effective, many organizations appoint formal coaches, but most coaching takes place informally. Indeed, the US Department of Labor reckons that 70–80 per cent of workplace learning occurs informally, and this is

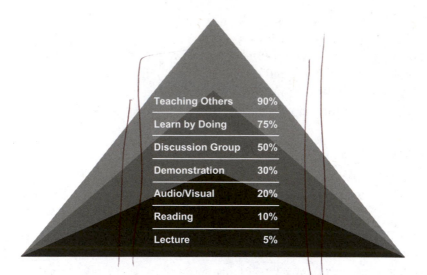

Figure 4.3 Average retention levels for different instructional methods

Source: developed by NTL Institute for Applied Behavioral Science, 300 N Lee Street, Suite 300, Alexandria, VA 22314, 1-800-777-5227.

plausible. Whenever we move into a new area of work, how else are we to learn if not by studying those who are doing the work already?

Organizations can do much to encourage people to learn from one another. In the United Kingdom, the Coventry Building Society recently selected five of its 50 call-centre employees and made them part-time coaches. For two hours every week, they listen in to their colleagues' efforts, then make observations and suggestions. Subsequent experience has shown that the number of calls fielded has gone down, but the call centre's performance has gone up.

Other businesses pair novices with experienced managers, or require managers to provide on-the-job coaching before they ever send anyone on a training course. At SAP North America, there is a 10–20–70 rule: 10 per cent of learning by formal training, 20 per cent from coaching and 70 per cent from on-the-job development. For training that builds not just engagement but practical, participative education, the ideal is to have line managers conducting classes themselves, so that the day-to-day problems and requirements of the business are fully explored. Facilitated lunchtime forums or informal networking events are other ways of getting line managers and newer employees to discuss current issues.

This is a practice we consistently employ within our own firm. All our coaching and training is done by line management. Everyone in the organization has a formal coach or counsellor who plays a key role in coaching and guiding people through their careers and aligning them with the right learning opportunities. The effectiveness of this coaching is assessed by the individuals themselves in the form of 'counselee' feedback surveys, and these then form part of the performance management criteria and expectations of their counsellors.

BUILDING AND CAPTURING CORPORATE KNOWLEDGE

One of the greatest challenges for any would-be learning organization is actually knowing what it knows – particularly the distinctive knowledge that makes it unique as an organization. This distinctive knowledge typically covers things like working practices, networks and relationships within the organization, special understanding of products, markets, suppliers, regulators, and above all, experience and memories stored within the organization.

Two contradictory factors make it harder for organizations to take stock of their accumulated knowledge and use it to greatest effect. First, the amount of recorded *irrelevant* information is rising exponentially thanks to the internet and email. It has been estimated that the total amount of available recorded information now doubles every five years, and that cycle time is reducing.

Second, *essential* knowledge within an organization is frequently fragmented, and tacit rather than recorded. Tom Davenport and Larry Prusack in their book *Working Knowledge* (2000) estimate that as much as 70 per cent of essential knowledge is unrecorded, and stored within the memories of individuals – what is commonly referred to as tacit knowledge. When these individuals disappear from the organization their tacit knowledge can well disappear with them.

In *The Man On The Flying Trapeze*, W C Fields demonstrated the importance of this kind of knowledge. He plays Ambrose Wolfinger, a downtrodden office worker. After many misadventures he succeeds in taking his first half-day's holiday in 25 years. Immediately, his firm falls into crisis with a major customer. His boss searches desperately for information in Wolfinger's cluttered desk. Wolfinger returns and immediately reels off from memory everything the firm needs to know about the customer – even his pets. Wolfinger is honoured and promoted – but what will happen when he retires?

So just when they are reeling under the bombardment of irrelevant information, organizations may be losing essential knowledge without even being aware of it. Knowledge management has therefore become a key issue for would-be learning organizations, but it had a somewhat uncertain beginning. Early initiatives in knowledge management, during the 1990s, tended to be over-formal. They were akin to electronic librarianship, and used highly developed taxonomies which people found hard to use and limited in value.

However, new tools of knowledge management and collaboration are now available which are less formal and better suited to capturing essential tacit knowledge. These tools in particular enable people to identify and access the sources of expert knowledge within an organization: the person who knows about, say, tax rules in Denmark, or the one who understands the details of a specific production process. This resource might seem elementary, but in many organizations it is surprisingly difficult for people to get hold of it.

Collaboration tools are growing rapidly across the internet, and are starting to grow within organizations, the so-called 'wiki' technologies we touched on in Chapter 2. While we, or at least our children, are using these readily at home, formal uptake and management across businesses is a little slower. We described some very innovative examples of how these tools are beginning to get used, and this will be an exciting and growing trend.

To be a learning organization you need to ensure simultaneously that knowledge moves freely and fluidly between people and that it is transferred and captured in a systematic way. This evolution of knowledge management – from a set of stand-alone repositories into a suite of capabilities integral to worker performances – is captured in Figure 4.4.

Collaborative and knowledge-sharing organizations reward people for sharing knowledge rather than hoarding it, and reflect this in their performance appraisal systems. They encourage knowledge sharing by technology, and both formal and informal processes, especially coaching, mentoring and brainstorming sessions.

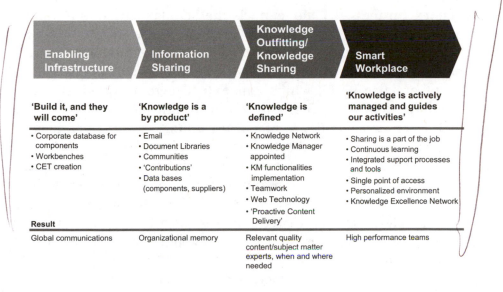

Enabling Infrastructure	Information Sharing	Knowledge Outfitting/ Knowledge Sharing	Smart Workplace
			'Knowledge is actively managed and guides our activities'
'Build it, and they will come'	'Knowledge is a by product'	'Knowledge is defined'	
• Corporate database for components • Workbenches • CET creation	• Email • Document Libraries • Communities • 'Contributions' • Data bases (components, suppliers)	• Knowledge Network • Knowledge Manager appointed • KM functionalities implementation • Teamwork • Web Technology • 'Proactive Content Delivery'	• Sharing is a part of the job • Continuous learning • Integrated support processes and tools • Single point of access • Personalized environment • Knowledge Excellence Network
Result			
Global communications	Organizational memory	Relevant quality content/subject matter experts, when and where needed	High performance teams

Figure 4.4   The evolution of knowledge management

This does require a special effort to identify and codify the unique knowledge people carry, especially imminent retirees. It is vital to codify knowledge against the competency models that describe and define the particular skills in different roles and workforces, which we went through in the previous chapter. If this information has been captured for employees as a matter of routine, then it will be easy to identify the impact of retirees and to understand the specific skills and competencies that you need them to pass on. If such information is not readily available, then you might interview such people formally, or invite them to write down what they think is most important to pass on to their successors. Their knowledge can then be passed on in many ways, not only formal training sessions and specific knowledge-capture initiatives, but also coaching and learning on the job, which will be particularly effective if the retirees are matched with a suitable protégé or other shadow.

Mapping and supporting the knowledge flows

It sounds like a daunting task to map and understand the largely informal flows of tacit knowledge around the organization. It is hard enough to prepare a formal organization chart with all the links in a complex business, let alone track the spontaneous or informal connections and collaborations between your people.

The first important approach is to strive to formalize these networks and collaborations through expert networks or communities of practice (CoP), which can extend across organizational boundaries. CoP were first chronicled by Etienne Wenger in his 1999 paper 'Communities of practice: learning, meaning and identity', and have been around for some time, particularly in professional services firms like Accenture. Unlike formalized training programmes, CoPs operate on an informal, largely voluntary basis as a network of people with similar professional or operational interests who share knowledge, solve problems, and advance the frontiers of understanding on topics at the intersection of personal and organizational benefit.

Today these networks are increasingly supported with collaboration tools such as SharePoint sites where knowledge, frequently asked questions and such like are captured in one source, edited and supported by the network itself. Webcasts and supporting tools are now commonplace in organizations: they allow easy and cost-effective means of sharing knowledge from experts to large groups through live learning sessions conducted virtually. Expert search systems that search skills inventories or even CVs to identify people with particular competencies are also now quite common, and other tools such as instant messenger (IM) programs as supported by Microsoft or AOL are providing other means to connect easily.

IM networks are themselves interesting insights into collaborative networks and teams, and often start out as classic examples of 'viral' technologies, where the adoption by users in an organization happens through word of mouth, or teams recommending it to each other as a means to connect better. Initially they may not even be supported by the internal IT organization, but spread nonetheless from users simply downloading the programs from the internet.

Analytical approaches to understanding knowledge sharing and collaboration across organizations have existed for a while. In our experience, they have not been in widespread use, but they may now be gaining more traction as the importance of corporate knowledge and collaboration is better recognized. These techniques come under the heading of social network analysis (SNA). A key strength of SNA is its ability to provide a picture of an organization which is independent of its structure. Based primarily on surveys, it maps the way people interact with each other within an organization and what they talk about. It thereby tracks the information flowing around the organization, and in particular, the elusive tacit knowledge which makes the organization unique. This offers great insight into its critical capabilities. It is not unlike the charts that soccer managers use to track their team's passing ability: SNA can track how people in your organization pass to each other, whether they pass long or short, which other people they pass to (or avoid passing to), and whether their passes are successfully completed.

LEARNING AT INTERNET SPEED: THE APPLICATION OF TECHNOLOGY TO LEARNING

The internet and steady reductions in the cost of information technology have dramatically enhanced the breadth of learning options in organizations. If (as we have argued) learning objectives are aligned with business needs and learning styles are aligned with individual abilities, technology has immense potential to fuel the learning organization. But it has not been easy to exploit the benefits of 'e-learning'.

In the late 1990s e-learning became a buzzword that was largely aimed at cost reduction. The logic was simple: if people can be presented with training at their PCs or laptops, then organizations could save vast sums in operating expenses for things like travel, instructor salaries and materials, and physical space and upkeep. Like so many breathtaking new ideas, e-learning initially failed to live up to expectations. Money was saved but learning did not happen any faster or better. The problem was it required a new way of structuring the learning, and simply mimicking a book online was generally less convenient and productive than having the book itself.

Recent years have seen a more sober approach, with a focus on balanced or 'blended' learning. Drawing on research into learning styles, more organizations now blend classroom-based, self-paced, web-enabled, and action-learning or simulation styles. Blended models offer distinct advantages that cannot be achieved through one approach alone, as described in Figure 4.5.

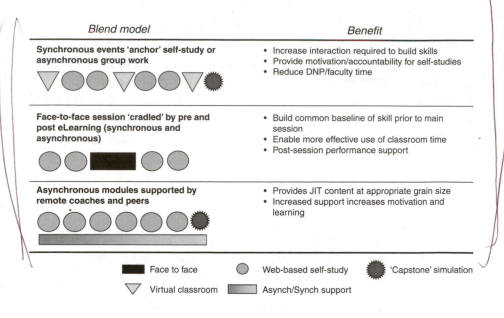

Blend model	Benefit
Synchronous events 'anchor' self-study or asynchronous group work	• Increase interaction required to build skills • Provide motivation/accountability for self-studies • Reduce DNP/faculty time
Face-to-face session 'cradled' by pre and post eLearning (synchronous and asynchronous)	• Build common baseline of skill prior to main session • Enable more effective use of classroom time • Post-session performance support
Asynchronous modules supported by remote coaches and peers	• Provides JIT content at appropriate grain size • Increased support increases motivation and learning

■ Face to face   ○ Web-based self-study   ✸ 'Capstone' simulation
▽ Virtual classroom   ▭ Asynch/Synch support

Figure 4.5   Advantages of blended learning

Learning techniques using technology have evolved into many more sophisticated forms. High-end e-learning involves simulating often complex activities, but takes advantage of improved learning retention as it mimics learning by doing. Simulations or action learning can involve online virtual coaches, high-fidelity gaming approaches and built-in assessments. Accenture developed many of the innovative approaches in this area of learning, and holds a wide range of patents.

The new collaboration tools mentioned above are blending with e-learning approaches and creating a whole new generation of integrated e-learning toolsets. They are bringing together the worlds of knowledge management and learning into much more of a continuum of learning – which after all reflects how people learn and use knowledge naturally.

As e-learning and the many new applications of technology provide people with greater opportunity to learn from each other more informally, the role of formal classroom learning is reducing and attracting a smaller proportion of total spending on learning. E-learning has really come of age, and has shown many advantages when used effectively. It is no longer focused on cost reduction but on effectiveness and uptake. E-learning modules can be used and reused countless times, and reconfigured with other learning modules to tailor specific learning programmes to individual needs based on specific understanding of competencies to be developed. Learning assets can be built into processes and workspaces, for users to access at any time they need to, or even be prompted to use by the application or transaction systems themselves.

We can now pull together learning and knowledge applications and assets with the application systems that employees use as part of their job tasks, into a single 'portal'. This provides a single integrated interface that provides everything users need, in a virtual workspace tailored specifically to their job and role, and even to them individually – what we term a performance workspace. Recent applications include workspaces within call centres that recognize user downtime and prompt people with short learning events. Knowledge captured about processes, customers, products or services can be presented to employees at the precise point they most need it. Examples include provision of voice-recognition technology, to identify key words as a call-centre operative talks to a customer, and then provide information direct to the operative's computer screen. Thomas Cook, the travel company, has used a technique like this to provide operatives with information on specific deals, or even information about particular locations and hotels, as they talk to customers. Imagine the level of customer service that can provide, and the sense of achievement for the employee.

Such embedded learning and knowledge truly brings learning to the point of need, and is allowing us to develop learning models that are much closer to how people best learn. We are finally able to break free from the shackles of that – literally – old-school paradigm of the classroom.

As e-learning has become more sophisticated, learning functions have been forced to evolve. Given some of the very specialist nature of skills required, which will include graphic design artists and specialists in e-learning content development, there has been a marked increase in outsourcing to organizations that provide these sorts of capabilities at scale.

PARTNERSHIPS IN NATIONAL EDUCATION

So far all of the discussion in this chapter has been focused on learning and knowledge initiatives within your organization. But of course you are not the only source of learning and knowledge for your current or potential workforce. Indeed you are almost certainly contributing a goodly sum in taxation to maintain your country's public education system, and as we observed in Chapter 1, the output from the educational systems is not proving sufficient to meet the ever-increasing demands of business. We shall therefore say a few words about the possibilities of partnership with that system.

Most, if not all, advanced countries offer businesses some opportunity to give direct support to the education system and exercise some influence on its output. Your organization might, for example, support research at universities, endow faculties and teaching posts, award scholarships and bursaries to students, give work experience to secondary school students, encourage staff to take up positions in school governance, enter sponsorship or partnership arrangements with schools, or offer teaching materials and regular educational visits. In considering all or any of such initiatives you need to keep two factors constantly in mind.

First, any such initiative needs to be integrated into your overall talent strategy – not a one-off piece of public relations or an attempt to recruit local labour on the cheap. A relationship with a school or a college should be a strategic resource, one that tries to develop or revive a source of essential talent.

Second, any such relationship needs to be a two-way relationship, in which the school or college is a genuine partner of your organization, not just a grateful recipient of your bounty. Schools and colleges rightly value their independence (which in many cases is established by law), and they are accountable to many different stakeholders. Moreover, academic freedom and intellectual inquiry are real assets to your organization, which you should always encourage. You should by all means seek to foster specific skills in school or college students, but they should also bring to you a willingness to argue, to challenge orthodoxy and embrace new ideas. By doing so, they bring you an infinitely richer source of talent and future growth than a set of highly qualified conformists.

The business sector certainly has every reason to engage with national systems of secondary and tertiary education. But even if they could be reformed successfully overnight, these systems could never do enough to meet the skills challenge faced by 21st-century organizations. First, there is an inevitable lag between the demand for new skills and knowledge from business, and the supply of qualified people from schools and universities. Before any new branch of knowledge can be taught, curricula have to be prepared, examinations devised, teachers, assessors and inspectors trained, students, children and parents prepared for new academic options, and, very often, earlier education has to be revised to give some grounding for the new skill. Even in ideal conditions, an education system moves too slowly for business needs.

Second, and more important, is the demographic factor. In most developed economies there simply are not enough young people to meet the demand for new skills (and those countries with a good supply of young people are often exporting them to those without). Even if businesses could persuade more young people studying media studies to switch to science, there would probably still not be enough scientists.

As we noted in Chapter 1, around 70 per cent of those who will make up the business workforce in 2020 have already left school or college. Those are the people who will determine whether you meet your talent needs or not. The most important element in that population is those working for you already, and that is why lifelong learning is the main focus of this section.

Lifelong learning

Although the necessity of lifelong learning is acknowledged by governments in advanced economies (the UK government has even had a Minister for Lifelong Learning), actual provision is extremely patchy. Figure 4.6 charts the variation in lifelong learning participation rates for the EU15 nations, showing Greece at the bottom, with around 17 per cent, and Austria at the top, with around 80 per cent. The total participation figures conceal strong variations by age group. Older people are far less likely to gain any new learning, despite calls from governments and business alike. Within the EU25 the participation rate for lifelong learning falls from 50 per cent for the 25–34 age group to less than 30 per cent for those aged 55–64 (according to Eurostat).

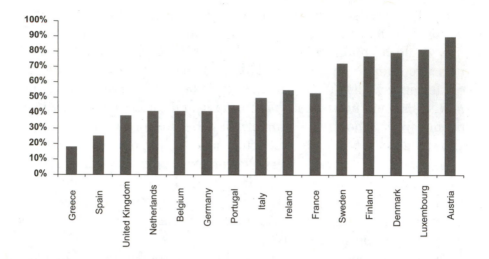

Figure 4.6 Lifelong learning participation rates for the EU15
'Lifelong learning' is defined as participation by people aged 25 or
over in any sort of learning activity
Source: Eurostat.

Clearly business has much to gain from boosting the participation
rates in lifelong learning, particularly in the lowest-rate countries and
among older people, to do more to promote retaining older people in
the workforce for longer. But it is not easy to deliver learning to
adults. Those in work, particularly those with caring responsibilities,
can rarely afford the time or money to attend full-time places of
education, or even one evening a week. Travel is often a barrier,
particularly for people who live far from colleges or training centres.
Some groups of adults, particularly the long-term unemployed and
those already retired, may need to be supported as they transition
back into training and learning.

Business therefore has a strong motive to help governments and
other education providers create new models of training and educational delivery. Virtual service provision and e-learning, and other
forms of home learning, can provide very powerful means to allow
people to learn in ways that fit their personal lifestyles and their
personal learning style. Many governments are indeed turning to
e-learning to deliver learning programmes to adults. For example, in

Finland the national strategy 'Education, Training and Research in Information Society' provides for a virtual school, polytechnic and university, which offer online training and education services independent of the time and place of study.

There are increasing examples of collaboration between business and higher education, which helps to extend the supply of talent to business. We described in Chapter 1 the incredible shortages of talent in IT services in India, and many Indian companies in this sector are developing creative ways to access talent early, and help to channel promising individuals towards their businesses.

Such an example was described by Fay Hansen in the journal *Workforce Management* (2006). The Indian multinational Zensar Technologies is addressing the shortage of managerial talent worldwide by partnering with business schools. Top managers invest a great deal of time at business schools, meeting new MBA candidates as soon as they are admitted, and maintaining connections with them throughout their time in the programmes. Yogesh Patgaonkar, associate vice president and head of HR, describes this strategy as catching them in the cradle. 'When they graduate, they come straight to work for Zensar,' Patgaonkar says. Zensar also pays for MBAs for technical workers who want to move into management. 'Outside of India, we run similar programmes to recruit and train both technical and managerial talent,' Patgaonkar says. 'We recruit from all of the premier campuses and use our own training centers so that employees continue to grow.'

Promoting adult learning also offers businesses a chance to combine corporate social responsibility with improving their access to local talent and skills. Training partnerships in local communities – like the one described in the box – have had an especially powerful effect in areas of high unemployment and social deprivation, where companies can be particularly effective actors in the process of urban regeneration (in collaboration with wider social partners).

Case study: Tesco

Tesco supermarkets in Ireland decided to build a new retail development in North Dublin in an area of particularly high unemployment. Tesco worked with the Northside Partnership, a locally based government-funded development company, as well as FAS (the national training body) and the Mandate Trade Union. The principal objective of the scheme was to offer training and work placements for up to 80 long-term unemployed people. Fifty-eight people successfully completed the training and received a nationally recognized retail skills accreditation. A quarter of the 350 jobs in the new store have now been filled by previously unemployed people from the local community.

Tesco has also undertaken a number of initiatives around the world in order to provide training and education opportunities for the local community. In Thailand, for example, Tesco has set up 50 scholarships for high school students from deprived backgrounds each time a Tesco Lotus Value store opens. So far 300 scholarships have been awarded in six provinces (www.tescocorporate.com).

Main source: BITCI (2005).

We shall return to this theme in the final chapter, as something that businesses, educational establishments and governments have an important shared interest in, as part of the response to building and developing the talent needed to sustain our businesses and economies.

DEPLOYING TALENT: MANAGING THE WORK STRATEGICALLY

Talent-powered organizations have well-honed capabilities in deploying talent to the mutual benefit of the organization and its employees. They assign and combine talent to ensure meaningful opportunities for individuals in roles and experiences that have strategic impact for the organization. High-performing businesses have institutionalized methods for matching and moving the best internal and external talent to the most critical positions for which they are well-suited, ensuring sufficient organizational capability to face current and future business challenges and opportunities.

Deployment from the perspective of talent multiplication is essentially about:

- creating the best possible match between employees' talents and aspirations and the strategic goals of the organization;
- making strategic use of assignments and experiences to further develop those talents to maximize employees' future contributions to the organization's strategic goals;
- expanding organizational capabilities by leveraging individuals' strengths, perspectives and experiences;
- shaping the composition, responsibilities and practices of teams to leverage the diversity of thinking styles, experiences and perspectives;
- encouraging and enabling the sharing of knowledge and best practice to encourage continuous renewal.

Deployment is also about matching the task and work requirements to the available talent, wherever that might be, so that in the end the organization has the right people performing the right tasks at the right time. This is the principal objective of staffing and scheduling, and other HR functions in organizations. Some organizations are more strategic about it, and some companies are better at it than others, but everyone is trying to match people and jobs on some level.

To this point, the implicit assumption has been that the task is to put people into jobs. Jobs were stable well-defined sets of duties and responsibilities. People were assigned to these jobs and they are moved around as required to fill jobs. However, with the changes in the context and nature of work and workers that we described in Chapter 1, this assumption no longer holds.

The deployment challenge remains the same, but the process for ensuring the right people are doing the right things is fundamentally different. Now, jobs or tasks can be moved to people as often as people fill jobs. More importantly, perhaps, technology increasingly allows work to be divided and distributed in novel ways. Work need no longer only be conceived of structurally in terms of organizational roles. It can now be thought of more dynamically, in terms of sets of tasks that can be segmented and sent around the world. Most enterprise resource planning (ERP) systems today support workflows that allow tasks to be segmented and tracked across a workforce. Products are being designed, developed and manufactured all over the place, with all the necessary information being sent electronically. If such complex products as airplanes can be developed through simultaneous engineering techniques, with parts being manufactured and assembled around the world and brought together to finally assemble the plane in a matter of days, as Boeing and Airbus now do, then any form of work potentially can be managed in this diverse, virtual way. Deployment is also therefore the process of defining and distributing those tasks.

To be able to do this effectively, you must have a very good understanding of current workforce skills and competencies. This is why understanding the competencies in your organization, an issue we reviewed in Chapter 2, is so critical. You also need to know where the right external skills are and how best to access them. Only then can you strategically match work to competencies in ways that multiply talent. Hence the analogies we have described to material supply chain planning and management.

There are two distinct dimensions to the deployment challenge: managing the work and developing talent. What types of work need to be done, and what talent can you access to do it? How are you managing the work that needs to get done today? What about the work that will be required down the line? What competencies are critical today? Have you predicted what competencies will be required in the future, so that you can begin to invest in building them or finding ways to access them? How are you developing your people through deployment?

Managing the work strategically increasingly involves 'following' or 'chasing' the sun. Organizations following the sun move work around the globe for a variety of reasons. Often, the workload simply exceeds the talent supply in a location, or around-the-clock customer service is required, or specialized skills are necessary that are not available locally. Emerging strategies for managing the work include distributing work globally, scheduling/rostering and 24-hour work teams.

DISTRIBUTING WORK GLOBALLY

With the right technology, organizations can transcend time and space and do work anytime, anywhere. Many kinds of work can take place almost anywhere, creating the possibility for global workflows that can be spread among many locations. Globally distributed work has been around for a while now for a number of types of work, such as customer service call centres, insurance claims processing, and accounting services. It is becoming increasingly prevalent for other more highly skilled occupations, including law and medicine.

Radiology offers an excellent example of this phenomenon. There has been an enormous growth in the global distribution of radiology work in the last few years. The proportion of radiology images that are read and interpreted offsite has grown dramatically as digital technologies have become more common. There are a number of reasons for this: a general shortage of radiologists, excessive workloads created by the growing popularity of powerful imaging technologies like MRIs and CT scans, and the rapidly growing need for already-stretched radiologists to read films at all hours of the night, as more and more emergency departments increase their utilization of imaging modalities.

Night work has been a prime driver for the global distribution of radiology work. Radiologists were being stretched too thin by the amount of work and the timing of the work. Some radiology groups are reporting a tenfold increase in the amount of night work in just five years. Because radiologists do a better job of reading images during daytime hours when they are well rested, many radiology groups have distributed images to be read in other time zones. Some have done this by outsourcing the work to vendors. Some radiology groups have set up their own shops overseas and staffed them with their own radiologists.

According to Michael C Beachley MD, chairman of the standards and accreditation board of the American College of Radiology, a significant advantage of virtual radiology is the ability for medical practices everywhere to access world-class specialists for help with interpretations – wherever those experts might be: 'Even in a moderate-sized practice, sometimes you'd just like to have the guy who wrote the book,' he says (Wiley, 2002).

Globally distributed radiology work also creates opportunities for accelerated learning for fellowship doctors by providing increased volume and more varied cases. Donald Resnick MD, a professor of radiology at the University of California at San Diego, attributes this to getting images from different types of practices: 'At one site you might have only chronic diseases, but at another place you might get only sports medicine, so all of a sudden these fellows are getting experience in [chronic diseases and] sports medicine. To me, the educational value is spectacular' (Wiley, 2002).

Another type of medical work now being distributed globally is clinical information and library resources. 'Chasing the Sun' is an international collaboration among medical libraries in the United Kingdom and Australia that takes advantage of time-zone differences to ensure medical practitioners can seamlessly access required resources, regardless of time or location. The concept relies on health librarians in different time zones providing expertise for an after-hours virtual reference service to clinicians. This first of its kind virtual network of health libraries ensures that expert clinical information is readily available to support patient care (Rockliff *et al*, 2005).

The benefits for organizations of distributing work globally go beyond simple labour cost savings to include access to previously unavailable capabilities or experience, flexibility to send the work to the most profitable talent supply, increased productivity, improved quality, greater information sharing and better workload balancing. There are often considerable benefits for employees too. The learning and experience gained by exposure to different types of work is invaluable for career development. Workload reductions for employees no longer responsible for the work sent to other locations allow those employees to maintain high performance and focus on high-value-added tasks. In addition, reduced late-night and early-morning time and schedule demands improve health and well-being, and create the potential for increased engagement.

SCHEDULING/ROSTERING

Rostering and scheduling provide more commonplace but highly practical examples of using talent to meet the demands of business need, as well as providing flexibility in working patterns for people. The airline industry has long had sophisticated means to manage its people to meet the demands of flight schedules and patterns, and there are now many automated tools that support this. Likewise, retailers are now increasingly exploiting this type of deployment capability to match their in-store staffing with the peaks and troughs of customer activity, as was recently reported for Wal-Mart. Done well, this can be of benefit to the employees too, to give them options in working around their own work–life needs.

TWENTY-FOUR-HOUR WORK TEAMS

Globally dispersed virtual teams allow organizations to effectively create a 24-hour work day by systematically passing work through teams around the globe. Thanks to ever-improving communication and collaboration tools and expanding global connectivity, the physical separation of geographically distributed teams is no longer the most significant barrier to productivity. It is time, not space, that now challenges virtual teams (Treinen and Miller-Frost, 2006).

Early adopters of the 24-hour work teams deployment strategy were mostly software developers and code writers. When team members are located around the world without a system for breaking down and handing off the work, team members are inevitably required to join meetings late at night or early in the morning rather than during the typical work day. With projects and tasks that follow the sun, members of distributed teams work in three separate time zones during their normal business hours. At the end of an eight-hour day, they hand over their tasks to other team members who are just starting their work days in the next time zone.

Deployment capabilities in talent-powered organizations go beyond managing the work. Deployment is also seen as a tool for development. In many ways, deployment is a continuation of development.

Segmenting work into discrete tasks that can be shipped around the world has its limits. Some work is simply not conducive to this type of deployment. More importantly, you must ensure that your strategies for managing the work do not inadvertently diminish workforce capabilities and engagement. We know from extensive research on job design, career development and employee engagement that stripping jobs of significance or limiting the range of career experiences will hinder development, lower performance and lead employees to disengage. Hence, you must be careful not to ignore the developmental needs of your workforce as you plan your deployment strategy.

Deployment strategies and processes must facilitate individual growth and development while enabling organizational flexibility and change. Firms need more than flexibility in the deployment of talent, particularly where employees' capabilities are most strategically important for the firm (as in knowledge-based businesses). Short-sightedness in this regard will hamper your organization's future competitiveness.

Capabilities in deploying talent involve job assignment and management succession systems that place people in jobs that will stretch them, in skill areas that have high competitive value for the company. Job assignments should balance the personal development needs of the employee and the strategic needs of the business. Talent-powered organizations structure developmental experiences that tap into employees' current strengths and also stretch them to maximize learning and development.

Development through deployment requires experiences that simultaneously stretch and support an employee. The more variety and challenge in employees' assignments, the more meaningful support and feedback they need from managers, coaches, team-mates and peers.

The strategic use of job assignments is one of the most important ways to develop talent, in particular the development of leaders. Research by Ayse Karaevli and Tim Hall (2004) has shown that a significant factor determining the performance of senior executives and their companies is the range of experiences the executives had during their careers. Exposure to a variety of corporate functions, industry sectors and types of roles (eg start-up, turn-around) helps to develop a variety of skills and competencies, builds the individuals' specific knowledge while increasing their adaptability and better prepares them for the future leadership roles.

Many high-performing companies such as IBM, Pepsico and GE are well known for their use of job assignments for development. Boeing is conducting research on the developmental outcomes of different assignments in order to map what kinds of learning and development come out of different types of assignment. With this knowledge, deployment decisions can be made to support the achievement of business objectives and the development of workforce skills and capabilities.

In this way, effective deployment brings your organization full circle in the talent multiplication cycle. Deployment is about bringing the work and the people together. In the process, mismatches and gaps become apparent, and require better and further redefinition of talent needs. This understanding then fuels the process of defining talent and competency needs, as we discussed in Chapter 2, and the virtuous circle of talent multiplication is complete.

SUMMARY

To become a talent-powered organization, you must multiply talent by developing and deploying the talent you have discovered. Talent development and deployment are key organizational capabilities that support talent multiplication and competitiveness.

Career development efforts in large corporations are too often limited to programmes that target people with high potential and future leaders. Given the demands of knowledge work and the increased strategic importance of human capital, broad investments in employee capability development should be a top priority for all firms.

Workforce development is a critical competency for all organizations in the 21st century, but it is especially vital in businesses and sectors where employees' knowledge, skills and capabilities are the main tools for creating value. Talent-powered organizations understand this and prioritize learning and development.

Deploying talent is becoming an increasingly strategic capability, with the proliferation of possible ways to organize work and access talent. Talent-powered organizations understand that deployment is not just about getting the work done (important though that is). It is also about developing your talent to increase your organizational capabilities and expand your strategic opportunities.

The way your organization deploys its talent will also have an enormous impact on employee engagement – the secret sauce of talent-powered organizations.

5

Engagement

Really great people make you feel that you too can become great.

Mark Twain (1835–1910)

We have dealt with many of the essential components of talent-powered organizations – a human capital strategy to address the new global workforce, approaches to recruitment that recognize talent market diversity, skills development and learning that best develop talent, and the ability to deploy talent to best advantage. But we still have more to do to achieve the high performance that any global organization requires. This is where engagement comes in.

WHY ENGAGEMENT MATTERS

Talent is the engine of the modern organization, and engagement is the mystery ingredient that can transform the engine's output. Talent-powered organizations have high levels of engagement which accelerate the performance of their people and make them deliver beyond their equivalents in peer organizations.

'Engagement' is a big word, incorporating many subsidiary meanings. It means motivation, commitment, passion, desire, ambition, trust, empathy, solidarity, inspiration, selflessness. It is the quality that persuades people to align their own interests with their organization's. It is what makes them want to work, to put the proverbial best foot forward, to go the proverbial extra mile. It is arguably the Holy Grail of high performance, but there is nothing mythical about it. On the contrary, as we shall show, engagement is identifiable, measurable, and responds to specific factors that we can influence and direct.

At the very least, there should be no dispute about the destructive effects of a lack of engagement. Having the best talent is worth little if they are not motivated or aligned with your business objectives, and yet there is much evidence to suggest that large segments of our workforces are disengaged, and the challenge is growing with attitudinal shifts across the generations, as we explored in Chapter 1.

We know intuitively there must be a strong link between engagement and performance. We know it for ourselves as individuals. Motivational studies have been a long time favourite area of research for psychologists, from the early pioneers such as Abraham Maslow, whose famous 'hierarchy of needs' developed in the early 1940s (Maslow, 1943) still has resonance for many business people today. Recent studies have demonstrated the linkage more directly. For example, the Corporate Leadership Council report of 2004 showed that highly engaged employees achieved performance 20 per cent above average. A Towers Perrin study in 2005 concluded after several years of surveys showing the link between engagement and performance, that a 5 per cent increase in total employee engagement correlated to a 0.7 per cent increase in operating margin.

The most comprehensive report we have seen was the ISR Employee Engagement Report in 2006 (2006b). It reported that organizations with highly engaged workforces performed up to 50 per cent better than those with low engagement. Based on surveys of over 664,000 employees worldwide, the study analysed companies' operating income, net income and earnings per share (EPS) over a 12-month period:

- In terms of operating income, the high-engagement companies improved by 19 per cent whereas the low-engagement companies declined by 33 per cent.
- Net income for high-engagement companies rose by 13 per cent; for low-engagement companies it fell by 4 per cent.
- In the high-engagement companies EPS grew by 28 per cent; in the low-engagement companies it fell by 11 per cent (Management Issues News Online, 2006).

These impressive findings leave little doubt that engagement is important to business performance, even if the precision of the numbers might be questioned, given the many other factors at work. The linkage might also be discerned in the results from the best-places-to-work surveys conducted routinely around the world and reported through respected periodicals such as *Fortune* magazine in the United States and the *Sunday Times* in the United Kingdom. Those companies voted by their employees as best places to work actually do seem to outperform their peers in share price growth.

However, in many of these findings we need to be careful to identify cause and effect. Are successful companies making their employees happier, or are the happy employees making successful companies? In the end, both are almost certainly true. The results of poor engagement are also visible, in high levels of absenteeism, valued employees quitting their jobs, and people harming customer service and other key business objectives.

The important thing to remember is that engaged, or highly engaged, employees may well be the exception. From the various engagement measures used across organizations today, it appears that many employees are not actively engaged, and some are actively disengaged – which means that many businesses worldwide could be underperforming because of lack of engagement.

Before we go any further, we should attempt a comprehensive definition of engagement, and seek to understand what is meant by 'highly engaged' in contrast to just 'engaged'.

WHAT ENGAGEMENT MEANS

The concept of engagement was not introduced to management literature until the late 20th century by Bill Kahn, who defined it as 'the simultaneous employment and expression of a person's "preferred self" in task behaviors that promote connections to work and to others, personal presence (physical, cognitive and emotional), and active full role performances' (1990). Put in more everyday terms, engagement is a measure of the degree to which people express their identity at work – not only who they are but who they would like to be. Engagement is therefore a complex phenomenon, defined physically, intellectually and emotively: 'I'm here, my mind and my feelings are on the job and with the people around me.'

An article in the wondrously named *Journal of Happiness Studies* (Schaufeli *et al*, 2002) identified the physical, intellectual and emotional components of high engagement respectively as 'vigour', 'absorption' and 'dedication':

- **Vigour:** highly engaged people are physically active in their work even if it is essentially sedentary. They are both physically energetic and mentally resilient. They put a lot of effort into their work, and sustain it even when they meet problems and setbacks.
- **Absorption:** highly engaged employees find their work engrossing and throw themselves into it without thought of time or surroundings or how they look to others.
- **Dedication:** highly engaged employees are dedicated to their work because they find it meaningful and fulfilling. Through their work they become better people in their own eyes.

Such behaviours are readily observable. An engaged workforce normally looks happier and busier. And as you would expect, research has confirmed that engaged employees have higher job satisfaction, work harder and perform better in their jobs than their less engaged colleagues. They have lower absenteeism and greater job loyalty. They have better relationships at work and build better teams. They are more likely to meet their organization's standards of behaviour and service to its customers.

In summary, engagement is a combination of heart and mind. It is a collective result of complex factors such as people's sense of identity and belonging, feeling valued and their emotional and intellectual connection with colleagues, and more extrinsic factors such as satisfaction in work content and the support they get to perform effectively. At the high end, engagement represents the degree to which they are aligned, confident and committed to achieving higher performance, and motivated to apply additional discretionary effort to their work; and at the low end, it manifests itself in low levels of responsiveness and energy, and high absenteeism.

An important and closely related concept to engagement is alignment: the degree to which employees understand and identify with their organization's goals, the linkage to their own objectives and abilities, and how they direct their energies to achieving them.

Without alignment, it is easy to see how even employees' positive engagement could be misdirected and wasted within an organization, but of itself it is also an important factor in building engagement.

In our own surveys for Accenture's High Performance Workforce Study (Accenture, 2003, 2004, 2007), mentioned earlier, we continue to find an alarming lack of confidence from the top executives of organizations in the alignment and understanding of their employees about corporate objectives. Our most recent survey found that only 20 per cent of executive respondents think that 75 per cent or more of their employees understand their company's strategic goals, and only 22 per cent of executives surveyed think that 75 per cent or more of their employees understand how they can contribute to achieving those strategic goals. That is not a very high degree of alignment, and this would certainly be a cause of low engagement. However, alignment in reality is in the hands of top executives to fix. We shall return to this important construct as we examine how to engender engagement.

CHANGING ATTITUDES TO WORK

But why is engagement seen to be so important today? In times gone by, this sort of discussion with top management would generally have been short and to the point. Something along the lines of 'We pay them to work, so they should work.' Now it is not that simple: the changing expectations and attitudes of the younger generations in the workforce, as we observed in Chapter 1, have made organizations treat people far more as individuals with choices as to where they use their skills, knowledge and energy. The increasing diversity of people across many dimensions is also forcing organizations to think more about the different drivers of engagement, and understand the different segments of their workforces.

Your challenge is to create conditions that encourage employees to engage and direct their effort and initiative to achieving your organization's goals. Among 12 global research organizations to have investigated this whole area of engagement (see Gibbons, 2006), the most commonly cited factors affecting engagement are:

- trust and integrity;
- nature of the job;

- ability to align individual effort with company performance;
- career growth opportunities;
- pride in the company;
- relationships with co-workers;
- personal development;
- relationship with immediate line manager.

Clearly, there is far more to engagement than interesting work for good pay. Personal relationships and the reconciling of personal and corporate goals make complicated demands on any employer, which we shall consider in detail later in this chapter.

MEASURING ENGAGEMENT

Having established what we mean, and why engagement can be a problem for so many in the 21st-century organization, we must look for a reliable measure of engagement. This is not easy. One of the most widely used measures of engagement was devised by the Gallup organization, and is published every quarter on the basis of the Q12 survey: 12 standard questions on engagement issues (see Gallup, 2001).

In overview, seven out of the 12 questions relate to the immediate personal contacts of the respondent in the workplace. Two of the questions relate to alignment – the relationship of the respondent's job to the goals of the organization, three questions highlight the importance of personal development, and three questions emphasize the need for workers to feel personally valued.

On the basis of the survey responses, Gallup divides workers into three categories: engaged, not engaged, and actively disengaged. The descriptor for 'engaged' is worth noting, as it sets quite a high bench-mark. Engaged workers are deeply committed to their jobs and their organization. Strongly energized, they exult in using their individual talent to fulfil the objectives of their organization. They make suggestions and launch new ideas. They enjoy taking individual responsibility. They strive constantly to improve their performance. They thrive on strong relationships with their managers and co-workers. They spread positive energy to their colleagues. (How many of these paragons do you have working for you?

Conversely Gallup defines 'actively disengaged' as being seriously unhappy with the organization, trying to spread that to others, and being resistant to change. 'Not engaged' is broadly neutral; these employees do their jobs but do not put in any additional effort unless pushed to.

In its inaugural Q12 survey, Gallup (2001) estimated that: no fewer than 24.7 million US workers – 19 per cent – were 'actively disengaged'. These disengaged workers took 3.5 more days away from work than other workers – an extra 86.5 million lost worker-days – and they cost the US economy between US$292 billion and US$355 billion in lost production.

In contrast, engaged workers (26 per cent of the workforce) were three times less likely to be planning to leave the company within the next year and nearly three times more likely to be planning to spend their entire careers with their companies.

Other research organizations like Towers Perrin, Hewitt and ISR have developed subtly different approaches to the subject. Because researchers and consultants offer so many ways to define and measure engagement, it is difficult to compare engagement levels across different surveys. Moreover, the reported levels of employee engagement often vary widely.

For example, in 2003 Towers Perrin reported engagement levels in the US workforce at 21 per cent, while the following year ISR reported them at 75 per cent (Towers Perrin, 2005a; ISR, 2004). Did the US workforce become miraculously engaged in a single year? In fact much of the range is attributable to the diversity in strategies and techniques used to classify survey respondents as highly engaged, disengaged or somewhere in between, as well as the categories that result. For example, the only employees that Gallup characterizes as 'engaged' are those who 'answer with a strong affirmative' to all 12 of Gallup's Q12 questions (ie all 5s on a five-point scale). This is a very restrictive approach given that at least one of the items could reasonably warrant a response below 5 from time to time, even for highly engaged employees (eg, 'In the last seven days, I have received recognition or praise for doing good work', or 'I have a best friend at work'). Gallup ends up characterizing a minority of the workforce (25–30 per cent) as engaged (Buckingham and Coffman, 1999).

Other engagement surveys are arguably more revealing. They seek to measure the actual components of engagement – the cognitive, emotional and behavioural facets of the connection between individuals and their work (see box).

ISR's approach to engagement measurement: think, feel, act

ISR (2006a) defines and measures three aspects of engagement: thinking, feeling and acting. The 'think' component taps into 'the degree to which the employee believes in and supports the goals and values of the company'. The 'feel' component assesses employee 'pride and emotional attachment to the company'.

The 'act' component is divided into 'Act-Extra Effort: the willingness of the employee to "go the extra mile" on the job', and 'Act-Stay: whether the employee is planning to stay with the company'.

ISR then uses a data-driven technique called cluster analysis to identify natural groupings of employee responses to survey items measuring four dimensions of engagement (think, feel, act-stay, act-extra effort). This approach yields four categories of engagement: 'highly engaged' (47 per cent), 'complacent' (14 per cent), 'less committed' (20 per cent) and 'fully disengaged' (19 per cent).

Highly engaged employees are defined as being positive on all four dimensions of engagement. Complacent employees are those that intend to stay but refuse to put in any extra effort, while less committed employees are likely to leave despite being average on the other dimensions. This latter group may be feeling external pulls like better offers elsewhere, a desire to relocate or changing career aspirations. The fully disengaged are relatively negative on all four dimensions – they are not intellectually or emotionally connected to the organization, exert the minimum required effort in their jobs, and are probably actively planning to leave the organization.

INTERPRETING ENGAGEMENT MEASURES

While measurement is important and these surveys are all in widespread usage, the scores in themselves give little guidance in deciding what action to take in response. What really has driven the scores? If a survey tells you that only 20–30 per cent of your workforce is apparently engaged, this would seem to be a major problem and you might expect to have very low performance and a lot of people walking out. But this is not usually the reality: you need to be pragmatic, and most important, to get behind the numbers to understand the real sources of engagement and what actions you can take. For example, it is hard for management to give people a best friend at work.

Organizational efforts to improve engagement often concentrate on increasing engagement among those who are moderately engaged or disengaged, or the complacent group ISR defines. But there are different ways of being disengaged. Some people stick around without adding much value, yet do not cause many problems for the organization either. Others stick around and wreak havoc. However, good performance management practices should flush out these sorts of individuals.

The value of differentiating types of engagement beyond the basic categories of engaged or disengaged should now be apparent, particularly since different groups of people become engaged or disengaged for different reasons. ISR found that engagement was driven by different factors for the highly engaged and complacent employees. Highly engaged employees responded more to factors like leadership and management effectiveness, organizational values, and opportunities to grow and make meaningful contributions. However, among complacent employees the biggest contributors to engagement were supervisor effectiveness, organizational focus on customer needs, and opportunities for long-term employment.

This suggests that organizations may need to target managerial interventions based on the patterns of engagement in the workforce. But it could also suggest that employee aspirations affect engagement: people expecting rapid career advancement respond to different factors from those content to take things at a slower pace. It is important to understand all the different drivers of engagement and to segment your workforce accordingly.

In our own firm's experience, the relationship with the supervisor or manager appears to be the key influence on engagement. In analysing data from our engagement surveys, we have found that over 80 per cent of the engagement score variance is attributable to the support from and relationship with the supervisor or immediate boss. At one level this is instructive and important, and it aligns with thinking about the importance of immediate leadership relationships but at another level it demonstrates weakness in the survey approach. There are other factors at play, but the measurement approach is not sufficiently sophisticated or insightful to bring these out.

We were therefore obliged to apply much additional judgement, using discussion with focus groups and other forums to get behind the range of engagement drivers in our organization. In reality there is no substitute for talking to employees, understanding what is concerning them and any sources of concern or unrest. Good managers and leaders do this continuously. Structured approaches to this are valuable, such as focus groups and employee advocacy programmes, and they signal to the employees that you take them seriously – provided also that they see some response and you are open with them about the conclusions from these soundings.

RELATIVE NOT ABSOLUTE MEASURES OF ENGAGEMENT

In view of the concerns about the validity of absolute engagement scores and categorization, you will almost certainly derive the greatest usable insight from engagement scores if you compare them across business units or entities within your organization. For example, suppose that a retail chain noticed significant variation in engagement scores between different retail stores. This could then be linked to performance measures such as sales growth to provide very valuable and actionable insight. Clearly the retailer would expect a higher-scoring store to outperform one with lower engagement: it could learn lessons from how that better-performing unit had managed to create a more engaged workforce. We have seen such analysis in a variety of organizations, which shows again that one of the biggest factors in building engagement in a high-performing unit is the effectiveness of its leader or management team.

There are some corporate-level drivers of employee engagement, such as trust in top leadership and the espoused values of the organization. However, in large organizations many of the management practices and behaviours that drive engagement are implemented at local levels: specific characteristics of employees' jobs (eg workload, degree of empowerment, input into decisions, autonomy); resources available to support employees on the job (eg training, technology); fit with job and career opportunities; workplace relationships (eg with co-workers, team members, manager); and compensation, rewards and recognition.

Hospital Corporation of America (HCA) has 190,000 employees providing healthcare services in the United States, United Kingdom and Switzerland. Its workforce is distributed among 182 locally managed hospitals, 94 outpatient surgery centres, and numerous imaging centres and physician clinics and offices. Despite measuring engagement levels for eight years, reading all the research, and consulting numerous experts, the company found its overall engagement levels unchanged. But the variations within its workforce were remarkable – ranging from 18 to 95 per cent. HCA concluded that 'they were trying – unsuccessfully – to force fit a single approach across the company' (SHRM, 2006).

HCA set out to figure out what its best units were doing right and learn from them to improve the low-performing units. It established criteria for high performance that included patient and physician satisfaction, productivity and retention, financial indicators, and employee engagement. It then identified facilities that had consistent or improving high performance over multiple years, and looked at the practices and behaviours that differentiated high- and low-performing facilities (Lewis, 2006). To narrow the engagement gap, HCA made its leaders more visible and improved communications; it improved staffing practices and made compensation and pay fairer; finally, it made recognition of employees and their contributions an integral part of the corporate culture.

The results have been impressive, particularly with the remarkable turnaround at the Medical Center of Plano (Texas). Between 1999 and 2004, this previously low-performing hospital managed to reduce staff turnover by 40 per cent and achieve a 43 per cent increase in engagement (on Gallup measures) while reducing costs and increasing profitability. The percentage of engaged employees rose from 18 per cent to 61 per cent, and the Medical Center of Plano has gone from the bottom of the barrel to having the second-highest engagement levels among all HCA hospitals (Robison, 2005).

DRIVERS OF ENGAGEMENT

Once you have diagnosed the areas in need of attention, you can concentrate on the primary drivers of engagement. As we have just seen, measurement tools will provide varying degrees of insight on these, but the variety of different drivers of engagement again illustrates the danger of oversimplifying approaches to improving it.

For catchiness, we list them as six Cs – content, coping, compensation, community, congruence and career. They are not mutually exclusive: quite the contrary, in a highly engaged organization all the Cs work together, like members of a sextet singing in harmony. They logically appear as something close to a hierarchy, not dissimilar to our old friend Maslow's, as shown in Figure 5.1. The building blocks of engagement are the more rational elements of the job or tasks, how well we support people in doing them, and whether we reward them fairly. The higher levels fall more in the emotional elements such as alignment of values, and then up to career fulfilment.

We now give a brief outline of each of the six Cs in turn, before commenting in more detail about each area. There are many links between the ideas here and other areas we have touched on, such as the concepts of employee value propositions, skills development, and the importance of line manager development, which we shall talk

Figure 5.1   Drivers of engagements: the six Cs

about more in the next chapter. Engagement is a central theme to the talent-powered organization, so it is not surprising it is pervasive across the whole field of defining discovering, developing and deploying talent.

At the basic level, the first C that drives engagement is the actual **content** of a worker's job. What physical and mental demands does it make? What sense of achievement does it offer? Does it offer any kind of learning or discovery? Is the work meaningful? Does the individual fundamentally find some level of satisfaction in his or her work?

This leads logically to the second C which is **coping**. Has the worker been given the means to cope with the demands of the job, and are his or her set goals and objectives achievable? These comprise not only the necessary knowledge, technology and training, but also a conducive workplace environment, supportive managers and colleagues, and working practices and processes that reduce effort rather than add to it. And do the demands of the job match with the work–life balance expectations and hopes of the individual?

The third C is **compensation**. In the first instance this is about whether the individual feels fairly rewarded financially for his or her contribution, at a rate which is reasonably market comparable. But it is also about other forms and symbols of recognition and compensation, which can be as basic as a pat on the back from the boss for a job well done. A closely related point then is whether the individual understands how he or she should be compensated through clear objectives and goals, understands how he or she was actually evaluated, and feels that process is fair.

The fourth C is **community** – what degree of positive social interaction and connection does the individual feel? To what extent is work fulfilling his or her social needs, providing an enjoyable experience

Figure 5.2   Pay and motivation

with some sense of fun and some ready identity with others? Is the physical workplace environment uplifting and supportive of social interaction? How well does he or she feel supported by work colleagues? Is the culture of the organization collaborative or confrontational?

The fifth C is **congruence** – alignment of core values and culture, and meeting the expectations of the individual, as well as alignment of objectives. Did the organization meet the expectations set through the employee value proposition and formally communicated or implied when the individual joined the organization or a particular unit? Are the espoused core values which the individual expects actually met through the actions and behaviours of supervisors and leaders?

The last C is **career** – alignment between the career and life expectations and aspirations of an individual in the short term as well as the longer term, and the opportunity he or she can see in the organization. It includes the notion of work–life balance since younger people, in particular, will look at career as part of their portfolio of interests, desires and aspirations in their lives. It also includes the degree to which individuals see the organization investing in them, how much they are able to shape their own destiny, and even build their CV – as well as their pride in the organization and identification with it. This must also reflect the alignment individuals feel with their boss or other persons evaluating their position and performance, and their confidence that these people understand their career expectations and aspirations.

There we have it. If we get all these right then we should have an engaged workforce. Some of the six Cs must really be dealt with at an enterprise level, but most are manageable at an individual or team level. It is very important to note that all six of these drivers are directly influenced, either positively or negatively, by the individual's immediate boss or supervisor.

CONTENT: SPICING UP JOBS AND WORK

We all have to work for economic reasons, but real engagement comes from a sense that the work context is somehow life enhancing. Work takes up a large proportion of our lives, sometimes too much, and we often identify ourselves through our work. If we did not enjoy it we would seek to change it – surely a primal instinct.

The content of work can be managed and impacted every day by the objectives or tasks we set. People today are looking for more ability to affect their own jobs, hence the rise of contractor or free-agent workers. But we can also affect this in our organizations, through for example letting employees have more freedom in how and where they do the work. The growths in flexible working, working from home and job sharing are all responses to this, and allow people to determine much more of how they work. With the growth of computer-based work, many jobs are open to this although sometimes some creativity is required in how we schedule or organize the work itself.

Sensitivity to employees' concerns about their jobs is a vital element. The best people to know how to improve a job or the work being performed are the people performing the work. Giving them more opportunity to have a say in how improvements can be made is a consistent feature in high-performing talent-powered organizations.

In talent discovery and in deploying talent, matching the content of work to the capabilities and preferences of the person is obviously important. As we explored in Chapter 3, when selecting possible recruitment candidates, using a skills or competency framework provides a better means of matching people and roles. If we understand the competencies required for a role, we can also look at means of altering the competency profile required by changing the role, for example, to allow us to access different pools of talent if our preferred sources of talent are proving too competitive. One particular pool of talent at which many organizations are starting to look at more with the ageing of workforces is older workers. In retail and customer service-oriented roles, as examples, older workers have shown greater reliability and loyalty. Their interest in people makes them well suited to these roles, and they are more readily engaged in this type of work than their younger peers.

COPING: THE IMPORTANCE OF SUPPORT

People need physical, intellectual and emotional resources to engage at work. They must have energy to invest. Obstacles or distractions that drain resources will limit the amount of physical, mental and emotional energy that individuals can bring to their work roles, and therefore reduce engagement. Energy and engagement are limited and renewable resources – if you constantly draw on people's energies they will burn out, but if you provide ample resources for coping with job demands and work–life stressors you can renew the energy stores that enable people to engage. As Tony Schwartz and Jim Loehr explained in their book *The Power of Full Engagement* (2004), fostering engagement is about managing both exertion (energy expenditures) and recovery (renewal).

Even the most dedicated employees cannot work indefinitely with unreasonable job demands, unachievable performance objectives, toxic managers and colleagues, tedious work processes, or misaligned or meaningless jobs. Often the most highly engaged workers are the most susceptible to burnout. They may perform at high levels for a long time, but constant strain will burn anyone out. It is a predictable human response to excessive and prolonged stress. Symptoms of burnout include fatigue, low energy, lack of motivation and an inability to concentrate.

Workplace stress and job burnout contribute significantly to decreased productivity and quality, increased absenteeism and turnover, and eroding workplace morale. The bottom-line impact of burnout can be enormous. Studies have shown that stress costs US businesses more than US$300 billion annually, while companies in Canada and the United Kingdom lose US$16 billion and US$7.3 billion respectively (HR.COM, 2006). As Maslach and Leiter argued in their 1997 book *The Truth about Burnout*, burnout represents an erosion of engagement wherein vigour melts into exhaustion, absorption becomes an inability to concentrate, and dedication devolves into cynicism.

Your organization can help employees cope with the demands of their jobs and their lives so that they have the ability to engage at work. It can do so by providing employees with all the critical organizational resources they need to perform their roles – and removing barriers that stop them. More than that, the resources provided to employees should encourage them to grow and develop. Obvious examples of such resources are adequate training and enabling technologies that can automate routine tasks, but the organization also needs to take into account processes and routines. How easy is it to order new toner for the photocopier? How easy is it to make a suggestion and ensure that the right person reads it?

Coping resources should address all the factors that drain or renew people's energies, and diminish or enhance their physical, intellectual and emotional engagement. At a physical level, that might include long hours, stressful travel, limited exercise opportunities and poor nutrition. At an intellectual level, it could mean removing confusion about tasks and priorities, helping employees to identify and achieve the urgent, and defer or delegate the non-urgent. At an emotional level, it could mean dealing with tensions between work and home demands, or addressing concerns about unethical or inappropriate practices.

Coping resources make it possible for employees to engage. Access to coping resources reduces the physical and psychological demands of the job, makes the work more meaningful, and conveys respect for the employees' performance needs. A lack of coping resources will keep employees from performing their jobs effectively, while also hindering personal development and quelling motivation.

Sufficient autonomy at work is one of the most critical coping resources that fuels engagement. A key task for your organization is to find ways of giving employees more control over their working processes and conditions, so that they can develop personally and enjoy greater freedom. This can include what tools and technologies they might use to support their work, particularly since these tools are changing so rapidly – with, for example, PDAs, webcasts, collaboration tools – and organizations are all trying to learn how to use these and best absorb them in the working environment. In a study on knowledge workers Accenture carried out in 2002 and published in the *Sloan Management Review* (Davenport, Thomas and Cantrell, 2002), we found that companies who were most successful in matching IT to their knowledge workers provided extensive training and coaching to help people select for themselves the technologies that best helped them in performing their role or tasks.

Case study: Best Buy

At consumer electronics giant Best Buy, employees create their own schedules, decide where they will work and how they will get their jobs done. The company has not merely introduced flexibility to the workplace, it has institutionalized it in the 'Results Only Work Environment' (ROWE). This goes way beyond tweaking existing schedules and practices or adding new 'non-traditional' work arrangements. The problem with such relatively superficial variations is that old norms and expectations around face time and productivity don't change at the same time. Managers end up using inappropriate standards to evaluate employees' engagement and performance. Employees can end up being punished for taking advantage of company programmes.

By creating an environment where exercising freedom is the norm rather than the exception, Best Buy has completely changed the organization's mindset and practices around deploying talent. As long as the work gets done and employees meet productivity goals, no one in the organization cares how, when, or where employees work. Sixty per cent of the 4,000 people working at corporate headquarters have adopted ROWE. The results have been impressive. Employee engagement scores have gone up (Best Buy uses Gallup's Q12) (Conlin, 2006), productivity has increased (a 35 per cent increase accompanied the switch to ROWE), and staff retention has improved. Moreover, employees report increased loyalty, focus and energy, and improved personal relationships (Kiger, 2006).

COMPENSATION: VALUING AND REWARDING PEOPLE

As noted earlier, the rational drivers of pay and benefits are still important, but the more emotional drivers and intrinsic rewards are also critical in building engagement. The emotional drivers include the idea of fairness – was my performance properly recognized and assessed, and is my pay and compensation therefore reflective of that? – as well as the wider sense of recognition that people seek for their contributions.

Pay and benefits must of course be enough to induce people to take a job in the first place. However, when we say a job is rewarding, we do not just mean financially rewarding. We mean one that offers much broader sources of satisfaction, such as feeling that individual effort makes a difference and is appreciated. And it must be clear to the individuals how their performance got measured and how this has directly influenced their pay and compensation.

A Hewitt survey in 2003 of *Asia's Best Employers* had some striking findings under this heading. Whereas 83 per cent of employees of the Top 20 companies said that performance had a significant impact on pay, among employees of other companies this figure was a mere 47 per cent. In these companies, most people expected to be paid the same regardless of the results they generated. This gave them little incentive to engage more and try harder.

Equally interesting was the finding that whereas 80 per cent of employees of the Top 20 companies said they received adequate recognition (beyond compensation) for their contributions and accomplishments, this figure was just 37 per cent among the rest. In the inferior companies, most employees felt under-appreciated.

Under-appreciated and unaccountable, paid the same regardless of results, is it likely that such employees will be engaged with their work or their company's goals?

Case study – Constellation Energy

To infuse a culture of high performance by individuals, CEO Mayo Shattuck revamped Constellation Energy's compensation system. Shattuck explained, 'We told everyone, right down to the lowest-level employees, we're going to hold you more accountable for our performance.' Constellation Energy abandoned its old compensation system based on pay grades, and created a new compensation strategy with a transparent relationship between performance and pay. In the new scheme, Constellation often sets base salaries below the median of the marketplace, but offers variable pay based on strong company and individual performance, which could take an employee's total compensation above the ninetieth percentile. The new pay practices are aligned with a new five-point scale performance standard.

Constellation Energy allows each business unit to customize its own performance rating system, but makes a clear linkage between individual performances and individual compensation. By 2005, Baltimore Gas and Electric (BGE) was the most evolved of its units. Every one of BGE's 3,100 employees – from managers to meter readers – participated in the business unit's incentive programme. Under this performance system, 50 per cent of an employee's performance rating is based on performance against individual goals, 25 per cent is based on demonstration of BGE's core values, and the other 25 per cent is performance of role-specific competencies. For example, leadership role competencies include customer focus, managing relationships, managing work, building high-performance teams, driving for results, advancing improvement and managing individual performance.

Constellation worked aggressively to align its compensation strategies with its business strategies for growth, and employs pay practices that are

> unique to the energy business. Shattuck and his senior vice president of human resources Marc Ugol took a hidebound company and introduced 'competitive' compensation practices to align human resources strategies aggressively with the business strategies for growth.
>
> Source: Thomas (2005a).

Recognition for contribution made is so important and often so simple. When someone does something right, and it makes a difference to the organization, an appreciative acknowledgement from the right person at the right time may be all that is necessary to ensure that the employee does more of the same. These are the circumstances in which one word may be a long-time guarantor of engagement. Conversely, one moment of neglect may disengage an employee completely and permanently.

At Campbell Soup Co, CEO Douglas Conant believes in 'celebrating what's right' in the company, and regularly acknowledges employees' efforts and contributions with hand-written thank-you notes. During his first six years at the helm, he has written more than 16,000 such notes. This humble gesture speaks volumes about Conant's respect for people and the value he places on acknowledging strengths and successes. This 'personal touch' and his openness to employee opinions and feedback create a culture of trust and respect for the individual, and is an important part of maintaining a high level of engagement amongst his employees.

With all of this discussion on compensation and reward, how feedback is communicated and how employees are communicated to regarding their performance is a significant source of engagement or disengagement. People today, particularly the younger age groups, expect direct feedback and support from their supervisors on how they are performing and how they can improve, including being clearly directed towards learning and development opportunities to improve their performance. This needs to happen on an almost continuous basis, and is critical to effective performance and employee development. The days of only receiving feedback at a stilted annual performance appraisal meeting should be long gone.

The most effective continuous performance management processes embody regular communication between employees and their supervisors about the employees' day-to-day performance. This type of developmental coaching can enhance performance and increase engagement. Research has shown that performance improves when supervisors coach their employees. One study of salespeople revealed significant improvements in productivity and performance when supervisors spent more time giving employees constructive, individualized feedback on performance. Coaching encourages and supports employee engagement as well. Managers and supervisors provide critical resources, and remove barriers, which not only helps employees perform successfully in their roles, but also facilitates personal development.

COMMUNITY: PUTTING THE FUN BACK INTO WORK

The idea that work and fun are not mutually exclusive still strikes some people as odd. We have all heard the 'old school' mantra that people come here to work, not to enjoy themselves. But people now expect work to be fun at least some of the time, and they believe that part of their line managers' responsibility is to create an environment that is enjoyable and fun to work in.

Best-in-class companies engage talented people by creating an employment 'experience' that is in tune with employees' needs and interests, and also consistent with people's expectations today about what constitutes an interesting and appealing work experience. Many Silicon Valley firms and high-technology companies have been trailblazers in this area, and while some of the early exemplars of casual, free-spirited, fun workplaces became casualties of the dot.com crash, this mindset is alive and well at high-performing companies like Google, Genentech and Yahoo! (which are numbers 1, 2 and 44 on *Fortune* magazine's 2007 list of the '100 Best Companies to Work For').

Google, the publicly held company behind the world's largest search engine, has more than 10,000 employees worldwide and generated more than US$10 billion in revenues in 2006. Despite their enormous success and projected rapid growth, founders Sergey Brin and Larry Page remain deeply committed to sustaining a corporate culture that is inspiring and fun and where people love to work, and this is a crucial part of the employer brand and value proposition of the company. Google attracts, engages and retains employees by explicitly promoting the fun experience of working there (see box for Google's engaging EVP). In addition to offering employees a chance to be part of a community of people doing meaningful work, the company treats family, leisure and personal well-being as important parts of employees' lives, and things that it can also directly influence. So it has blurred the line between work and life, and expresses this directly in its values and employee value propositions.

Besides the appeal of working for an industry-leading firm, 'Googlers' can bring their kids to work, enjoy weekly roller hockey games in the parking lot, park their scooters and pets in their cubicles, work out in the gym and take a sauna or get a massage afterwards, and sit down at the grand piano that's in the company's lobby when the musical urge hits. All this and more is available right within the Mountain View, California 'Googleplex'.

Organizations seeking to create a compelling community that encourages engagement would do well to look at examples like this, and consider how they could provide more to their employees in the form of an inspiring employment experience.

Case study – Google

'Enjoy what you do, where you do it, and the people you do it with.'

'What is it that you really want to do? Your master plan, not just your 5-year plan. At Google, our strategy is simple: we hire great people and support them in turning their aspirations into reality. We work hard here, and play here, and dream here. Googlers are bright, passionate people with diverse backgrounds, coming together to create a unique culture. One where the open exchange of ideas is encourages and thinking beyond the norm is expected, no matter what position you happen to hold. Working at Google is as much a mindset as it is a job.'

Top 10 Reasons to Work at Google
1. **Lend a helping hand.** With millions of visitors every month, Google has become an essential part of everyday life – like a good friend – connecting people with the information they need to live great lives.
2. **Life is beautiful.** Being a part of something that matters and working on products in which you can believe is remarkably fulfilling.
3. **Appreciation is the best motivation**, so we've created a fun and inspiring workspace you'll be glad to be a part of, including on-site doctor and dentist; massage and yoga; professional development opportunities; on-site day care; shoreline running trails; and plenty of snacks to get you through the day.

4. **Work and play are not mutually exclusive.** It is possible to code and pass the puck at the same time.
5. **We love our employees, and we want them to know it.** Google offers a variety of benefits, including a choice of medical programs, company-matched 401(k), stock options, maternity and paternity leave, and much more.
6. **Innovation is our bloodline.** Even the best technology can be improved. We see endless opportunity to create even more relevant, more useful, and faster products for our users. Google is the technology leader in organizing the world's information.
7. **Good company everywhere you look.** Googlers range from former neurosurgeons, CEOs, and US puzzle champions to alligator wrestlers and former-Marines. No matter what their backgrounds Googlers make for interesting cube mates.
8. **Uniting the world, one user at a time.** People in every country and every language use our products. As such we think, act, and work globally – just our little contribution to making the world a better place.
9. **Boldly go where no one has gone before.** There are hundreds of challenges yet to solve. Your creative ideas matter here and are worth exploring. You'll have the opportunity to develop innovative new products that millions of people will find useful.
10. **There is such a thing as a free lunch after all.** In fact we have them every day: healthy, yummy, and made with love.

Source: http://www.google.com/jobs/

The other interesting aspect of community is the workplace environment itself, and the impact that can have on engagement. This has been much studied, and working environments have been experimented with for many years. Closed office spaces have given way to open working environments where even the most senior employees may end up with desks or cubicles like their staff.

Much of these workplace designs are intended to improve social interaction. For sure if the old office space was a series of enclosed offices with frosted glass doors, then having something more open plan sends a very different signal and makes managers appear much more accessible to their employees. Brighter décor, and more facilities for people to interact such as coffee bars and relaxed seating areas would seem to facilitate a better sense of community. However, the evidence is a bit mixed on the success of such workplaces actually improving creativity and engagement. If the bosses do not use open-plan spaces with relaxed seating, this will suggest to other people that they might be frowned on if they sit there themselves. Many open spaces get filled in by more cubicles as various teams or departments seek to expand and lay claim to the space that no one seems to own.

The impact of the behaviours and actions of the more senior people is crucial in making the notion of community work well with investment in office space that facilitates openness and more social networking. They have to live the values that experiments in open-plan offices seek to espouse. This is a key part of the idea behind congruence, which we shall discuss next.

CONGRUENCE: ACHIEVING ALIGNMENT FROM TOP TO BOTTOM

Congruence is crucial for engagement because it represents how the employee sees the cultural and core values expressed in the actions and behaviours of leadership. Are the promises and expectations set as part of the employee value proposition being met? If employees are to feel good about their organization, they must know that the same sense of values and alignment goes right to the top. In a highly engaged organization people know that its leaders are walking the talk and there is strong cultural alignment.

There is a natural sequence from the organizational beliefs and values through to actions and behaviours, and each chain in the sequence needs to align, much like the vertebrae in a spine need to align for a person to stand straight. The sequence is illustrated in Figure 5.3 in a model developed by Javier Bajer, former CEO of the UK Talent Foundation and now CEO of Possibilate, a UK-based consultancy.

An example of how this works in practice is shown in Figure 5.4. The processes and policies that define the intentions, promises and actions make the cultural values real, but they must be executed consistently. If in the example shown the organization failed to carry out its defined and communicated processes and employees saw that actions were therefore inconsistent with intentions and values, it would lose their trust.

To ensure that these processes are being carried out effectively, they should be measured. Performance measures that focus attention on

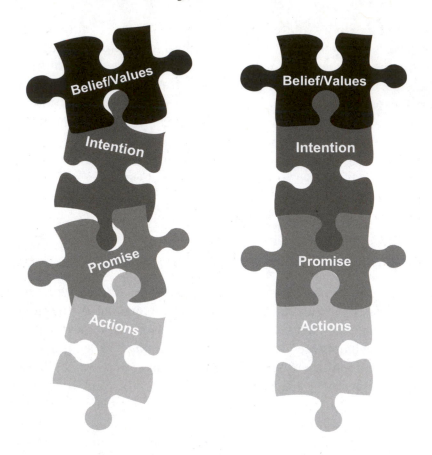

Figure 5.3 The chain from belief to action
Reproduced with the permission of Possibilate Limited.

the execution of processes, and surveys that test the feedback and response from employees such as satisfaction surveys and 360-degree feedback, should complete the chain.

Visible leadership gives a constant reminder of the objectives and values of the organization, and is also an essential part of alignment. Employees will be watching for behaviours and messages that reinforce the values, and seeing that first hand from their bosses and leaders is very important and reassuring – provided of course that those leaders are using consistent language and behaviours.

Authenticity in behaviours is absolutely essential. You cannot perform on the corporate stage acting something you do not believe in – you simply cannot keep it up and you will be found out. Nothing

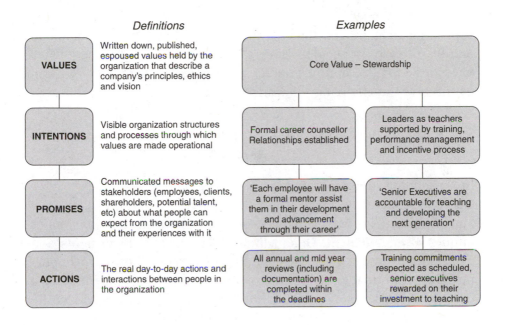

Figure 5.4 The chain in practice, from belief to action
Reproduced with the permission of Possibilate Limited.

is more guaranteed to break trust and confidence. That means that leaders must personally align the organization's espoused values, their own values, the promises they make and the actions that follow. A simple but effective tool developed by Possibilate called the Leadership Alignment Tool© or LAT allows individuals to test this alignment for themselves, and then take positive actions to realign where needed.

As we have previously explored, younger workers are much more sensitive to all these points than previous generations. They are generally much less tolerant of dissonant behaviours and have higher expectations of their direct leadership. For example, they will not take many cues from a leadership team that proclaims a belief in diversity but does not reflect that in its own makeup. They enjoy the opportunity of direct contact and having their voice heard, and they have much less respect for hierarchies. Ethical behaviours, respect for diversity and informality are traits they look for in their managers. They are looking for immediate role models, not so much at the head of the organization, but people they can directly relate to.

Since engagement is influenced so strongly by the immediate line supervisor or manager, then all these issues have to be understood and learnt early in people's careers before they manage others. They need to be taught, and in Chapter 7 we shall see how everyone can get involved in engaging the workforce.

CAREER: PROVIDING OPPORTUNITIES FOR ACHIEVEMENT AND BALANCE

In developing and deploying talent, a key task of leaders is to give employees opportunities to stretch themselves so that they can grow and develop. The very existence of such opportunities is a major builder of engagement. Organizations need to find placements and assignments for people to achieve this while contributing to important organizational goals. In other words, people development is not a peripheral, 'make-work' activity but a central objective for the entire organization. It is also therefore vitally important that leaders understand the hopes and aspirations of the people who work for them, and are able to align opportunities that meet those aspirations for their most talented employees. A great source of disengagement is the feeling that your boss does not understand you or understand where you want to go. Employees themselves also have a significant responsibility in making their aspirations and expectations known.

Moving people around the organization can keep them engaged and help them to meet their career aspirations within the organization, stopping them from having to look elsewhere. Marriott Hotels, for instance, keeps its managers engaged by providing many opportunities for development and advancement. Aside from the traditional functional and horizontal moves (moving from a limited-service property to a similar position in a full-service hotel, for example), managers can apply for lateral and 'diagonal' internships with other functional areas. Marriott Information Resources recently launched a programme that creates mentoring relationships, which allow senior leaders to learn about and contribute to areas of the business outside their comfort zone and current areas of expertise. Marriott prefers to promote from within, and views these programmes as a way to cultivate tomorrow's senior leadership (Thomas *et al*, 2006a).

UPS often deploys its own star performers to start strategic initiatives. For example, in the early 1990s, when it wanted to move down the supply chain, UPS recognized the untapped opportunity to capitalize on its own core business and deep knowledge of the customer. Instead of going outside for logistical support, it searched in-house for high performers to launch a service parts logistics initiative. UPS Service Parts Logistics now manages US$1 billion in contracts for multinational customers such as IBM, Hewlett Packard and GE Medical, and is a critical part of the integrated package of services that UPS offers its customers. The 30 UPSers who were deployed to the initiative were able to expand their own skills and experience while making meaningful contributions to the business (Thomas *et al*, 2006b).

Another very important part of understanding Career is the challenge people increasingly feel about balancing their work and life commitments and interests, and leaders need to be aware of this. Employees must feel that working and personal life are mutually sustaining rather than in conflict. This highlights one of the key current challenges of employee engagement at the stages of development and deployment: work–life balance. If your organization's employees use this term regularly it is a sign of potential trouble. The term actually implies that 'work' and 'life' are different things, and worse still, that they are opposing forces.

It might be better to talk of 'work-as-life' initiatives. Paraphrasing Clausewitz, one might then say that 'work is the continuation of life by other means'. This might encourage organizations to think about the challenge of making their employees identify their work more strongly with their personal goals. A successful 'work-as-life' initiative would be one that allowed employees more time and energy for *everything* they want to do in life, fusing these ambitions in a way that delivered maximum value to themselves and their organization.

As we saw earlier in talking about Google, newer companies particularly in the high-technology sectors have started out with a very different view of how to manage the seeming conflict of work and life and blur the boundaries between them. Technology itself is making this happen more and more, as we find ourselves 'always on' or always reachable, with access to work and colleagues anytime, anyplace, anywhere. Organizations are all learning how to deal with this, as we are as people. Technology can provide many advantages for work and life flexibility, but it is also easy to abuse and therefore create more stress. There seems little doubt that this will continue to be a growing trend in how we work, and the virtual workers and other shifts in working patterns we reviewed in Chapter 1 are here to stay.

Bringing work and life closer together is arguably most important for the mid-career professional who might easily stagnate if not presented with new challenges. As we noted before, middle managers who are typically the mid-career employees are a very vulnerable segment of the workforce, and often have among the lowest levels of engagement. They have all the concerns of where they are going and whether they are in the right place to achieve their goals and ambitions, at the same time they have added responsibilities at this stage in their lives. The surveys we have carried out on this cohort of the workforce have consistently shown that around two-thirds of middle managers would seriously consider moving jobs, and at any time up to one-third are actively considering or reviewing other options. This is indicative of high levels of disengagement.

So mid-career rejuvenation is becoming ever more important to re-engage with mid-level managers who might otherwise leave. People are spending more of their lives working, not more time in retirement. Employers who find ways to sustain employees' energy and enthusiasm throughout these newly extended careers will reap significant returns. As Mary Catharine Bateson observed, 'Careers, like marriages, can grow stale. Technical training updates obsolete skills, but renewing aspirations is a greater challenge' (Bateson, 2005).

A small but growing number of companies have found that sabbaticals from corporate life can stimulate personal growth and professional development for mid-career professionals, while also benefiting the company and society. Silicon Graphics, Adobe Systems, Wells Fargo and Hallmark Cards all encourage the use of sabbaticals to rejuvenate employees by providing them with time for activities that draw on underused skills, develop new talents or inspire creativity. Regardless of how employees spend the sabbatical time, they inevitably return re-energized and recommitted to their work.

Arrow Electronics, one of the world's largest products and services provider to the electronics industry, offers sabbaticals of eight to 10 weeks to employees after they have reached seven years of service. Kathy Bernhard, director of management development, explains, 'We tend to run people really hard. There's a lot of travel associated with many of these jobs, and it's a high-stress, high-change industry, so it's really just a chance for people to get recharged' (Schettler, 2002).

However, the sabbaticals are not simply a career break for the employees who take them, they are also a career boost for the employees who step in to cover for colleagues on sabbatical. 'We get a lot of bang for the buck,' Bernhard says. 'Not only does the program serve as a retention tool for people who have the opportunity to go on sabbatical, but it also serves as a developmental tool – and in some ways a retention tool as well – for people who get to do sabbatical coverage. In a sense, everybody wins.'

GAINING MORE INSIGHT ON ENGAGEMENT – SEGMENTING THE WORKFORCE

As we have seen, people today have many options in how they interact and communicate, how they spend their time, and how they seek fulfilment. What is engaging for one person can be the opposite for another, and all the drivers of engagement we have discussed will vary by segments of the workforce.

Organizations have far greater diversity in their workforces, crossing cultural and geographic boundaries. Yet most of them persist in trying to manage people the same way. Flexibility is frequently regarded as synonymous with cost and complexity. Indeed, because it has been a mantra of business for so long that standardization means efficiency, most organizations have re-engineered and systematized themselves towards that goal.

But managing people in today's world demands flexibility, not standardization. That means that organizational and HR capability must be significantly improved to support flexibility in work contracts, work locations, ways of working. We shall explore the implications of this for HR and support functions in Chapter 6, but let us start with a little bit more science in understanding what people actually want, and what managers need to think about in creating opportunities for them to achieve it.

We have already discussed how we can learn from the disciplines of marketing to create compelling employee value propositions for groups and individuals, and exploit channels to market them to potential employees. In this context we have consistently spoken of segmentation, and this is also a critical construct for engagement.

Tesco, the leading UK-based retailer, wanted to understand engagement and retention issues in its workforce. As a retailer, it readily understood the importance of customer segmentation, and applied it to its workforce to understand the different aspirations and expectations of each segment. Working with Lynda Gratton from the London Business School, an authority on people implications of strategy, Tesco surveyed its workforce and concluded there were five primary behavioural and attitudinal segments, as shown in Figure 5.5. By understanding motivations and needs by segment, Tesco could begin to tailor the employment proposition to enhance overall engagement and commitment levels and improve retention.

With this sort of insight, approaches to managing the drivers of engagement can be much more targeted. For example, in the areas of content and coping, for those who are in the Work–Life Balancers category, providing options to work from home, flexible hours working or part-time arrangements for periods of time would all be very relevant. For those that Live to Work, these will assume much less importance and they will be interested in career – how can they advance? Are their career expectations well aligned with the options for them to progress, and understood by their line manager?

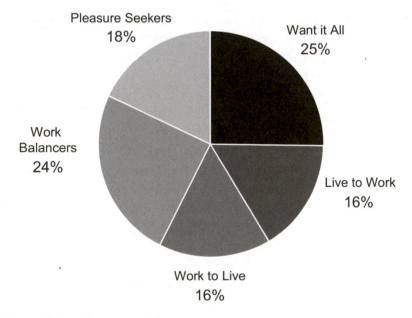

Figure 5.5   Tesco workforce segments
Adapted from Gratton (2003).

For people in the category of Work to Live, their motivation is much more likely to focus on compensation. They will be much less concerned with long-term career and positioning, and will really be looking to maximize their financial reward for working. Pleasure Seekers and those who Want it All are more challenging. Community is certainly a major part of what will drive them – do they get the fun and the social networking out of the job that they want, and can they relate to their managers as people, not just as co-workers or technical experts? These groups may have lower loyalty to their organization because their expectations are high, and if they do not get what they want in many different areas they are likely to go.

It is essential to devise strategies and options with flexibility to adjust to the needs of different sections of the workforce. As with all issues around talent today, we have to be able to focus our strategies and actions at a much more granular level than we have in the past, with a thorough understanding of how the six Cs of engagement apply to different groups of people.

It is self-evident, for example, that career factors will vary by age, just as work–life balance issues change by age and circumstance. Other attitudinal dimensions of the workforce will also make each of the six Cs more or less important to individuals, including their level of ambition and aspiration (of which their education background is often a strong indicator). To understand the workforce segments requires the usual marketing techniques of surveying and focus groups, but with a much greater sophistication than is usually employed, in both the survey and analysis of results. Engagement surveys have typically given organizations far too little insight into differences across workforce segments. As noted earlier, if a survey can explain only one major driver of engagement it will not reveal the importance of other drivers for different workforce segments.

Some interesting tools are emerging that can help with some of these analyses. A Sydney-based company, Change Track Research (CTRE), has created a very powerful surveying and analytical approach to understanding the drivers of change. As its research progressed, it became clear that the factors that most influence the progress of change are similar in characteristics to the broader factors that influence engagement. Indeed, one of the dimensions CTRE measures for managing change is engagement of the workforce. The analysis also picks up leadership at different levels, and identifies a very important construct of 'turbulence' – how many concurrent changes are happening, and how much confusion and concern this generates. Many organizations would recognize such turbulence as an important issue in the levels of motivation and engagement.

The fundamental observation noted by Warren Parry, CEO of CTRE, is that in all organizations, across the many dimensions in CTRE's analysis, people always cluster in clearly observable groups. Each group will have some common demographic elements – not surprisingly, some recurrent groupings are defined around attitudes and concerns at top management versus middle management. However, it is also easy to observe other factors at work across organization units. The different groupings can then be characterized, much as Tesco was able to do. For example, in analyses within Accenture we could characterize some groups as 'sleepy in success', while others appeared to be in a 'crisis of confidence' or 'battling it out'. Clearly we needed a different strategy to engage each of these groups.

Such analytical techniques can start to provide much greater insight in addressing not only engagement, but other issues such as leadership capability, willingness and ability to change. These are the most difficult areas of talent to understand, but the most critical for high performance.

THE KEY INGREDIENT OF ENGAGEMENT – THE LINE MANAGERS

As we have observed throughout this review of engagement, and indeed in so many other areas of creating a talent-powered organization, much falls on the shoulders of the line manager. They are the people to whom the majority of employees report, and who can most impact the drivers of engagement. Yet too often this crucial part of our organization is sadly neglected.

How often are line managers appropriately qualified and trained, aligned with corporate vision and goals, able to enthuse others with the vision, and imbued with the necessary people skills to bring the best out of those in their charge? To pose the question is to know the likely answer, yet these are the fundamental leadership skills that all organizations need, and which we so often complain we are short of in our own organizations.

We are talking for the most part about those who are commonly known as 'middle managers', a term that has in itself a distinct undertone of disparagement. It almost implies mediocrity, limited ability for decision making, people who will never become strategists and leaders. The Russian language has a synonym which captures these implications: *tchinovnik*.

For the moment we shall abandon the semi-derogatory term 'middle manager' in favour of the more neutral 'line manager', which in most organizations means someone who is expected to deliver a certain specified output from the staff for whom he or she is responsible. If the target is met or outperformed, the line manager will be rewarded, whether or not the staff are performing to their maximum commitment and capability.

Line managers and supervisors explain and transmit the objectives of the organization to their staff. If they cannot understand those objectives there is no hope that the staff will do so – however many mission statements or top-level strategic communications they receive from above. If line managers concentrate simply on achieving their given target, there is every likelihood that they (and their staff) will miss some target that is equally important, or will overlook some wider objective that is even more important.

The Gallup Q12 questions mentioned at the beginning of this chapter focused strongly on the immediate personal working environment of employees – on which line managers are the biggest single influence. Study after study has suggested that the biggest single factor in deciding whether people like their jobs or detest them is their relationship with their immediate supervisor or line manager. It also takes us back to that vital ingredient in our definition – the 'emotional' connection between an employee and his or her organization. The Corporate Leadership Council report of 2004 showed that emotional drivers such as relationships with one's manager and pride in one's work had four times greater impact on discretionary work effort as did rational drivers such as pay and benefits.

The extent to which organizations are failing to make the most of this vital resource is shown by Table 5.1, from the 2003 Towers Perrin survey. Here we see that a mere 18 per cent of supervisors and foremen are 'actively engaged' in their work, and so are an almost equally shocking 25 per cent of directors and managers. There is a huge drop in engagement scores from the top of organizations to the

Table 5.1 Engagement across job levels
Source: Gibbons (2006). Data source: Towers Perrin (2003).

Job level	Actively engaged (%)	Actively disengaged (%)
Senior executives	53	4
Directors/managers	25	10
Supervisors/foremen	18	15
Specialists/professionals	16	18
Non-management salaried	14	20
Non-management hourly	12	25

mid-levels of management. No wonder they do not do such a great job of motivating those beneath them!

Line managers are the people who can have the most impact on ensuring that each of the six Cs is working for each employee. As to content, line managers can make the daily routine of a job enriching or stultifying. As to coping, line managers can deliver or deny the tools for their workers to do their jobs, and they can make workers feel confident and empowered, or humiliated and enraged. As to compensation, line managers have the power to make workers feel recognized or neglected, or even cheated. As to community, line managers can create a sociable, collaborative atmosphere in their unit or an atomistic, hostile one. They can encourage or wither personal relationships with their people. As to congruence – the line manager is the representative of the values and behaviours of an organization. He or she has the power to make employees believe or disbelieve in its values and in its sincerity. As to career, line managers can make workers feel that they are progressing or regressing.

If you have any doubt about the influence of line managers, or that the negative depictions could be true in reality, go back to the description of the demented Kurt as reported on Vault.com in Chapter 3, page 102. Then we should ask ourselves the question, how is it that such managers can exist and to what extent do they exist in our own organizations?

They do exist, and there are many of them, and they are a significant cause of low engagement. It is true to say that people join organizations, but they leave managers. But it is also true to say that they exist because organizations and senior management let them exist, and do not do enough to train and develop this key segment of the workforce. There is in general far too little training of line managers on key leadership capabilities of people management and development, understanding of their business's strategy and direction, and other general leadership areas such as how to effectively manage change. We let the famous 'Peter Principle' continue to operate, with people being promoted to a level beyond their competence, and then do not do enough to support them. It is no longer good enough (if it ever was) for managers to be in their position because they had the best technical or functional knowledge of their area, if they cannot also perform as leaders.

SUMMARY

If there is a single lesson to take away from this chapter, it is to focus on the strategic role of line managers in building engagement. Do everything you can to make them take responsibility for building engagement, and give them the training and support they need to do it. Make clear that they will be judged on their success.

To succeed in this, you will of course have to ensure that line managers themselves are engaged. So begin by applying each of the six Cs to them. Do they have satisfying jobs? Do they have enough support, especially training, to cope with their existing demands, let alone the new challenges of building engagement in others? Are they fairly compensated and fully recognized for their contributions? How do they feel about their own careers and personal development? As to congruence – line managers almost certainly know your organization well. Do they identify with its values? Do they have faith in the way the organization applies those values? If your line managers cannot give a satisfactory answer to each of these questions, your organization has almost no hope of building an engaged workforce.

However, line managers also need one further resource. They need a clear strategy, created and sustained by senior leaders, and a clear understanding of their role in delivering it. In our next chapter, we shall discuss how to embed good systems and align mindsets and efforts to build and sustain a talent-powered organization.

6

Embedding and Sustaining Talent Power

No matter how good you get, you can always get better.

Tiger Woods (1975–)

In the preceding chapters we explained how organizations that build distinctive capabilities in defining talent needs, discovering sources of talent, developing talent potential, and deploying talent in the right place at the right time will outperform competitors. When these capabilities are aligned with each other and with business strategy, and when investments in each area are measured and tracked, talent can multiply and power your organization to high performance.

In the first half of this chapter, we explain the importance of understanding and measuring how talent contributes to your organization's performance. Experience reminds us that 'what gets measured gets managed'. Talent-powered organizations measure investments in talent processes and capabilities to ensure that they are defining, discovering, developing and deploying talent in ways that create value for themselves. We present a robust measurement framework that can focus your organization's energies and investments as you build your talent power.

Of course, embedding and sustaining talent multiplication capabilities is not simply a matter of measurement. It requires robust and integrated processes that support all aspects of talent management

throughout the employee lifecycle, and it requires complete alignment of mindsets and efforts within the organization. Talent multiplication happens in the course of the daily business of the organization
as employees engage in their work activities, create and innovate
together, and interact with customers and clients. For this reason,
everyone in your organization must be involved in multiplying talent
– from top leaders to HR, to line managers, to employees. Therefore
the second part of this chapter focuses on the need to:

- **maintain visible leadership** that keeps your organization permanently focused on talent as its top priority;
- clearly **encourage and reward line managers for their performance** in nurturing talent;
- ensure that **HR departments and training organizations are
  modernized** and retain the capabilities to act as the expert advisors, supporters, adjudicators and enablers of discovering, developing and deploying talent in the organization.

MEASURING TALENT'S CONTRIBUTION TO BUSINESS PERFORMANCE

Robust measures of talent or human capital are essential to all the
stakeholders of an enterprise. Top management and leadership must
understand where and how investments are necessary in improving
the performance of the workforce to drive greater business value, and
it is equally essential for every line manager to understand how the
competencies of their teams line up and how well they are performing
against specific organizational objectives. HR leaders need a deep
understanding of gaps and needs in talent across the organization,
and where and how investments need to be made, and they must be
able to present the business cases for investments that talk about
value outcomes, not just possible cost savings in process improvements. Outside investors or stakeholders also need more visibility. As
we explored in earlier chapters, given the contribution of human and
intellectual capital to future business value, outside stakeholders need
some better frameworks for assessment.

Measurement to date has generally focused on costs of human
resource administration activities or some measures of process effi-

ciency. These are the easiest aspects of talent management to measure, and are well supported through benchmarks such as from the Saratoga Institute. Cost metrics for people-related processes are important to track, especially where the operating model for HR requires cross-charging of HR services to business units, such as through a shared services model, which we shall review later in this chapter. However, since so many HR functions still work with fragmented systems, processes and capabilities, it can be challenging simply to get reliable cost data.

In the end, cost data of this type point only to efficiency of processes, and not to effectiveness or value. Since costs of human resource administration activities are actually a small component of overall organizational costs (typically in the range of 1–3 per cent of selling, general and administrative (SG&A) costs) then even if administration activities are very efficient, the overall savings to the organization are small. And if you have efficient first-quartile cost-benchmarked recruitment processes, for example, but those processes are not giving you the right people, then that efficiency is valueless.

Different surveys across many organizations continue to show that despite the wide recognition today of the importance of business outcome measures related to workforce investments, there is a significant lack of actual measurement or agreed frameworks. For example, research by the Chartered Management Institute in the United Kingdom found that there was a wide divergence on what senior executives and directors of UK companies thought was important to measure, and what was actually being measured: for example, 60 per cent of respondents thought succession planning important, but fewer than 10 per cent thought they were effectively measuring it. There was a similar dichotomy on managers' effectiveness mapped against departmental performance (over 60 per cent thought this important to measure, fewer than 10 per cent thought they were achieving this) (Scott-Jackson et al, 2006).

Our own research in this area suggests that measurement of the effectiveness of HR and training support, and the impact of investments in people on business performance, is generally unsatisfactory, although it is now receiving much more attention. Among the key findings of our High Performance Workforce Study (Acenture, 2006, 2007) were:

- nearly 40 per cent of respondents said they had no formal measures to gauge the impact of their HR/training efforts on the performance of their top three workforces – 39 per cent said they had such measures but only for some HR and training initiatives;
- customer satisfaction and retention, employee attraction and retention, and employee productivity are the most common outcome-based metrics;
- 59 per cent of respondents said they used margin/profitability to measure the business impact of HR and training efforts;
- 50 per cent used revenues/sales pipeline to assess HR/training effectiveness.

The study also separated out what we termed 'human performance leaders'. Only 9 per cent of the surveyed population rated the performance of their top three workforces at the highest level, rating them 5 out of 5, and they rated the performance of their HR and training functions highly. To illustrate these leaders' accomplishments more fully, we compared their responses and experiences with those of respondents from 'laggard' companies, which account for 54 per cent of our overall survey sample. We defined laggards as those companies in which none of the three top workforces is performing at the highest level (ie, received a performance rating of 5). In comparing the two groups on the subject of measurement, 35 per cent of the leaders had formal measures for gauging the impact of all HR/training support activities versus 19 per cent of the laggards, and 65 per cent of the leaders used margin or profitability as a measure to gauge the success of the HR function's performance, versus 56 per cent of the laggards.

TOP-LEVEL PERFORMANCE MEASURES

At the highest level, measures of organizational performance for all public sector organizations or NPOs will always include profitability. Given the reality today of the high proportion of value and market capitalization tied up in intangibles, associating talent with profitability would seem to be a sensible top-level business performance measure. The simplest measure would be profit per employee. Total profit is in the end the result of the total number of employees and how much profit is attributable to each employee, so it would be valuable to make these measures visible to contribute to greater understanding of organization performance. Although they may be difficult to compare across industries, especially for those that are more or less capital-intensive, such measures would illuminate the key part of intangible value, which is such a large constituent of total value, and reveal how it is changing. Alongside other traditional measures such as return on invested capital, they would provide more total insight into performance.

Organizations can improve profitability and performance by investing more capital, or increasing or reducing their investment in and cost of labour – in its simplest form, by adding or shedding staff. Clearly, if profitability per employee is rising, that would show good use of talent in either circumstance.

Accounting measures will give visibility to capital invested, but as cost of labour now accounts for such a large part of the cost base (for service-based companies these costs will be the largest single cost category, and typically will be of the order of 60 per cent or more of the total cost base), then we should also give visibility to cost of labour – how many employees and the average cost per employee. Other basic measures of the health of human capital within a business include attrition or staff turnover rates, absenteeism rates, engagement levels or feedback from employee satisfaction surveys, average length of employee service, and total training days per employee and levels of training investment as a proportion of employee costs.

None of these top-level measures are difficult to obtain for any organization, although they are rarely reported. We would advocate them as basic measures that all organizations should track, which if done consistently would provide greater insight into what is really driving performance today and expectations in the future, for all stakeholders.

In the same study by the UK Chartered Management Institute quoted earlier, its surveys of wide samples of top executives came up with five key human capital measures seen to be most significant in impacting future financial performance. These were consistent for both UK-based and international company executives. The measures were:

- leadership;
- staff motivation;
- training and development;
- performance improvement;
- pay and reward structures.

These measures are broadly similar to the basic measures of human capital described above, with the exception of leadership. There is no doubt that this is a critical measure of the health and future value of an organization, but it is challenging to measure objectively. The study proposed various measures focusing on aspects such as top team reputation, assessment of percentage of managers with necessary leadership capability, and percentage of managers ready to assume a greater role.

There is no doubt that more and more organizations are trying to measure key aspects of talent and link these to performance outcomes, using these as part of their internal measurement or balanced scorecards. For example, a number of years ago Sears, Roebuck and Company built some sophisticated statistical analyses to link talent to financial performance. Sears, a large North American retailer, mapped the relationships between human capital practices, employee attitudes, customer attitudes and behaviours, and revenue. It saw exactly how its employees' attitudes to the job and the company drove customer service, which in turn influenced customers' satisfaction with the shopping experience and the likelihood that customers would recommend Sears to friends and family as a good place to shop (Weatherly, 2003, citing Becker *et al*, 2001: 124). Customer enthusiasm promoted customer advocacy, which is directly linked to revenue growth and is a key driver of profitability at Sears. Through the research and analysis, Sears found that a 5 point improvement in employee attitudes would lead to a 1.3 point improvement in customer satisfaction, which produced a half per cent increase in revenue growth (Huselid, 2005; Weatherly, 2003). Investments in specific human capital processes that improved how employees felt about their jobs and the organization would increase customer referrals and enhance business results.

Other organizations such as SYSCO Corporation (see box) and Royal Bank of Scotland (RBS) have built on this idea, also focusing on establishing the linkage between improvement in people measures, such as engagement and employee satisfaction, and improvement in sales and customer service. RBS is one of the leaders in the measurement of people and their relationship to business performance, and as Neil Roden, group director HR, says, they are trying to further develop ideas that came from organizations such as Sears – 'we're trying to take that one step further by saying if you can get your people scores up by a certain figure, this is what it will do to your business output measures'.

Case study – SYSCO Corporation

SYSCO Corporation is a US-based Fortune 100 global food-service marketer and distributor, with a turnover of US$33 billion and 50,000 employees across 172 operating units. As executive vice president and chief administrative officer, Ken Carrig makes sure SYSCO's human capital strategy supports the business strategy. Much of the value SYSCO provides to customers is a function of the strong relationships its associates form with customers.

SYSCO tracks key financial, operational, customer and human capital metrics for all of its autonomous operating companies. The three critical human capital metrics are work climate and employee satisfaction, productivity (measured as employees per 100,000 cases sold) and retention. After several years of measuring and analysing these key metrics, SYSCO has been able to link effective talent management practices to business results (Cascio, 2005). The operating companies with highly satisfied employees had higher revenues, lower costs, and superior customer loyalty and employee retention (Cascio, 2006). This is a causal relationship, such that employee satisfaction leads to customer satisfaction, which drives long-term profitability and growth (Cascio, 2005).

SYSCO has demonstrated empirically that effective talent management drives employee satisfaction and employee retention, so it routinely measures and manages seven dimensions of the work environment that are related to employee satisfaction: leadership support, front-line supervisor, rewards, quality of life, engagement, diversity and customer focus (Cascio, 2006). Under-performing units are identified and helped to improve. Talent retention improved from 65 per cent to 85 per cent in six years, and saved the company nearly US$50 million dollars in the process.

MEASURING THE RETURN ON INVESTMENT IN TALENT DEVELOPMENT

Besides payroll, the largest investment in people is usually in learning and development. Measurement in this area, as we noted in Chapter 4, is usually limited to input measures of things like training attendance and training days provided, or soft assessment measures of whether recipients of learning 'enjoyed' the programme or feel that it has somehow 'helped' them in their work. Measures that evaluate learning as a strategic investment, and look to establish return on investment (ROI), would be more insightful and more valuable to decision making.

Since Accenture invests heavily in learning, we set about developing a robust learning ROI model built on outcomes for which good data could be found. These elements include recruiting, retention and performance. Performance was defined as 'per-person margin' and measured as the person's bill rate times the number of hours billed minus the cost of that employee over the same time period. Per-person margin is widely accepted in the firm, and in similar services companies, as a measure of personal contribution to company performance. A simple conceptual model was developed as shown in Figure 6.1.

The Y-axis of the model, 'contribution', can be defined in terms of whatever activity is most meaningful to a company and particular workforce. For Accenture, the contribution measurement is the per-person margin. The X-axis represents employees' time with the company. The presumption here is that the longer the employees are with the company, the more they contribute. Based on a review of the research literature, it was assumed that if the company offered training, people would remain with the company longer, hence the longer dotted line versus the short dashed line which represents no training. In addition, people's speed to competency and contribution would be faster and higher when they were offered training, as represented by the higher and steeper slope of the dotted line versus the dashed line. The overall effect of training on the business should be the area under

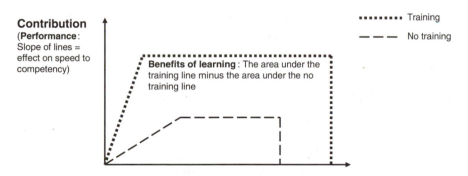

Figure 6.1   The Accenture Learning ROI model
Source: Vanthournout *et al* (2006).

the line for the company that trains, minus the same area for the company that does not provide training. This very robust model holds up to statistical analysis. The team used the total hours of training employees had received as an independent variable. They controlled for factors that might confound the relationship, such as experience, inflation and business cycle, and they used per-person margin as the outcome or dependent variable. This allowed them to calculate the effect of training on performance while controlling for factors that might cloud the picture.

The ROI for Accenture was calculated as the net benefit of training based on the assumptions above divided by the non-payroll costs of training. The final return on investment turned out to be an impressive 353 per cent. The firm could take this number to the outside world of investors and say confidently, 'Investment in human capital is important. Learning investments are not just the "right thing to do" for our people. They make strong financial sense.'

MEASURING PROCESS EFFECTIVENESS – THE CONCEPT OF MATURITY

Assessing how well an organization develops and manages its human capital assets is not an easy task. Human capital processes are among the 'softest' processes in an organization. Even when a human capital process does have a tangible metric associated with it – like 'time to hire' for recruiting or 'training dollars per employee' for learning – these measures address only the efficiency of the process, or the input costs. They tell us little or nothing at all about the effectiveness of the process – how well the activity is carried out and how reliably it achieves its intended impact.

One very important contributor of understanding about processes is the concept of maturity – a measure of robustness, integrity and consistency in application of those processes. All organizations will say that they have the major talent management and development processes in place in some form – performance management, succession planning, rewards and so on. The real question again is how effective these are, and whether they are well designed, well documented and understood (by both the people applying them and the recipients or employees), consistently applied, and effectively integrated with each other. In other words, are the processes institutionalized and does the organization have the commitment and ability to perform the processes consistently? If it is carrying out performance management, are the means by which people are being assessed visible, fair and consistent; do the results clearly link to rewards; can it also link performance shortcomings to learning and development programmes? Integration of this kind is necessary for the most effective and impactful processes, and it needs to be assessed consistently against some reliable benchmarks.

The concept of process maturity and measurement has been widely applied in the software industry in particular. The pioneering work of the Software Engineering Institute at Carnegie Mellon University in the United States from the late 1980s created the Capability Maturity Model (CMM). This has been widely applied, and has proven very important in helping the software industry to arrive at standards to distinguish among vendors, according to the reliability and repeatability of core processes associated with the development, testing and release of software. The developers of the CMM carried their work further, to include what they refer to as the People Capability Maturity Model or P-CMM (Curtis *et al*, 2002), applying the same sort of thinking to the maturity of people processes.

P-CMM is an approach that allows people-related processes to be evaluated against a five-point maturity scale that ranges from basic level 1 to optimizing level 5, with managed, defined and predictable as levels 2 to 4. Each maturity level has defined characteristics for how processes are designed and implemented. The P-CMM framework has been much less widely adopted than CMM, but in recent years it has had some application, especially in the aerospace, software development and IT services industries which had already adopted CMM. It has been used and applied notably in India, where there is such fast growth and fierce competition for talent in the IT services industry. Most of the major players there have gone through the certification process, which is very detailed and thorough and are recognized at level 5. To be level 5 you must have very mature, embedded processes that integrate consistently. The processes assessed through the P-CMM framework are comprehensive and include:

- staffing (includes recruiting, selection and planning);

- managing performance;
- training;
- compensation;
- work environment;
- career development;
- organizational and individual competence;
- mentoring and coaching;
- team and culture development.

P-CMM points to the use of competency frameworks as a central construct in mature and integrated processes. Even at the lower levels of maturity, it is a common theme to have a competency framework with ability to assess competency and having competency-based practices. It highlights the good practices of process measurement as the means to verify that processes have been performed consistently, and reinforce accountability for their execution.

Level 5 certification requires a high level of capability in people-related support processes. Its adoption by IT services companies in India demonstrates the degree of sophistication in people management they have had to develop in order to attract and retain their people. Assessed this way, these organizations today have some of the best talent management capabilities in the world.

However, P-CMM is time consuming and requires a lot of effort to apply, and it does not measure the linkage to business performance and outcomes. It is assumed that high levels of maturity in people processes and practices improve outcomes. However, Bill Curtis, one of the original authors of P-CMM, has carried out further research over several years through longitudinal analyses of data at the same companies. He has been able to show, in the example of software development, that higher levels of maturity of processes lead to significant reductions in defect and rework rates as organizations mature from the lower levels up to level 5, and significant improvements in programming productivity. Evidence from Accenture also confirms that high levels of process maturity do equate with better employee retention and engagement, and we are engaged on further research in this area ourselves.

The key linkage that we are seeking is between investments in people and people development processes, and business outcomes and performance. Understanding this linkage is crucial for improved decision making and prioritization of how to drive high performance in a talent-powered organization.

MEASURING INVESTMENTS IN HUMAN CAPITAL – FROM PROCESSES TO PERFORMANCE OUTCOMES

It is essential to provide good information to managers at all levels on the effectiveness of the talent management or human capital support processes, and on how investments in people are resulting in useful business performance outcomes. It is a familiar concern to hear managers complain that they 'have all these data but no real intelligence'. You need to measure what matters, but to know what matters you must establish a firm connection between business or organizational strategy and human capital strategy, as we discussed in Chapter 2. Otherwise, you will measure to no avail.

In other words, you need to have a clear sense of how talent leads to value. Talent-powered organizations understand how their workforce talent and their human capital capabilities contribute to the achievement of the firm's strategic objectives and create value for the firm. For these high performers, it is impossible to talk about how the business achieves its objectives and creates value for stakeholders without talking about talent's contribution. At Southwest Airlines, the leading low-cost airline in the United States, workforce capabilities are essential to executing their 'low-cost operations and high-quality customer service' strategy. Business guru Tom Peters (1994) once described Southwest's formula for success in this way: 'Cost, cost, cost, customers, customers, customers, and people, people, people. Any three-year-old can understand it.' An organization's formula for success must be powerful, but it need not be complicated.

Any approach to measurement needs to link talent to value. For example, in Figure 6.2 we distinguish four levels of measurement arrayed in a causal flow, very similar to the structure we described in Chapter 2 of linking business strategy through to HR strategy, which controls many of the underlying processes of talent management. At the top are an organization's **strategic objectives**. These can be depicted many different ways: what matters is that they are measurable.

Directly beneath are the levers or drivers of greatest influence in achieving those objectives; these are commonly referred to as

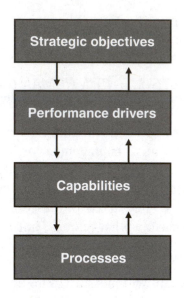

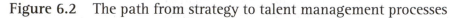

Figure 6.2   The path from strategy to talent management processes

'**performance drivers**' in the management literature. They are few in number, and vary in importance depending on the markets in which a given organization competes. For example, according to Michael Treacy and Fred Wiersema, authors of the business standard, *The Discipline of Market Leaders* (1997), most businesses elect to compete on the basis of product leadership, operational excellence or customer intimacy. Each basis for competition relies on a different prioritization of innovation, product quality, productivity and customer satisfaction.

Beneath the performance drivers are the **distinctive capabilities**; these are the human and organizational competencies that most distinguish the critical elements of success for the business and, for example, make it possible to be innovative, produce high levels of quality, ratchet up productivity or keep customers satisfied.

Finally, at the base of the model are the **processes**, activities, practices and programmes that fuel the creation of those distinctive capabilities. Capabilities like creativity and engagement do not come about of their own accord; they are themselves the product of enabling conditions, deliberate managerial effort and robust supporting processes. Successful innovation may be impelled by higher levels of engagement, but as Chapter 5 has just shown, engagement cannot be taken for granted in the first place.

Framing the issue in this way allows you to work your way from top to bottom, or from bottom to top. You can start with strategic objectives or from an assessment of the underlying processes. Either way, the key is to focus on the path through which value is created, not measure elements in isolation. It is only with this understanding of the links between talent management and performance that organizations can measure and invest in processes and capabilities that will directly affect whether they achieve their strategic objectives.

A FRAMEWORK FOR PRIORITIZING AND MEASURING HUMAN CAPITAL INVESTMENTS

Various models have tried to make the linkages from underlying processes to outcomes, or as we saw earlier in Chapter 5, linkages between particular aspects of talent such as engagement and overall business performance. Most of these models seek to link from basic HR-type measures to some measures of business value or outcomes, including Bassi and McMurrer's model of human capital dynamics (2007); Boudreau and Ramstad's (2005) HC Bridge Framework, which links from efficiency to effectiveness and impact; Becker, Huselid and Ulrich's HR scorecard (2001); Kaplan and Norton's strategy maps (2004); and Gallup's 7S path to business performance (Coffman and Gonzalez-Molina, 2002). The challenge with all the various approaches is to track the complete value chain, from human capital processes to human capital capabilities, to key performance drivers, to business results.

Over the last few years a framework has been developed that seeks to track the full value chain to provide a better assessment of how effectively an organization's human capital processes create value. This framework, called the Human Capital Development Framework (HCDF) (Benton *et al*, 2004; Cantrell *et al*, 2005), draws on best practices in the fields of human resource development and learning, as well as state-of-the-art measurement techniques. It enables an organization to:

■ determine its strengths and weaknesses in 13 key human capital processes;

- prioritize and track investments;
- target those interventions most likely to have the greatest overall impact on its business results.

The framework assesses, benchmarks and determines the relationship between elements in four distinct areas, shown as tiers in Figure 6.3:

- Business results, or the financial measures of organizational success, such as capital efficiency, revenue growth, return on invested capital and total return to shareholders (Tier 1).
- Key performance drivers, or the intermediate organizational outcomes, such as customer satisfaction and innovation, that are typically captured on a balanced scorecard (Tier 2).
- Human capital capabilities, or the most immediate and visible people-related qualities that human capital processes produce, such as workforce performance, employee engagement and workforce adaptability (Tier 3).
- Human capital processes, or the specific practices and activities organizations undertake to develop their human capital assets, such as performance appraisal, workforce planning and learning management (Tier 4).

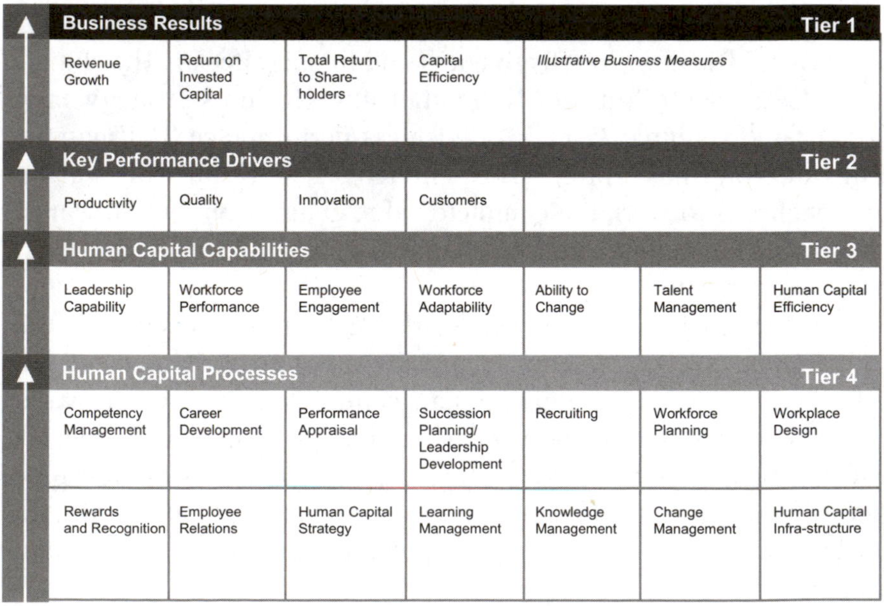

Business Results				Tier 1		
Revenue Growth	Return on Invested Capital	Total Return to Share-holders	Capital Efficiency	*Illustrative Business Measures*		
Key Performance Drivers				**Tier 2**		
Productivity	Quality	Innovation	Customers			
Human Capital Capabilities				**Tier 3**		
Leadership Capability	Workforce Performance	Employee Engagement	Workforce Adaptability	Ability to Change	Talent Management	Human Capital Efficiency
Human Capital Processes				**Tier 4**		
Competency Management	Career Development	Performance Appraisal	Succession Planning/ Leadership Development	Recruiting	Workforce Planning	Workplace Design
Rewards and Recognition	Employee Relations	Human Capital Strategy	Learning Management	Knowledge Management	Change Management	Human Capital Infra-structure

Figure 6.3 Accenture Human Capital Development Framework
Source: Benton *et al* (2004).

These processes were carefully chosen, based on previous research and our thinking and experiences concerning the programmes and practices most likely to affect workforce performance and business results. They include not only core HR processes such as recruiting, career development and competency management, but broader human capital processes as well, such as workplace design, learning and training, and knowledge management. The framework explicitly assesses the maturity of each process, drawing on some of the thinking that was developed through P-CMM: the extent to which it uses best practices, how well it supports employees, and its reliability and repeatability.

Tier 4 measures in the HCDF and the P-CMM are similar in many respects, and HCDF uses the construct of maturity in assessing the human capital processes, but what makes the HCDF distinctive is its direct linkage to organizational attributes and business outcomes. Mature processes are capable, robust, world-class in their operation and finely tuned to the business model of the organization that employs them. This distinction is important: mature processes provide the greatest benefit when they are aligned with the business model. Maturity scores in Tier 4 result from the combination of quantitative and qualitative information collected from a survey sample of human resource executives and employees who answer questions related to the following three dimensions.

Human capital best practices

The degree to which an organization incorporates best practices in each process area can tell us much about the effectiveness of the process. Best-practice questions also serve to assess the completeness of the underlying practices for each process, and the degree to which technology and other resources are used to maximum effect. The definition of each best practice represents the collective knowledge and expertise of Accenture specialists and academic researchers as to what constitutes highly effective, state-of-the-art performance. Sample best-practice questions for the career development process are listed in Table 6.1.

Execution and support of the process

The HCDF also adopts the assessment of maturity of processes as a key measure of effectiveness and robustness of processes. It incorpo-

Table 6.1 Sample best-practice questions for the career development process

---

Questions include the extent to which:

- the organization provides employees with access to web-based tools (24 hours a day, 7 days a week) for:

  ○ documenting career development plans and skill gaps
  ○ identifying appropriate training
  ○ recording and reviewing feedback

- the organization provides employees and supervisors with access to web-based tools (24 hours a day, 7 days a week) for viewing the career paths and associated job descriptions for all jobs in the organization

- employees use feedback from others (ie multi-rater feedback) on their strengths and weaknesses as input into their career development plans

- employees have career development plans that describe such things as development activities (eg job experiences of training) and/or possible future roles

- career counselors (ie supervisors or team leaders) review employees' development plans, looking for such things as realistic career goals, development activities and timelines

- employees meet with their career counselors to discuss their progress against their career development plans.

Source: Cantrell and Benton (2005).

rates key areas of assessment, including the extent to which an organization has:

- people (including human resource managers, supervisors, and/or employees) with the skills and abilities necessary to support and use the processes;
- clearly defined goals for each process and management support of their pursuit;
- clear and consistent policies for each process;
- measurement and continual improvement of the processes.

Employee use of the process

The HCDF also seeks to understand the employee perspective. Data obtained from employees serve two purposes: as a cross-check for the reliability of the data provided by human resource executives, and as an assessment of the effectiveness of the process in supporting its end users. Sample questions addressed to employees for the career development process include:

> To what extent does your organization's career development process provide you with the talent you need to meet current and future business needs?

> To what extent do you have a career development plan that provides you with clear guidelines for achieving your career goals?

The tool offers organizations guidance on which human capital processes to invest in, and enables them to begin to evaluate the return on their human capital investments – a metric that is critically important yet largely unavailable. For example, researchers used the HCDF to determine which human capital capabilities and processes would need to be enhanced if an organization sought to improve its ability to innovate (see Figure 6.4). From data collected in over two dozen applications of the HCDF, researchers could show that the most direct path to improved innovation began with effective and mature processes in rewards and compensation, employee relations, workplace design and knowledge management. These, in turn, enhanced employee engagement – and employee engagement turns out to have the highest correlation with the level of organizational innovation. The HCDF therefore suggested that if an organization really depends on innovation, its best bets in spending money on people would be on rewards, employee relations, workplace design and knowledge management.

This framework has been implemented with organizations in a variety of industries around the world (see box). Based on a growing database, the framework has established empirical links between specific human capital investments and business results. It enables organizations to diagnose their strengths and weaknesses in key human capital processes, benchmark their performance against others, and track performance changes over time. Most importantly, the framework enables executives to assess their

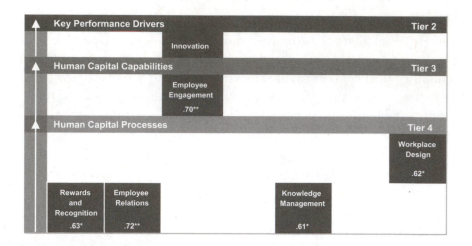

Number at bottom represents the correlation (r) with the element at the next tier
*r = .05   ** r = .01

Figure 6.4   Drivers of engagement and innovation

capacity to achieve superior business results through investments in human capital.

Case study – SAP America

SAP America, the North American sales and services division of enterprise software giant SAP, embarked on a new business strategy in 2002 in order to turn around its declining revenue and market share. SAP America's future depends on its ability to deliver a steady stream of innovative software applications to its customers and to tailor them to their targeted market segments. Executives therefore wanted to ensure that the company focused on the human capital processes that could help it innovate. As president and CEO Bill McDermott put it, 'The people component of executing our strategy was by far the most important. If we didn't get that part right, we wouldn't win. And we were in this game to win.'

SAP used the HCDF to gather empirical, quantifiable data to establish priorities human capital investments. The framework results showed that the company would be best served by focusing investments on a limited set of human capital processes: learning management, human capital infrastructure (eg the firm's HR processes) and succession planning. These three processes were identified as those that would have the greatest impact on workforce performance and thus business performance. SAP subsequently invested in three aspects:

- identifying clear learning and training requirements for its job families and ensuring that managers work more with employees as coaches and mentors to develop learning plans;
- improving the accuracy and user-friendliness of processes involving payroll and benefits administration, with an HR call centre to boost employee satisfaction and engagement;
- establishing processes to give managers a clearer picture of people who might later qualify for key positions, and to ensure that high-potential individuals received development plans to help them build their skills.

One year into the turnaround efforts, many initiatives were paying off in improved process and capability scores. According to senior vice president of human resources, Terry Laudal:

> The framework is immensely useful because it gives us something the HR community is generally lacking: a common language and vocabulary for what we do. It frames human capital processes in terms of business results, providing a professional toolkit for our HR team members to speak with business executives about the value of human capital investment and the contribution to the bottom line.

Case study – SKM and human capital

Sinclair Knight Merz (SKM) is an Australian company that provides consulting services in sectors including the environment, infrastructure, building and property, and power and mining. In this industry, companies compete largely on the basis of their people – specifically, their knowledge, skills and the ability to provide excellent client service. SKM was looking for ways to increase its ability to manage and grow its workforce capabilities. The company used the HCDF to identify ways of enhancing its human capital capabilities.

SKM's human capital processes were among the strongest ever analysed using the framework. However, the analysis did more than just confirm existing strengths. It also identified a number of areas where further improvements could gain the organization vital competitive advantages in workforce performance. For example, although the HR function had many best practices in place, executives were surprised to learn how few employees in non-managerial roles knew about them. This finding prompted HR to increase its communication to staff.

The framework results have also prompted SKM to review its methods of recruiting top talent, and put in place an internal capability in key geographies. This initiative has been immediately effective; it has reduced time to recruit key staff, increased the firm's ability to handle large recruiting assignments, and significantly increased the satisfaction of managers with the HR recruiting service.

THE TRANSFORMATION AND REORGANIZATION OF HR

The HCDF and all the other measurement techniques commonly used show clearly that underpinning the value drivers of human capital are the human capital or talent management processes. It is impossible to drive up the performance of people consistently if the basic support processes are inconsistent, poorly applied, or poorly structured and enabled.

Most of these processes are the responsibility of the HR function. However, as we indicated in Chapter 2, HR is too often poorly positioned and lacking in some of the capabilities that are needed to optimize these processes, and is therefore not always well placed to achieve the necessary improvements leading to real talent multiplication.

The HR function has been receiving a lot more attention and investment in the last few years than it probably ever did in the past. It is HR's moment in the spotlight. Leading organizations everywhere are looking at how to significantly improve the capabilities and value added of the function, for all the reasons we have explored throughout this book, and many are well down this path. Many global organizations are in the process of scaling up their HR capabilities and seeking to manage their people consistently across all parts of their organization. It is part of the essence of a truly global business, or indeed any business that runs across different locations and organizational entities, to manage and develop its people through consistent and proven practices and processes. Visibility to the total workforce, mobility of people around organizations, and the focus on distinctive competencies and critical workforces, all require this.

We also described in Chapter 2 the evolutionary journey of HR and the organizations it supports, and compared this to the journey frequently undertaken by the quality and IT functions. The journey begins with improving the capabilities and focus of attention from administration and control, ultimately to adding value and enabling talent multiplication.

However, HR has often found it hard to shift its focus of attention and capability from administration. HR still tends to concentrate on transactional and administrative activities – payroll, personnel administration and record keeping. As Jac Fitz-Enz, founder of the Saratoga Institute, the HR benchmarking organization, said in 2000, 'Only 10 per cent of current HR contributions add value. The other 90 per cent is transactional nonsense.'

Working with a wide range of HR organizations, our own research has shown that even where HR has organized itself to split out the roles of more specialist HR personnel to focus on more 'strategic' activities, the department still spends most of its time on administrative or trans-actional types of activity. This is shown in Figure 6.5, based on a wide range of activity analysis data from many different organizations. Although it may be transactional, of course this work has to be done. The issue is how to best do this work to ensure that it is done as efficiently as possible and in a focused part of the organization.

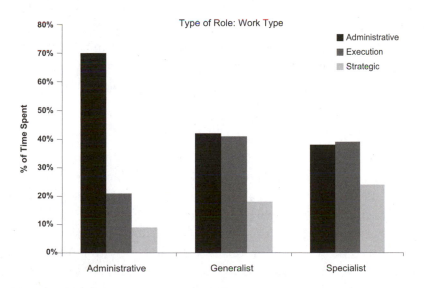

Figure 6.5 HR activity analysis

THE KEY PILLARS OF EFFICIENT AND EFFECTIVE HR CAPABILITY

Most transformations and reorganizations of HR have included a number of common elements. As we have seen, a primary goal is to focus transactional activities and to improve the value added of HR. We shall look at four basic building blocks or pillars:

- **Harmonized processes and policies** – consolidation of processes and policies to consistent formats and approaches, leading to more consistent management of people.
- **Integrated HR systems and information** – a consolidated database of information providing 'one truth' for HR information, and integrated systems to support integrated processes.
- **Shared services** – consolidation of administrative and transactional activities into a common or shared service structure that supports the rest of HR across the business, supported by an integrated service management measurement framework.
- **Focused and improved capabilities and governance** – organization of the activities into specific areas of capability to ensure focus, with improved governance to ensure adequate oversight and appropriate management of all parts of HR across the organization.

These areas are to a large extent interdependent – it is hard to have good shared services, for example, unless the processes and policies are harmonized, and likewise it is hard to reorganize HR to provide more focus without these two aspects coordinating. Each area is worth some further exploration, given the importance of the HR function to enabling a properly talent-powered organization.

HARMONIZATION OF PROCESSES AND POLICIES

HR-related processes and policies, in all but the most centrally managed organizations, have evolved as the business itself has evolved. When new organizational entities came into being, or parts of organizations were devolved or acquired, the people management processes tended to come or go with them. They therefore grew up in many different ways, with different standards and policies that reflected management's views at the time. Organizations often have many different pay schemes, performance management processes, recruitment processes and channels, reward programmes and so on.

This makes it difficult to compare, measure, and provide consistency of best practice to managing the talent across the organization.

Getting more alignment on processes and policies is essential for consistency and efficiency, but the evolution of these processes often makes it difficult to achieve agreement on this. HR is one of the few functions on which every line manager and business leader is likely to have an opinion. Many leaders across the different parts of organizations relish the elements of empowerment they have, and their ability to manage their part of the business as they see fit, and this is usually true in their thinking about people. The common refrain of 'You don't understand – we're different' has been heard thousands of times as organizations seek to get more consistency. Yet in the area of HR or people processes, good processes are not only consistent, they are able to flex where they need to support what truly needs to be different or localized. Bring together the common elements, execute them in a common way, and allow for variation where it is really needed.

So the management of sales people, their reward and compensation programmes and so on, will be different from those required for the people operating machinery on the factory floor, but the administration of these activities can be done together, allowing the best people to support both of these groups of employees in a consistent way. However, to make this happen requires compromise and understanding of the organization's ambitions for the common good. Objectives such as the ability to take a consistent view of people across the business, consistent assessment of skills and competencies, and consistent measurement and data, are much easier to achieve if processes and policies are more standardized.

There is now some documentation and understanding of what might be regarded as best practice process flows from various sources and case examples. We use these extensively to provide a baseline against which to compare existing practices, and this is usually a better startpoint than arguing over which particular version of the various existing processes across the organization is the best.

Best-practice process re-engineering is now also well understood, and should be applied – things such as having process owners (an issue to which we shall return in considering HR organization), process measures, process documentation and training, and good structure and workflow. Measurement of processes should include the concepts of maturity we discussed – how consistently they are being executed, how well integrated they are – as well as whether or not they are meeting efficiency and cost targets.

Since HR processes often involve different people at different times, workflow and understanding process integration are essential. We have noted before that integrating the key talent processes is an essential part of talent multiplication. Employees need to see and understand how the process of objective setting is linked to performance management, and how that connects to rewards, and where and how they then need to focus on learning and development to improve their performance. They also need to understand how their careers are developing, and how performance assessment, skills and competency needs, and opportunities to learn the new skills they require for new roles can best be achieved. Skills and competency frameworks that underpin this integration are essential in providing a common language and context.

These are crucial connections, but they happen all too rarely today. In many of the organizations we have studied, concern or dissatisfaction with their people arises most significantly when there is no visibility across these processes. As we noted in earlier chapters, clear performance feedback and recognition of developmental needs, together with the support that the organization can provide, are becoming ever more important to the new generations of workers.

INTEGRATED AND COMMON HR SYSTEMS

HR has rarely received good investment in systems, and often missed out on the wave of enterprise management systems that first swept through organizations in the 1990s. HR itself was usually unable to articulate the need, or business case for investment or the IT organization had other priorities, and it has therefore generally been left with a legacy of poorly integrated and fragmented systems.

This is reflected in the multiplicity of spreadsheets and local databases that have grown up in support of local management need, or to plug the gaps of the poor information and functional support provided by the various HR systems. Without proper systems, not only are the processes described earlier poorly supported and inefficient, but the data or information needed to understand talent and value are missing. Without data, HR credibility with business leadership is compromised and weakened.

Today, the major enterprise system or ERP vendors – dominated by SAP and Oracle/Peoplesoft – have broad-based and flexible HR systems platforms that have been implemented in every type of business. They incorporate many of the best-practice processes in HR, and provide off-the-shelf integration across these processes, and into other systems such as finance. The sales of these systems are accelerating as organizations consolidate their HR processes and look for more integrated HR systems platforms. There is much interest and investment in the HR systems marketplace, and there are also many niche solution providers, providing richer functionality, in particular for the higher-value HR processes such as recruitment and resourcing, performance management and learning. Consolidation is happening and will continue as this market matures. IDC, Gartner and other analysts all see growth in these markets of 8–10 per cent or more per year for some time to come, and in some regions of the world the growth rate is significantly higher as organizations seek to catch up.

One area of modern HR systems is providing better enablement of talent processes and integration across organizations. It is generally

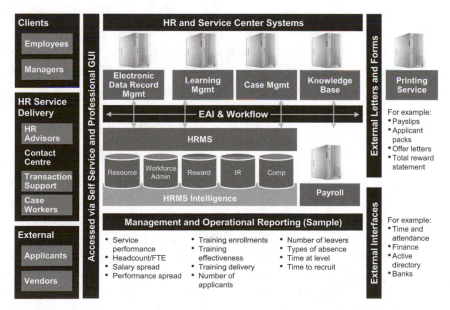

Figure 6.6   Depiction of integrated HR systems

titled eHR – a moniker for e-enabled HR. Since many HR processes directly engage people and managers, it makes much sense to provide more ability for them either to perform directly parts of those processes, or to access directly and more easily information that is relevant to those processes. So-called 'self-service' has emerged in many organizations as a response, but also as a means to drive greater efficiencies. For example, rather than employees having to send a note or make a call to someone in HR to update personal details such as address changes or bank account details, they can do it themselves directly into the system. This assures them that the details have actually been recorded, and allows them to check current information; it also removes a simple administrative task from HR.

Self-service and e-enabled HR processes need to be well designed to ensure ease of use for the range of likely users, and their implementation and uptake need to be properly communicated. They must also be supported by well-designed and consistent processes, and their assimilation into the organization must be carefully managed. Users, whether line managers, employees or outsiders, have to see and understand the value of such processes to overcome the natural resistance to using them, and the belief that they are a means to reduce cost for HR but add tasks to everyone else.

HR SHARED SERVICES

The idea of shared services for support functions is far from new, and many organizations have shared services in some form, typically as part of finance, procurement and IT functions as well as HR. When executed well, shared services provide consistent support and capability in administrative and transactional processes in a cost-efficient way to the rest of the organization.

The concept is essentially to bring together as far as possible common activities into one place to execute them consistently and efficiently. The activities that can most benefit from this are the more administrative and transactional tasks, from payroll-related processes to personnel data management and the administration of higher-value functions such as learning and resourcing. Moreover, much HR information and query support can be provided from a shared service centre, such as information on HR policies and procedures, and standard HR reporting.

Connection to the rest of the HR function and the managers and employees is then provided through a contact centre, or through self-service technologies. Since the HR processes need to work across the shared service centre and the rest of the organization, there needs to be workflow-type technology that facilitates the passing of casework, for example from the line HR organization to the shared service centre.

Well-run shared service centres filter the work coming in to the centre to ensure that it is processed efficiently and effectively. The more experienced HR personnel in the centre will be assigned the more complex case work, whereas basic queries or administrative activities can be done by less trained or less skilled staff. Effective use of self-service can also filter out many minor activities from the centre.

Organizations with multiple locations and across multiple geographies inevitably have to consider how many shared service centres they should have and where to locate them. In the last few years there has been a clear tendency to consolidate into a small number of centres, with their location essentially determined by considerations such as language support and time zones. As more and more big-name organizations like P&G, BT, and Unilever are forging a path in moving these centres to low-cost locations across the world such as India, confidence and capabilities are increasing, allowing more radical restructuring of HR support in this way. Cost has prompted further consolidation and location of centres to low-cost countries: the cost savings can be very considerable, at least 20 to 30 per cent on current operations for most businesses.

However, these programmes of change are not for the faint-hearted, and require significant effort and investment to make them happen successfully. Given also the difficulties in setting up new centres in the low-cost locations of the world, and the issues of availability of suitably qualified resources to staff these centres, there has also been a significant growth in outsourcing these centres to other organizations.

As we noted in Chapter 1, the favourite locations for these types of business processes are rapidly becoming crowded. Staff costs rise, issues of staff recruitment and retention grow, and without the scale to be able to respond to these pressures and move work around or open centres in other cities, these can make life difficult. Outsourcing service providers are locating HR capability across many centres around the world today; they are constantly looking at locations and flexing the support infrastructure to be able to move work around.

Figure 6.7 shows some examples of processes and how they might split between different parts of the organization.

With the additional complexities of split tasks and processes, and the need to ensure that the shared service centre is operating effectively and efficiently, it is essential to have good measurement and management. A comprehensive service management framework that covers all of the HR processes should provide:

- **planning and prioritization** – identification and prioritization of service requirements according to business objectives;
- **service reporting** – enables the delivery of an agreed, defined, measurable and continuously improving service;
- **visibility** – measurement of service performance against agreed-upon key performance indicators and service level agreements, and regular reporting and review of measurements;
- **improvements** – identification of areas for improvement based on feedback and measured performance trends;
- **flexibility to change** – a controlled and formal, but not bureaucratic, change mechanism.

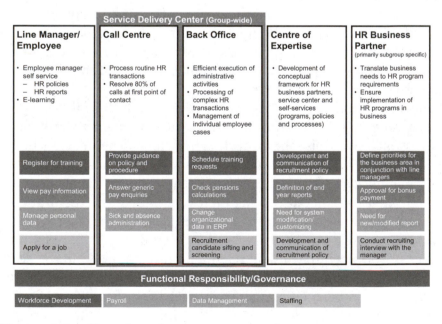

Figure 6.7 Shared service process examples

Without such a framework, it is easy to lose sight of the objectives and inefficiencies can easily build up. In particular many organizations have found that work intended for transfer from the line HR organizations to the shared service centre does not move completely, or starts to creep back. Shadow organizations build up and duplicate work and effort, and key cost-saving objectives are then lost.

The changes in behaviours required from both HR people and the employees and line management should not be underestimated. For many HR people, administrative and measurement work is their 'comfort zone', while employees, and line managers in particular, need to let go of the old ways of working where they were accustomed to high-touch HR support or the ability to walk in to the HR department to get their questions answered. Again, good measurement raises the visibility of how well the newly defined processes and organization are working, and will show if and where the change is incomplete.

Case study – Levi Strauss & Co

The business challenge

San Francisco-based Levi Strauss & Co (LS) is among the world's largest apparel marketers and most widely recognized brands. In 2003, LS's senior management launched a company-wide effort to reduce costs and refocus the business on profitable growth. This required a transformation of HR, not only to reduce costs of the function, but also to better enable the strategy and management of talent across the organization.

The HR transformation programme

The company set about a major change programme for HR from early in 2004, including consolidation of HR systems, processes and transactional activities into shared service centres, tightly defined performance metrics and a service management framework. Many of the administrative operations were outsourced, to allow the company to focus its attention on transforming the higher-value functions and capabilities of HR internally. In April 2004, Accenture assumed responsibility for all HR administrative operations for LS's active and retired employees in North America, including: recruiting; training design, development and administration; benefits administration; leave of absence; compensation; customer service; HR administration; expatriate and relocation; performance management administration; and HR systems and applications.

High performance outcomes

LS now enjoys a cost-effective, employee-centric approach to the delivery of HR services, complete with improved service levels, predictable fixed costs and tangible savings. Overall HR costs at LS have fallen by 35 per cent, and the HR organization offers more and better tools, processes and services. Standardized, practice-based HR processes are now in place across North America – processes that are enhancing employee data quality, reporting and analysis. LS's HR organization is also better positioned to support company leaders in their quest for profitable growth: for example, by helping executives select the right talent, emphasize the right capabilities, and develop creative solutions to motivate and reward people. The net effect is a new level of high-quality, cost-effective HR service, with flexible, scalable processes that help deliver more savings and stronger business support.

IMPROVING HR ORGANIZATION AND CAPABILITIES

When the more administrative and transactional activities are located in shared service centres, the rest of the HR function is able to focus more on the high-value-adding and business-facing processes and functions. The best-practice HR organization is disciplined and organized according to capabilities. Experienced, business-oriented HR professionals work closely with the business functions and leaders, able to understand their needs and to relate these directly to talent and people-related needs and capabilities. A common term for these roles is the 'HR business partner'.

Higher value and complex specialist HR capabilities are brought together into centres of expertise, to consolidate the deep expertise and provide consistent support to the rest of HR and the business. These can include areas such as recruitment, resource planning, compensation planning, industrial relations and employment law, but also some of the additional capabilities that HR is more often developing such as organization design, change management, and HR intelligence and reporting. Learning and development, as already discussed in Chapter 4, is a critical and significant function which should be consolidated and brought together under a senior leader who may be a peer of HR or report to the head of HR depending upon personalities and organizational style.

Figure 6.8 shows the basic elements of an HR organization that is organized around capabilities to provide the most efficient and effective support to the organization and employees.

For all the elements to come together, and for this model to work, strong governance and oversight of HR is required across the enterprise. Many HR functions have developed with a devolved governance, where the corporate HR leadership has varying degrees of influence but often not direct control of HR across all the business divisions or entities. The shared service centres and centres of expertise should all report centrally, and have service level agreements and key performance indicators that allow the business entities to manage and measure the services they need. The business partner roles should have joint accountability to the business entities they support, and to corporate HR to maintain oversight. Finally, given the way in which HR processes can be split across the HR organizational components, strong process governance is required. Process owners for the key HR processes need to be established and have a level of importance, and credibility, equivalent to business entity HR leaders and other direct reports to the corporate head of HR.

Figure 6.8 HR organization

Case study – Unilever

The business challenge

Unilever is one of the largest consumer goods companies in the world, with revenues of €42 billion. One in every two households in the world has a Unilever brand in its home; every day, 150 million people in 150 countries use Unilever's products. Unilever's mission is to 'add vitality to life'.

In 2005 Patrick Cescau, the new Unilever CEO, instituted the One Unilever programme, targeted with delivering annual savings of €700 million through the implementation of a unified and streamlined operating model for the company. As part of this, Unilever established a global HR transformation programme with the aim of commercializing and streamlining HR, providing line managers with new/enhanced self-serve tools, increasing access to global workforce data, leveraging benefits from Unilever's global scale and delivering savings of at least 20 per cent.

The HR transformation programme

In May 2006 Unilever signed a seven-year business process outsourcing agreement to help it transform its HR operations in 100 countries. Accenture as the outsourcing partner will provide recruitment, payroll administration, reward administration, performance management, workforce reporting and core HR administration. Accenture will also provide vendor and content sourcing and development, programme planning and delivery, learning system hosting, and management and administrative services.

The HR processes and systems are being redesigned to support more common ways of working and shared service operations globally. Support across Unilever's three geographic regions will be provided through six shared service centres, with some high-touch services remaining in the local business entities, such as some instructor-led training and recruitment interviewing. Unilever is retaining key areas of capability around high-value HR processes and all of the HR business partners who work alongside business leadership.

Organizing HR in this way will focus on the need for upskilling or new capabilities. The business partner roles, for example, really require very business-oriented and capable people who also have expertise across the broad range of HR functions, at least at a high level, and familiarity with policies and processes. In the past, HR has not always been the function that has attracted the best and brightest. At the University of Michigan's Ross School of Business, which has one of the best faculties in the United States for organizational issues, just 1.2 per cent of the 2004 graduates joined an HR organization (Hammonds, 2005).

For the most part, HR professionals in the past have not considered training in business-oriented skills to be that important, and HR functions have usually not demanded it either. The US-based Society for Human Resource Management (SHRM) carried out a survey in 2005 asking HR professionals what they felt was important from the range of academic courses and subjects for a successful career in HR. No fewer than 83 per cent said that classes in interpersonal communications skills had 'extremely high value'. Employment law and business ethics followed, at 71 per cent and 66 per cent respectively. Change management and strategic management were much lower at 35 per cent and 32 per cent, and finally finance was at only 2 per cent.

For HR to change and become a fully integral business function, it needs more business-qualified and savvy people, alongside deep specialists in core areas of talent management. The days of HR being the place for generalists or non-business-oriented people are rapidly disappearing.

'Business acumen is the single biggest factor that HR professionals in the US lack today,' says Anthony J Rucci, executive vice president at Cardinal Health Inc, a big healthcare provider. Rucci was the HR executive who led the work at Sears we mentioned earlier, seeking to establish the links between employee commitment, customer loyalty and profitability; before Cardinal Health he was head of HR and strategy at Baxter International, another healthcare company. Such people are becoming more common as leaders of HR. Much has happened in functions like IT in the past, business-experienced leaders are increasingly moving into senior roles in HR, sometimes as part of their 'tour of duty' as they gain experience across the organization. This can only be a good thing, and will encourage the spread of experience and ideas of talent management between the HR function and the other business functions and entities. Developing common understanding and accountability for the development of talent is one of the key aspects of being a talent-powered organization, and achieving talent multiplication. We should next examine what collective responsibility for talent development and multiplication really means.

EVERYONE'S RESPONSIBLE

Talent multiplication capabilities must be embedded in the activities of the organization and sustained by everyone. Discovery of talent cannot be left to the HR function alone – line managers and employees must see the identification of new talent sources as their responsibility too. Formal learning activities are necessary but not sufficient for developing your talent. Everyone in the organization must contribute to building the capabilities of others through everyday activities like performance feedback and coaching, and knowledge sharing, as well as mentoring and developmental relationships. Every manager and supervisor has the opportunity to deploy talent to create value when he or she assigns people jobs and tasks. Every employee can pursue developmental experiences that contribute to the business by proactively taking on new responsibilities or getting involved in activities outside of his or her normal role.

Talent power is created by everyone in an organization, but the virtuous cycle of talent multiplication is set in motion by leadership. Visible leadership on talent issues is absolutely necessary to ensure that everyone in the organization understands that talent is mission-critical. Leaders must also cultivate a talent mindset in the organization, to create the momentum that sustains talent multiplication and powers performance.

THE IMPORTANCE OF VISIBLE LEADERSHIP

Leaders need to take responsibility for talent issues because – as we have stressed constantly – talent is strategic. Leaders have a multitude of competing claims on their attention and energy, and for that reason alone they need to prioritize talent issues by dedicating significant time to them. By giving priority to talent issues, leaders can signal to everyone in the organization that talent is strategically important to the business.

The most recent Accenture High Performance Workforce Study from which we have previously quoted, showed that companies we defined as leaders had a much higher level of involvement of their leaders directly in people and talent issues, as Figure 6.9 shows.

Above all, leaders – not specialist functions like HR – decide what issues are strategic. They not only set strategy for their organization,

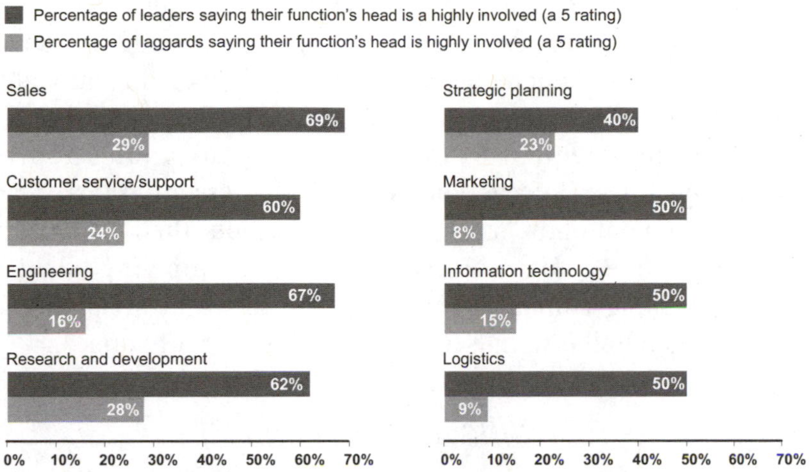

■ Percentage of leaders saying their function's head is a highly involved (a 5 rating)
■ Percentage of laggards saying their function's head is a highly involved (a 5 rating)

Sales
69%
29%

Strategic planning
40%
23%

Customer service/support
60%
24%

Marketing
50%
8%

Engineering
67%
16%

Information technology
50%
15%

Research and development
62%
28%

Logistics
50%
9%

0% 10% 20% 30% 40% 50% 60% 70%

0% 10% 20% 30% 40% 50% 60% 70%

Figure 6.9 Human performance leaders are more likely to have the heads of their top functions deeply engaged in talent management initiatives
Source: Accenture (2007b).

they decide the building blocks and determinants of strategy. Leaders alone have the power to make long-term strategic decisions take priority over short-term interests. This is particularly important in the field of talent, since the rewards for investing in talent are less apparent to markets than those of other decisions. There are fierce pressures on company leaders to produce good-looking short-term results.

Bill Zollars, CEO of YRC Worldwide, is one leader who has resisted these pressures to keep his company firmly focused on its talent strategy:

> The one thing that I probably underestimated was the short-term focus that public companies now have to deal with in terms of Wall Street. I knew it was crazy, but I had no idea how crazy it actually is. It's really gotten to the point where long term to most analysts is next week.
>
> (EIU, 2006)

Zollars is one of a growing number of top executives who have taken personal responsibility for talent issues within their organization. He was one of 20 CEOs or COOs of major global companies interviewed in an Economist Intelligence Unit Survey, 'The CEO's role in talent management'. The survey found that 14 of the 20 were devoting at least 20 per cent of their working time to talent management: seven of these were giving it between 30 and 50 per cent. However, their efforts were not typically guided by a formal talent strategy directly linked to their company's major goals or embedded in their business planning processes. The 20 leaders generally engaged instead in selected supporting activities where they believed that they could add value.

A major focus of leadership is to direct the human capital strategy and capabilities required to execute the organization's top-level strategic objectives. However, before even that essential task, leaders need to create a common belief system throughout their organization, in which everyone is focused on growing and multiplying talent, and assumes the same commitment to achieve this. Put simply, leaders need to create a 'talent mindset' as we described in Chapter 2.

CREATING A TALENT MINDSET

When an organization has a talent mindset, the objective of multiplying talent unites the individual and collective efforts of all its people, and directs its practices, culture and ambition. In J M Keynes's memorable phrase, it becomes part of the organization's 'animal spirits'.

This mindset is built on two shared beliefs. First, people recognize that talent is vital to the organization's immediate and future needs, and their own, and that talent sets them and their organization apart from others. Second, people recognize that they can contribute personally to increasing the talent available to their organization. Based on these shared beliefs, organizations with a talent mindset shape and achieve a shared vision, align it with customers and other stakeholders, and constantly raise their performance and value. In the words of Annette Law, manager of organizational development at UPS, 'Your vision is where you want to be and talent is the engine to get you there' (Morton, 2005: 8).

To build that talent mindset, leaders must look first to establish a high-performance environment. They set high expectations and highlight their achievements, both individually and collectively. They make decisions based on critical skills, attitudes and values which foster talent. They should then develop the right talent capabilities by identifying the sources of talent development, investing in them and managing them, and monitoring and building on their results. They diffuse roles, responsibilities and authority to stretch their people. They constantly seek and create opportunities for all their people to do what they already do best, and discover other things they might be able to do.

All of these tasks require visible and committed leadership from the top, as demonstrated by Ken Chenault of American Express. An excerpt from the Conference Board's profile of American Express in its 2005 report on talent management strategies appears in the box.

American Express Company: 'Mindset begins at the top'

CEO Ken Chenault's vision is for the company 'to be the world's most respected service brand' with centralized strategy development and the creation of a range of integrated initiatives. A decentralized line-of-business structure then provides implementation and further interrelationships. The lines of business are global, so a global talent management framework is being developed to support them.

In keeping with this customer-focused vision, American Express subscribes to the employee service profit chain philosophy, which links employee satisfaction to customer satisfaction. This aligns the company's employment brand to the belief that motivated or engaged employees create satisfied customers. When employees commit to the employment brand, they contribute their best talent, skills, and ideas and play a critical role in the organization's success.

The CEO drives this talent mindset. He recognizes that 'people are the company's greatest strength.' He spends 30 to 40 per cent of his time on leadership issues, working directly with leaders. His involvement includes leading a twice-yearly CEO summit, where top talent meet with him for two days to work through a significant business issue. He also dines quarterly with top talent and annually has several chairman-led sessions during which talent is discussed. He is personally informed about how employees feel – he listens and is very approachable. Not only does he play a visible and active role with all employees, but he also has similar requirements of his staff. There is clearly a top-down emphasis on talent.

Source: Morton (2005: 28).

GIVING PEOPLE MANAGEMENT BACK TO MANAGERS

The most critical task is to integrate human capital management practices into the very fabric of business. The way to do that is to ensure that line managers, to whom the majority of people in any organization actually report, take on proper accountability and responsibility for talent management.

On some level, this is just common sense. A line manager's role has always been to coordinate and direct people and resources in pursuit of business results. Furthermore, as we have already highlighted, an employee's immediate manager matters most to his or her performance and engagement. And yet common-sense messages often get lost in the clutter of large organizations. Debra Hunter Johnson, a vice president of human resources at American Airlines, told us how good intentions eventually disconnected too much of the day-to-day responsibility for people management from line managers:

> Over time, as human capital management became a centralized specialization under the domain of HR, we started taking away some of the managers' people management responsibilities so they could 'focus on the business'. Although numerous benefits were achieved by this, we have gone overboard, and it is time we give people management back to managers where the biggest performance improvements can be made.

Beyond the common-sense premise, however, lays the major question – how does an organization accomplish this change? The principal ways being used by companies to give a significant boost to workforce performance through hands-on talent management include shifting active people management responsibilities back to line managers, creating the expectation that managers ought to be teachers and trainers, and measuring the effectiveness of line managers in managing and developing talent. We consider each in turn.

Managers actively managing talent

There is no question that over the years line managers have become frustrated by new demands on their time that seem to have little bearing on employee performance. Too often, HR departments have offloaded precisely the wrong kind of people management work onto their managers, asking them to perform administrative duties in the name of 'empowered self-service'. This shifting of tasks often over-burdens busy managers with work and reduces the time they actually have to manage their people.

Managers' responsibilities and impact on talent are vital in a number of ways. First, they should provide frequent, informal and personalized career counselling, feedback and recognition for their employees – even more essential with the expectations of the younger cohorts joining the workforce. At Procter & Gamble, for example, managers frequently work with employees to define the ideal 'destination jobs' they would like to obtain, and to create plans to help them get there. At TD Industries (a mechanical and electrical systems contractor) and Microsoft, formal performance reviews are supplemented by systems in which managers and employees can confidentially record frequent, informal feedback. Jessie McCain, managing director of human resources at TD Industries, describes the informal communications as 'live, organic, incredibly messy working documents that encourage frequent, honest, and specific feedback at the point of need'. Their existence means that issues are discussed and resolved on an ongoing basis rather than once a year under formal, often uncomfortable, circumstances.

Similarly, companies that are especially focused on development do not wait until the end of the year to reward their employees with bonuses or raises. Instead, they offer frequent, informal and tailored recognition and praise. The North American division of SAP, for example, established a values-based rewards programme to encourage its managers to reward performance throughout the year. Using simple templates, managers give their employees everything from an email of recognition (which also goes to the employee's colleagues and superiors) to small gifts (movie tickets or a gift card) and larger corporate recognition awards and bonuses in the form of trips, cash or extra time off.

A second way leading companies develop employees is by treating them all as valuable – not just the so-called stars or high potentials. In these organizations, mentoring and stretch assignments are not just for leadership candidates. At Microsoft, for example, nearly every employee has a mentor. And not coincidentally, every manager is considered an HR manager (*Canadian HR Reporter*, 2002). The company employs a web-based matching tool that provides employees with potential mentors (using blinded profiles) every five to six months. By working with mentors, every employee is challenged to avoid complacency and to explore untapped skills and areas of interest.

The same is true for companies that offer stretch assignments or job rotations regardless of an employee's level. Tom Hennigan, COO of Victorinox (owner of Swiss Army brands), feels that he maximizes both the long-term and short-term performance of his people by placing them in stretch assignments. He often pairs two people in the same assignment so that they can learn from each other and avoid the mistakes that can come when going it alone in a new situation. And at

Nike, cross-functional and cross-divisional movement is seen as especially valuable. Line managers periodically get together to discuss where their people might best fit in new stretch opportunities in other parts of the organization or under the supervision of other managers. Although the process started out to target only leadership candidates, many divisions of the company have now adopted it to support all employees.

Measure and reward what matters

Line managers are no different from anyone else. They need new incentives to take on new responsibilities. Without them, they will not get beyond 'an individualistic results orientation that makes managers more likely to stomp on their employees in order to maximize short-term results than develop them for the long-run benefit of the business', as one manager at a company with well-recognized but rarely used HR best practices and programmes described its approach to people management.

Organizations often attempt to hold managers accountable for talent development by making sure they complete activities and follow processes, paying scant attention to the outcomes the activities and processes are intended to achieve. Managers dislike being policed, and thus will often just go through the motions when tasked with the requirement to complete performance appraisals or send their employees for training. A more thoughtful approach is to concentrate on outcomes, which is why at Marriott, one-third of a manager's performance rating is based on employee engagement scores; at Procter & Gamble, managers' compensation, stock options, performance ratings, and assignments are tied to their success in recruiting, developing and retaining high-performing employees; and at Becton Dickinson, managers are assessed on whether they are 'net exporters of talent', a metric indicating how many of their employees have been promoted into management in other parts of the company. Likewise at Accenture, one-third of all managers' and executives' performance is based on talent development, and is critically appraised through 360-degree feedback and peer reviews.

In addition to giving managers more responsibility, leading organizations are also using horizontal and vertical integration to create advisory groups on people management. Men's Wearhouse, a leading US retailer, and one highly successful technology company in our study have each integrated the performance consulting and coaching roles into a core business group such as operations or a strategic council of business leaders. Not only does this approach ensure that talent management is taken seriously by line managers (as the command to do so is not just another HR directive), it is also more likely to lead to practices that are relevant to line managers' needs, since people from the business with real management experience are involved.

Other companies have created permanent workforce performance groups composed of people from multiple functions. BT has its 'Workstyle Consultancy Group' and Sun Microsystems a 'Workplace Effectiveness' group, for example. Others like Cisco have created cross-functional task groups composed of representatives from HR, IT, finance and workplace resources that are responsible for project-based workforce performance improvement initiatives. Some organizations have tried to transform HR itself into a group that takes on the primary role of supporting managers in improving employee performance. This approach tends to be more successful when people from the business are brought into HR (or people from HR are rotated into the business), and when HR is transformed into an internal consulting function that coaches not just senior executives, but all managers with supervisory responsibilities.

Teach and develop line managers to be better people managers

Having established the importance of measuring the performance of line managers in how well they manage and develop talent, we must also think about how we develop them to improve this performance. As we observed in Chapter 4, the majority of line managers typically receive little training or development support to enhance their professional and leadership skills. Surely the most important leadership skill, and one that is core to every business, is the management of people and development of talent, yet so little is done in any formal way to improve that skill for the average line manager. People are promoted into roles where they need to supervise and manage others, often based on their technical or functional prowess, and their organization then relies on whatever natural talent they may or may not have for managing its most critical resources.

Looking ahead, the demands on line managers are going to increase as workforces become more diverse, more virtual, have higher expectations and different attitudes to work and employment. Managing multi-generational teams, with mixes of geography and ethnicity, work styles, and rewards and compensation requirements, brings on a whole new set of challenges. If workforce engagement today is in some state of decline, and we know that immediate line managers and supervisors are the most significant influences on engagement, and they also impact individual and team development, then we must put more in to supporting them and teaching them how to manage people in this new world.

There are several areas that we would strongly advocate as core training and development needs for line managers in every organization:

- self-awareness – understanding their own leadership styles, developing their perspectives and teachable points of view, understanding what they need to improve and focus on;
- team management skills – providing vision and inspiration, setting direction, empowering others, dealing with ambiguity, understanding and managing diversity;
- people management – giving performance feedback (good and bad), coaching and counselling, understanding learning and development needs and opportunities, understanding total rewards, sensitivity to diversity;
- managing change – change management practices and techniques, importance of leadership, aligning stakeholders;
- project management – creating business cases, resource management, project control and reporting;
- understanding the organization's strategy – understanding the key objectives, strategies, and challenges being faced by the organization, the competitive imperatives, and how these relate to the line manager's area of responsibility.

This last point is vitally important in addressing the issue of alignment and understanding of the strategy, which is seen as a significant issue by top management as we have previously discussed. However, while this should be a formal part of manager development and training, it is not sufficient to rely on this alone. Top-down communications are clearly a very significant part of getting alignment on everything from strategy to core values, and they are worth reviewing as one of the final elements of embedding and sustaining talent multiplication and a talent mindset.

FAILURES OF COMMUNICATION

In all talent management areas – definition, discovery, development and deployment – communication is an essential resource for organizations seeking to build alignment as well as engagement. Sadly, most organizations fail to sufficiently communicate their key strategies, values and motives to their employees, and thereby miss the chance to foster some of the key motives for engagement. When business leaders do not take enough time to explain their strategic goals to their employees, should they be surprised that those employees are insufficiently aligned with corporate strategy? Yet executives continue to fall into this trap – as demonstrated by repeated surveys in recent years. Time after time, executives have complained about insufficient strategic understanding among their workforces, only to admit in the next breath that they make no special effort to consult that same workforce or confide in them.

Hewitt's 2003 survey of the Best Employers in Asia shows the vital difference between top employers, which do make the effort, and the rest, which hardly do at all. Among the 20 best employers, CEOs communicated their business strategy, goals and results to employees on average 16 times a year. Among the rest, the average was only six times a year. Not surprisingly, then, only 57 per cent of employees outside Hewitt's top 20 said they got enough good information about their company's business results and performance; and only 72 per cent said they had a good understanding of their company's business goals.

This means that employees of most Asian companies receive a high-level insight into how their firm is doing just once every two months. Consequently, nearly half of them feel under-informed, and more than a quarter do not really understand what the company is aiming at. They are anything but aligned.

Engagement, of course, must be a two-way process, and it is no surprise to find that the same survey reveals that whereas a healthy majority of Top 20 employers genuinely consult their employees, making use of their ideas and making them feel valued, among the rest, only 36 per cent of employees believe their opinions and suggestions are heard and acted upon.

Is this failure of communication a purely Asian problem? Certainly not. Towers Perrin's Global Workforce Study of the same year (2003) showed that engagement levels of employees fell the lower down they were in the hierarchy, and that only one-third of global respondents believed senior management communicated openly with them. A mere 40 per cent said senior management acted in a way that was consistent with their own personal values. Could lack of engagement be any more fundamental than that?

Marriott, the hotel chain, actually builds communication into its assessment of its intangible value. Certainly, the modes, volume, content and style of an organization's communications all have a key role to play in aligning and engaging employees:

- in content – telling people what their jobs are about;
- in coping – telling people what resources are available to them, and making them feel supported or stressed;
- in compensation – making people feel understood, recognized and valued (or not);
- in community – helping to promote interaction and interchange;
- in career – making people understand (or not) how the organization matches its processes and its needs and objectives to their career goals;
- in congruence – defining the organization's values and showing how individual behaviour can reflect them.

Good communications help all the wheels run smoothly and together; bad communications do the opposite. 'Good' communications for building alignment and engagement are:

- clear;
- self-contained (it is infuriating and inefficient if employees cannot understand a communication without referring to another);
- carefully rationed (employees should not be overwhelmed with instructions or exhortations);
- as personalized as possible (even mass communications can make employees feel that they are being individually addressed).

By communicating regularly and effectively, organizations can achieve better alignment around their core values and priorities. As we commented from the outset, there can be nothing more important than to communicate the importance of talent to the whole organization, and to create a talent mindset across the organization.

SUMMARY

The measurement and alignment of talent management activities sustain the virtuous cycle of talent multiplication. The power of the talent multiplication model lies in the dynamic integration of capabilities in defining, discovering, developing and deploying talent, and the alignment of those capabilities with business strategy.

Talent-powered organizations treat talent not simply as another resource to be managed, but as a strategic asset to invest in. They make strategic investments in human capital processes to build the organizational capabilities that multiply talent and create value. They regularly measure the impact of their investments in people on business results.

HR is organized around capabilities, and focuses the administrative and transactional activities in shared service centres. Measurement of all HR processes and activities is in place, including agreed service levels and key performance indicators. Consolidated HR systems provide a solid base of talent-related data and information.

Everyone in the organization must be involved in multiplying talent. Leaders of talent-powered organizations take a visible role in talent management. They understand the strategic issues involved in using people's talent to gain sustainable competitive advantage. They think about these issues systematically, and give them their maximum priority and attention. They ensure that other leaders do the same – making talent multiplication part of their daily responsibilities and equipping them to achieve it. In talent-powered organizations, CEOs devote a significant amount of their time and energy to talent management initiatives.

Talent management needs to become everyone's responsibility in every organization. While top leadership and HR involvement are essential, a talent mindset and capabilities must be embedded and sustained throughout the organization. In talent-powered organizations, everyone in the organization identifies and nurtures talent in ways that enhance performance.

7

Next Steps and the New Imperatives

Knowing is not enough; we must apply!

Goethe (1749–1832)

'Action this day!' was Winston Churchill's imperative during the Second World War. It meant what it said, and Churchill demanded a report on how it was executed. The last six chapters should have convinced you that talent issues have the same urgency for your organization. In this concluding chapter we set out a talent agenda, based on the five imperatives we set out in the first. This agenda is strategic and long-term – but like Churchill's it can and should begin with 'Action this day!' In some places we have directed the call at specific parts of your organization – especially leaders. But we have extended the messages beyond top leaders to all stakeholders and all parts of the organization, since talent management is a collective responsibility. Action this day! is for everyone.

The structure of this chapter is simple: we begin by drawing together in one place the key actions needed to build a talent-powered organization. We then identify the top tasks for critical stakeholders. We emphasize the must-do's for organizational leaders, line managers, finance staff, HR professionals, employees and governments, including regulators. We close with some thoughts on what comes after talent multiplication.

BECOMING A TALENT-POWERED ORGANIZATION

There is no simple formula for becoming a talent-powered organization, but throughout this book we have tried to identify the core principles and practices of talent-powered organizations. Five principles stand out.

TALENT IS THE SINGLE MOST IMPORTANT FORCE CREATING STRATEGIC VALUE FOR YOUR ORGANIZATION

Executive leadership – creating the vision

Strong leadership involvement in talent management is absolutely necessary to create a talent-powered organization. Leaders must demonstrate to their entire organization that talent is at the top of their personal agenda. You should communicate a personal vision, for all its members to share, of the strategic importance of talent and of their commitment to provide opportunities for talent to grow and multiply in their organization. Their aim should be the creation of a talent mindset within the organization that animates core values related to people and gives them meaning and direction.

Developing a human capital strategy

Leaders must demonstrate understanding of the key components of their strategies which depend on developing and using talent to gain sustainable competitive advantage. You must identify the distinctive competencies you need to nurture and grow, and to think about talent holistically, aware of how it underpins every effort by every part of their organization to fulfil its strategic goals. You should be aware of current gaps and shortcomings, and upcoming talent and workforce challenges, and how well the organization is aligned and engaged behind the strategic goals.

With these in mind, you should create a human capital strategy which recognizes the specific demands for talent required by those goals, what you need to change in creating a high-performance culture, what leadership capabilities you will need, and how the organization is promoting or impeding the intended strategy.

Such a human capital strategy entails:

- understanding the drivers of high performance for the organization and recognizing the key sources of value creation;
- thinking through the demands of leadership, talent, organization and culture in executing strategy, and where the gaps are from today;
- identifying talent and the segments of the workforce that are most critical to the execution of strategy today, and over the next five years;
- recognizing the areas of talent that are most at risk from retirements, shortage of skills and new competitive pressures;
- identifying present and potential sources of talent, appraising options, and creating a talent supply chain for sourcing talent.

Leaders should demand the data necessary to inform these decisions and priorities, and support investments in talent.

Measuring the value of talent

Because such a high proportion of total business value is now represented by human and knowledge capital, organizations need more comprehensive and robust measurement to make good judgements over ongoing investments in talent and capabilities. At the top level, balanced scorecards must include good measures of people which highlight their contribution to business outcomes and economic success, as well as the general health of the talent pool in the organization.

Measures such as profit per employee can be good overall indicators of how investments in people are paying off. Together with workforce measures such as levels of engagement, headcount growth, attrition and absenteeism rates, average payroll, levels of investment in learning and development, and leadership capacity, they can give good insight into the progress or needs in development of talent in the business. When linked to key business drivers such as customer service and innovation, they can provide much-improved understanding of where and how to invest in improving business performance through talent.

Talent supply chains and 'right sourcing'

Many more options and new ways of accessing talent now exist, together with new ways of working. Your organization must think strategically about how and where to access talent to meet the future demands of the enterprise. Creating or extending talent supply chains in developing parts of the world requires particularly careful consideration. Evaluate realistically whether your organization has the resources, knowledge and capabilities to access this talent competitively, and what might happen if you have to upscale or downscale rapidly in response to future demands.

Leadership talent becomes even more stretched as the workforce expands and diversifies. As you think through the talent supply chain, it is vital to understand the current leadership bench strength, what future leadership skills are going to be needed, and options to address the gaps and to develop a clear and regularly updated succession planning process for all the senior and critical leadership positions.

You therefore need to examine all the options for accessing the specific talent or mix of talents you need to execute your strategy. This is the concept of 'right sourcing': picking the options that offer the maximum gain to the business strategy. In particular it entails:

- examining the costs and benefits of new talent locations, including a thorough understanding of their local cultures and regulatory frameworks;
- understanding of more diverse pools of talent and how to access them, together with implications for existing sources of talent;
- exploring the possibilities of working with partners or outsource service providers in new locations who can provide access to new talent;
- assessing the possibilities of contingent labour forces, including new collaborative networks and 'free talent'.

The virtuous cycle of talent multiplication

Having started with the right mindset and clearly articulated strategy and objectives, talent-powered organizations multiply talent by building distinctive capabilities in defining, discovering, developing and deploying talent. These talent multiplication capabilities need to be internally consistent, mutually reinforcing, and aligned with business strategy to fuel the talent-powered organization. To reinforce the linkages in the talent cycle and to understand talent at the right levels, you need to think about these key principles:

- measuring all the critical aspects of talent in each part of the cycle;
- understanding talent at a 'granular' level of competencies, and using a competency framework to integrate the different elements of the talent cycle;
- integrating all the processes associated with talent management and development, and taking a holistic approach;
- segmenting the workforce through different dimensions appropriate to the different parts of the talent cycle to provide greater insight and understanding.

Defining talent is a capability in identifying and articulating the organization's critical talent needs for each area of the business, in particular for the mission-critical workforces. The human capital strategy provides the basis for talent definition at the highest level. Defining talent is an ongoing process. It requires continual matching of business requirements with talent availability and development needs, so that gaps are clearly understood, and specific strategies and approaches to address the gaps are developed. This involves:

- continually assessing current and future talent needs, with a focus on the most strategically pivotal segments of the workforce and the mission-critical jobs;
- matching available talent sources with demand, and highlighting specific requirements for future talent and skills, and identification of the potential sources of talent;
- providing ongoing evaluation of the current state of talent, challenges and issues such as attrition rates, levels of engagement and productivity measures, with clear measurement and data on the key performance indicators for the workforce.

Discovering talent is a capability in identifying and sourcing talent to best enable and propel the execution of an organization's chosen strategy. This involves:

- systematically and continuously evaluating options and channels for sourcing the required talent and competencies, including the existing talent and competencies of the current workforce;
- putting in place robust and integrated processes to attract and recruit talent, with clear messages and value propositions that establish your organization's specific appeal to the pool of talent you want to access;

- continuously evaluating current employee value propositions for relevance and integrity.

Developing talent is a capability in continuously developing individual and collective skills, knowledge and behaviours to expand the organization's capabilities and its strategic advantage. This involves:

- investing in building employees' talents to achieve the organization's purpose and strategic objectives;
- building a more integrated capability and culture of learning and organization with clear outcome-based measures to align direction;
- coordinating learning investments and building a broader capability using technology-enabled learning and knowledge sharing to make learning more efficient and more effective;
- integrating development into the daily work of the organization through work roles and special assignments, and through relationships at work, particularly with line managers.

Deploying talent means building a capability in putting the right talent in the right place at the right time to allow the organization to execute its current strategy and prepare for future challenges or opportunities. This involves:

- institutionalizing methods which match and move internal and external talent to the places where it is best suited;
- creating the best possible match between employees' talents and aspirations and the strategic goals of the organization;
- combining and recombining talent within the organization to enable the sharing of knowledge and best practices to encourage continuous renewal;
- shaping the composition, responsibilities and practices of teams to leverage the diversity of thinking styles, experiences and perspectives.

The virtuous cycle of talent multiplication is under way.

Strong leadership creates a shared vision of talent multiplication and removes barriers to its fulfilment. A human capital strategy is in place and well designed to serve the organization's overall strategy.

Dynamic human capital capabilities are in place, sustained by the right mindset.

Talent needs are being defined and talent sources are being discovered, in light of current and future strategic goals.

Talent is being nurtured and developed to fulfil employees' aspirations and advance the goals of the organization.

Talent is being deployed where it can make the biggest contribution to immediate needs and where it can be grown to meet future needs. People are engaged and invested in achieving high performance. Future leaders are being groomed.

Talent is now multiplying. The virtuous cycle is in motion. The organization is increasing skills, adaptability, learning, flexibility, innovation and performance. It has a more engaged workforce which is delivering greater productivity, higher quality, innovation and customer satisfaction. In the process, the organization has made itself more attractive both to its existing talent and to potential additions. Current employees are using their strengths to drive performance, and new talent is being drawn towards the organization. Performance continues to improve and possibilities expand. Talent is creating value.

DIVERSITY IS YOUR BIGGEST ASSET

The extraordinary complexity and multiple paradoxes embodied in today's global talent market – especially the combination of local scarcity and global abundance – have created talent pools of unprecedented diversity in age, gender, ethnicity, geography, work arrangements, attitudes and career expectations. Your organization can accept diversity as a forced response to labour market pressures or new regulation, or it can embrace and leverage diversity deliberately as a means for competitive gain. To achieve this, you will need to be able to attract and retain more diverse talent than you have in the past. Your leaders and managers will need to be properly equipped and supported to engage more diverse people and teams, and taught how to manage the various different issues that arise, including greater use of virtual teams and capability.

Identify the specific competencies you need

To make best use of diverse talents, your organization must develop a deep understanding of the specific and general competencies necessary to achieve its strategic objectives. You must be able to model those competencies to map out skills, knowledge and behavioural needs for critical workforces, and use this understanding to source the right talent efficiently and effectively. You also need durable processes for assessing competencies and proficiency levels to identify current gaps and future needs.

Working the channels

Having identified diverse talent sources and determined your competency needs, you must make sure that your marketing and recruiting efforts enable the discovery of diverse talent. First and foremost you need to be clear on the value propositions of your organization, and how those appeal to different segments of the talent market. Establish your 'brand' as an employer to convey compellingly what it means to work for your company, and what candidates and employees can expect. Be sure that the promises you make in the recruitment process match the reality of working for your company, and that these are consistently conveyed through all the channels – online, recruitment agencies, direct recruitment, informal or word of mouth. With the widespread use of interactive technologies and information sharing, the power of word of mouth is enormous, and negative information about you as an employer can seriously damage your recruiting abilities. If you consider outsourcing all or part of your recruitment process, do not base the decision on short-term cost savings: decide instead whether an external partner can do the best job of finding you the critical talent you need.

Attracting diverse workforces: tailoring the EVP

In order to attract a diverse workforce you need to combine a strong brand as an employer with a strong personal appeal to the talent you hope to hire. As far as possible you need to offer a customized employee value proposition (EVP) to every worker, offering options that allow people to choose a personally meaningful way to contribute to the organization's objectives, as well as when, where and how they get their work done. Rewards can be offered using a menu-driven approach which allows people to pick the types of benefits they value most, and also change to their choices at different stages of their lives. You need to cast your EVP wider than traditional offers of money or promotion, particularly for younger workers, for whom job content and high-quality relationships, especially with managers, are all-important. A sense of corporate responsibility is increasingly important in the EVP, especially for younger workers. Talent-powered organizations offer employees compelling and customizable value propositions that lead them to be widely viewed as the best companies to work for.

LEARNING AND SKILLS DEVELOPMENT ARE CRITICAL ORGANIZATIONAL CAPABILITIES

The knowledge economy constantly redefines the skills it demands from the workforce. It requires ever-greater competencies; it turns the ability and the willingness to learn into cherished qualities. A talent-powered organization is both a 'learning' and a 'teaching' organization: it has mastered how to invest in learning and development and knowledge-management capabilities, and how to use them to accelerate skills building and improve competitiveness in all its critical workforces. It has also inculcated a culture of knowledge sharing and teaching, where more experienced employees pass on knowledge to others, formally and informally, so that the whole organization moves forward.

Learning faster, learning better

Learning and development is targeted and demonstrated around seven key principles:

- learning with purpose: align learning initiatives closely with your strategic goals;
- learning with impact: measure the business contribution of your learning effort;
- learning with outreach: spread the benefits of new learning to suppliers, customers and other partners of your organization;
- learning with leverage: promote learning in places where it is most critical;
- learning with integration: integrate learning with other human performance systems and functions;
- learning with variety: blend learning methods for greatest impact;
- learning with maturity: achieve maturity in the design and delivery of leadership courses.

Building and capturing knowledge

One of the greatest challenges for a learning organization is knowing what it knows – the informal as well as the formal knowledge that it uses to create value. Knowledge management, as it has come to be known, has evolved from the library-type function of old, to a capability that connects people and diverse sources of knowledge and expertise across and beyond the organizational boundaries. While the central repository still has value in maintaining the structured knowledge and learning of the organization, information must now be accessible in an instant, shared among its users and creators, and subject to challenge, test and enhancement. Essential to this new state of affairs are technology-enabled learning and knowledge sharing – new forms of collaboration tools, expert search capabilities, and modularized learning content available at the time and point of need by diverse groups of users. Learning is a continual process, through coaching and mentoring, blended formal and informal learning enabled by technology, and learning and development opportunities are a critical part of the employee value proposition. They are therefore a great way to engage people.

ENGAGEMENT IS THE KEY TO HIGH PERFORMANCE

What engagement means and why it matters

Engagement is a combination of heart and mind. People who are engaged exhibit a high level of energy and emotional connection in their work. They invest additional effort, and persist in their efforts despite challenges or setbacks. They are dedicated because their work is meaningful and provides them with ample opportunity to use and develop their competencies and their strengths. They gain social esteem and satisfaction from their work, and clearly identify with it.

Highly engaged employees are more satisfied with their jobs, and they work harder and perform better in their jobs than their disengaged colleagues. They have lower absenteeism and are more loyal to their employers. They have better relationships at work and build better teams. They are more likely to meet their organization's standards of behaviour and service to its customers. Above all, when properly aligned, engaged employees improve the organization's productivity, customer service, innovation and profitability.

Engaging employees has become more important as organizations become increasingly reliant on talent. At the same time, changes in attitudes about work and life priorities, the rise of knowledge work and workers, and new options for when and where people work, have made engagement more difficult to achieve, and a more complex issue. To understand engagement, you must recognize that different segments of the workforce have different needs, aspirations and expectations. Engagement cannot be solved with one initiative, but requires a holistic understanding with real insight into different groups and individuals.

Measuring engagement and understanding the drivers

Measures of engagement among workforces are very important. Although they vary in how they categorize levels of engagement, they all point to the same conclusion: organizations with highly engaged workforces perform significantly better than those with low engagement. Assessing engagement realistically entails being able to compare it between different parts of the workforce and link it to performance metrics and outcomes. Many engagement measures give limited insight to the real drivers of engagement, so further analysis is usually required. However, the most important influence on engagement today is the line manager or supervisor, so comparisons between engagement scores, team performance and leadership scores at this level can help to identify where attention is needed.

Having measured where and how engagement may be affecting your organization's performance, your task is to drive it up where it is most needed. That means evaluating the impact and effect of the six key drivers of engagement – the six Cs:

- **Content:** are the physical and mental demands of jobs reasonable? Is the work meaningful to the worker? Are there opportunities for learning and development? Do employees have enough control over the work tasks to perform their jobs successfully?
- **Coping:** has the worker been given the tools, knowledge, working environment and sustaining relationships to meet the demands of the job?
- **Compensation:** do all the rewards of doing the job, particularly the value and respect given to the worker and recognition for good performance, match the sacrifice of his or her time and energy?

- **Community**: to what extent is work fulfilling an individual's social needs, providing a sense of purpose, enjoyable interactions with others, and a sense of fun?
- **Congruence**: are your actions and practices aligned with the expressed values and purpose of your organization?
- **Career**: can workers see a career path in your organization which matches their personal goals for different life stages?

The importance of the line managers and supervisors

Line managers have the most direct contact with employees, and hence have the most impact and influence on employee engagement. People join organizations, but they leave bad managers or supervisors. With greater workforce diversity and a greater mix of work content and methods, building engagement has become more complex. Organizations must ensure that their line managers are responsible and accountable for engaging their people, and measure and reward them appropriately for their performance in managing and developing their people – an area where they need much more training and support than in the past.

TALENT MULTIPLICATION IS EVERYONE'S JOB

In talent-multiplying organizations everyone assumes responsibility for developing and nurturing talent. The HR function provides much of the enabling processes and support for talent management, but is not ultimately responsible. HR should also provide the information to the organization to ensure it understands the talent issues and challenges, the investments in talent and progress on performance improvement. It should be a source of expertise in talent management and development

Measure so you can manage

No matter how often leaders repeat the message about the strategic importance of growing talent, it will not become common practice until it is measured and managers are rewarded for it. But measurement by itself is not enough; there must be a clear empirical link between talent and value creation. For these reasons organizations must use measurement approaches that start with business strategy, and identify key performance drivers and the related workforce and organizational attributes that generate their impact on that strategy. Then they must properly resource the processes that create those attributes.

Such a strategy also requires new frameworks and metrics to capture the contribution of human capital to the creation of intangible value, which has now become by far the greatest source of value for any business organization, and to guide future human capital investments. Developing such new metrics requires a joint effort by Human Resources, Finance and IT, which will have to step outside their existing framework of skills, including present accounting conventions. Together they will need to:

▪ map the causal links between the organization's human capital/ talent resources, key performance drivers and business results;
▪ use data and metrics to guide the right decisions on talent; then
▪ use a selective scorecard to measure return on talent investments and keep the organization focused on high performance.

Modernize the HR function

Evidence from many organizations today suggests that the HR function needs to improve its efficiency and effectiveness, and to provide greater value in addressing the issues of talent and workforce development. At the same time, the level of attention on HR is at an all-time high as organizations struggle with the new paradigms of talent and global competitiveness. HR has had lower investment in systems and technology than most other functions: it often has fragmented processes and systems which have evolved with the organization. In consequence, HR cannot provide best support to the business and/or consistent support to employees at a time when their needs and demands are rising.

Investment is needed to:

▪ provide more integrated and functionally rich systems to give better support to talent processes providing more consistent information to the business, and allowing for greater flexibility in how talent is supported across the organization;
▪ harmonize processes and policies to provide more consistency in how people are managed and developed across the organization;
▪ reorganize the HR function to focus administrative and transactional activities into shared services and higher-value HR capabilities into centres of expertise;

- upskill the HR business partners who work directly with the business leaders to understand business requirements and support on all aspects of planning and development of talent.

Many options now exist to locate the administrative shared-services part of HR in low-cost locations and countries to provide more significant cost savings to offset the investment costs of transforming HR. However, taking advantage of these locations requires new capabilities, and many organizations are sourcing these capabilities from specialist firms which have the existing infrastructure and scale needed.

Once the essential building blocks of a high-performing HR function are in place, it can respond better and more flexibly to the needs of different workforce segments. Good metrics and information give greater credibility to the function, and allow it to act more strategically and therefore to better fulfil its critical role in the talent-powered organization.

CRITICAL TASKS FOR KEY STAKEHOLDERS

We have set out a wide-ranging agenda for organizations and the various stakeholders who have an interest or impact on talent. In reality, we are all stakeholders, whether we are leaders, managers, employees, investors, regulators or in the public service.

In this final section, we have aimed to pull together the key messages and imperatives for the different stakeholder groups – a checklist of ideas and actions we can all take in our different roles and responsibilities in managing and developing people and the talent we need to successfully build our businesses and organizations.

BUSINESS LEADERS

Business leaders have a primary role in creating the mindset and context for creating truly talent-powered organizations. They need to:

- understand the issues and changes happening in the world around talent, skills and the nature of work;
- set these issues in the context of their own business and business strategy;

- provide the vision and passion around talent and its strategic importance to the organization and its future – to put talent issues at the top of their agenda;
- spend personal time on this agenda, and in particular take direct responsibility in the development of leadership within the organization, particularly at the senior leadership levels;
- expect that the business strategy will be supported by a human capital strategy for accessing and using the talent needed to achieve high performance;
- demand robust information and insightful measurement of talent that defines how value is being added, where investments need to be made, and where the current gaps and issues are;
- ensure that the specialist functions, particularly HR and learning, have the skills, capability and credibility to drive real talent multiplication in the organization, then position these functions strategically within the core leadership team of the business;
- ensure that the whole organization is focused on multiplying talent, and enable a culture of learning and teaching to produce sustained high performance;
- ensure that line managers have the resources to manage diversity and build engagement;
- build alignment and engagement by practising visible leadership, spending time with critical personnel and job functions throughout the business, explaining and communicating the vision and strategy time and time again;
- ensure that regulators and governments are aware of obstacles to successful talent strategy, and engage with them in opportunities to overcome those obstacles.

LINE MANAGEMENT

Line managers have the most direct impact on talent across the organization simply because most of the people work directly for them or with them. Their role in talent development and engagement is therefore critical. They need to:

- be aware of their personal responsibility for talent development, especially in managing diversity and building engagement, and the skills and behaviours they need;

- understand the organization's strategy, goals and objectives, and their role, and their team's role, in achieving them;
- understand the competencies and capabilities of the people that work for them, together with the business needs and talent requirements to fulfil the goals and objectives;
- make clear the support they need, particularly in terms of information, communications and time for personal contact, in meeting these responsibilities;
- accept that they themselves will be judged and rewarded by clear standards of performance in developing the talent for which they are responsible;
- understand their own leadership and people management capabilities and shortcomings, and work actively to improve on them;
- understand the needs and aspirations of those who work for them, and provide enriching and sustaining work experiences for their staff;
- provide clear feedback on performance, clear guidance on developmental needs and how to take advantage of learning opportunities;
- act as coach and mentor, and actively pass on their knowledge and learning to others;
- become authentic personal representatives of the values of the organization;
- take responsibility for their own careers and developmental needs, and make these clear to others who are in a position to support them.

TALENT MANAGEMENT FUNCTIONAL LEADERS

Human resources, learning and development are the functions most directly focused on the development and management of talent. They have the specific responsibilities to enable the practices and processes across the organization to support talent multiplication, and to provide the information the business needs to carry out its wider role in this context. They need to:

- understand the issues and challenges of talent in general, and specifically as it relates to the organization;

- be able to articulate these challenges, and opportunities, in business terms, and express the business strategic imperatives in people and skills terms;
- understand the most important value drivers of talent in the organization, the critical workforces, the key competencies, and be proactive in developing strategies to enhance them;
- provide the data and information for the business to assess accurately the current workforce and talent issues, gaps, and critical requirements, the investments needed and the expected returns, and the options available;
- act as a sounding board to the people in the organization, being aware of their issues and concerns;
- provide efficient administrative support to the business for all areas of talent management;
- understand and meet the regulatory and reporting requirements for human capital in all areas of the business;
- have deep competence in the core functional, professional and legal areas of HR, and learn to properly advise and support the business leaders;
- provide high value-adding capabilities to the organization in critical areas of talent and organization such as resourcing, compensation and reward, workforce engagement, learning and development, change management and organization design;
- work alongside top management in the organization as credible members of the business leadership team.

FINANCE LEADERS

Finance is increasingly aware of the issues of people and talent, and the value they contribute to the organization in financial terms. Finance leaders are engaging more closely with the talent management leadership, and are increasingly concerned about measurement and regulatory issues of talent. They need to:

- move beyond the limits of conventional accounting, and collaborate with HR leadership to develop new metrics to value human capital and guide human capital investments within the organization;

- consider what metrics can provide more insight to external stake-holders on the talent and organizational capital of the business, and encourage the development of standards;
- support talent management functions in developing stronger skills and knowledge in finance and key business fundamentals.

EMPLOYEES

Employees themselves have many responsibilities in how they engage, perform and support the achievement of the organization's goals and objectives. These run alongside the responsibilities they have to themselves in extending their knowledge and skills base and developing their own careers, as well as those of their colleagues. They need to:

- articulate their needs and desires for learning, development and advancement for satisfaction and meaning in work in ways that their supervisors and the organization can understand and respond to;
- be proactive and take full advantage of the opportunities given to them for learning and development;
- seek to understand clearly how their performance contributes to the achievement of the organization's objectives and how they are rewarded as a result;
- be open and honest, and willing to listen and learn from performance feedback;
- collaborate and share knowledge and learning with colleagues, and be good team members;
- understand their own sources of frustration or disengagement, and coach and guide their supervisors in helping them to be resolved.

GOVERNMENTS AND REGULATORS

Governments and regulators play a very significant role in many aspects of talent. They provide the environment in which businesses operate, and in which they can access and employ the right talent. Regulators need to adapt and respond to the many rapid changes in the world of talent. They need to:

- understand and be aware of the talent trends and demographics affecting business and the workforce at large, and how these specifically relate to the national or regional workforces they impact;
- support appropriate movement of work and talent across national borders with both inward and outward investment to help address workforce shortfalls;
- work with business, educational institutions and non-governmental organizations to identify the critical skill gaps, and create educational and labour market policies that maximize national talent pools and productivity, both for foundational skills and in further education;
- embrace the idea of two-way partnerships between business and government in the design and delivery of critical new skills, and allow more autonomy for educational establishments to innovate and respond to skills needs in the business world;
- encourage more uptake in adult education and lifelong learning programmes to help enhance the relevant skills and to retain competitiveness in the current workforce;
- support investment in providing training and education through new technology-enabled channels in order to maximize the accessibility of services and engage those who are outside formal education;
- encourage the increase in commercialization of research, with better linkages between business and academia to help improve the transfer of ideas, skills and technology between the two sectors;
- ensure that employment law and policies, for example around pensions, encourage all segments of the workforce to provide their talent – especially younger workers entering the workforce, and older workers who want the option to continue to work;
- work proactively with business, the accounting professions and the financial community to develop deeper insight and measures for assessing talent and intangibles to set new standards in business reporting.

INVESTORS AND EXTERNAL STAKEHOLDERS

In commercial enterprises as well as the public sector, those who advise or support organizations from an external perspective also play a role in providing insight or pressure on organizations to understand their human capital better.

Non-executive board directors have a responsibility to the organization and its shareholders to ask management how it is building human capital, and how well it understands and is responding to the internal and external talent issues. They also have a responsibility to ensure the organization is meeting relevant regulatory and legal obligations. They can help and advise on how organizations should gain insight, learn from others and improve their overall management of talent.

The investor community, financial analysts and others all play a significant part in keeping a focus on talent in both quoted companies and privately owned enterprises. There is broad understanding and awareness of the limitations of traditional financial measures in providing insight into the significant contribution of intangibles to the future value of enterprises. This community can play a big part in demanding more measurement and standards, as well as in the development of those measures directly.

CONCLUSIONS – BEYOND TALENT MULTIPLICATION

In their marvellous study of entrepreneurs in different fields, *The New Alchemists* (1999), Charles and Elizabeth Handy noted that at some stage in their early years someone, somewhere told them that they had a special talent. Sometimes it was a teacher or a grandparent or a first boss. What mattered was that someone gave them what Freud called 'the golden seed': confidence and succour that germinated into a vision, then an experiment that worked, and finally an organization that engaged and enrolled others in a common pursuit.

In a complex, connected world replete with material and intellectual interdependencies that seem to draw us together tighter by the day, networks of talented people will soon stand alongside individuals as the newest alchemists. Individuals will still matter. But communities of collaborators will rise in importance – not as anonymous crowds, but as networks of people that form to address problems of interest, significance and value, and then dissolve once they have found a solution that can be routinized or even automated.

The golden seed of the future will, in many respects, resemble the golden seed of the past. Individuals will still nurture individuals, and close personal relationships will incubate great talent. But individuals will be much less likely to labour in isolation from one another. Even the most introverted will find that the internet and its successors will provide them with the opportunity to multiply the resources available to them, and the impact that they can have on the world around them.

We suggested at the outset of this book that state-of-the-art talent management has evolved from a system of personnel control, to one of people development, and now to talent multiplication. Current organizations that have found it possible to multiply talent through effective definition, discovery, development and deployment will likely find themselves profoundly affected by the processes they have helped set in motion. They will themselves become networks of talent – forming and reforming in response to opportunity, technology, and social and political change. We believe that beyond talent multiplication lies an exponential increase in creative capacity.

So we also recognize that this evolution is unfinished and there is still much to learn. We are all on a journey to discover how to access, engage, develop and channel human potential to create organizational value, and new ideas, new approaches and new challenges are emerging all the time. We are truly in a new age of globalization and talent, and the promise that technology is finally beginning to really show in unlocking the potential of talent everywhere. These are exciting times.

The focus of management attention, of academics, of technologists, of educators and of governments, is turning more and more to this great challenge. It will go way beyond the competitiveness of organizations to become the key issue in competitiveness of nations in the future. Clearly we have only just begun to imagine the potential of talent power.

References

Accenture (2003) *The High-Performance Workforce Study 2002/2003*, Accenture Research Report

Accenture (2004) *The High-Performance Workforce Study 2004*, Accenture Research Report

Accenture (2006) *Driving High Performance through Mission-Critical Job Families*, Accenture Learning Research Report

Accenture (2007a) *Skills for the Future*, Accenture Policy and Corporate Affairs, in conjunction with the Lisbon Council

Accenture (2007b) *The High-Performance Workforce Study 2006*, Accenture Research Report

Accenture Learning (2005) *The Rise of the High Performance Learning Organization: Results from the Accenture Learning 2004 Survey of Learning Executives.*, Accenture Learning Research Report

Ballow, John, Burgman, Roland, Roos, Goran and Molnar, Michael (2004) *A New Paradigm for Managing Shareholder Value*, Accenture Institute for High Performance Business, Wellesley, Mass, July

Bassi, Laurie and McMurrer, Daniel (2007) Maximizing Your Return on People, *Harvard Business Review* 85(3), pp 115–23

Bateson, Mary Catharine (2005) The HBR List: Breakthrough ideas for 2005, *Harvard Business Review* 83(2), p 50

Becker, Brian E, Huselid, Mark A and Ulrich, Dave (2001) *The HR Scorecard: Linking people, strategy, and performance*, Harvard Business School Press, Boston, MA

Bennis, Warren G and Thomas, Robert J (2002) *Geeks and Geezers: How era, values, and defining moments shape leaders*, Harvard Business School Press, Boston, MA

Benton, James M, Cantrell, Susan and Vey, Meredith A (2004) Making the right investments in people, *Outlook* 3, pp 64–73

Bersin & Associates (2007) Statistics, benchmarks, and analysis of the US corporate training market, *The Corporate Learning Factbook 2007*, 11(1), January

Boudreau, John W and Ramstad, Peter M (2005) Talentship and the new paradigm for human resource management: from professional practice to strategic talent decision science, *Human Resource Planning*, 28(2), pp 17–26

Buckingham, Marcus and Coffman, Curt (1999) *First, break the rules: what the world's greatest managers do differently*, Simon and Schuster, New York

Business in the Community, Ireland (BITCI) (2005) Tesco Ireland Employment Programme Case Study, in *Inspiring Excellence: Best practice in corporate responsibility in Ireland*, vol 2

BusinessWeek (2005) The rise of a powerhouse, December

Canadian HR Reporter (2002) Interview with Frank Clegg, president of Microsoft Canada, in 'CEOs talk', 16 December

Cantrell, Susan (2006) The workforce of one: an overview, Accenture Institute for High Performance Business Research Note

Cantrell, Susan, Benton, James M, Laudel, Terry and Thomas, Robert J (2006) Measuring the value of human capital investments: the SAP case, *Strategy and Leadership* 34(2), pp 43–52

Cantrell, Susan, Benton, James M, Thomas, Robert J, Vey, Meredith A and Kerzel, Linda (2005) *The Accenture Human Capital Development Framework: Assessing, measuring and guiding investments in human capital to achieve high performance*, Accenture Institute for High Performance Business White Paper

Cantrell, Susan and Benton, James M, (2005) *The five essential practices of a talent multiplier*, Accenture Institute for High Performance Business Research Report

Cantrell, Susan and Foster, Nicole Di Paolo (2005) Techniques for managing a workforce of one: segmentation, Accenture Institute for High Performance Business Research Note

Cappelli, Peter (1999) *The New Deal at Work: Managing the market-driven workforce*, Harvard Business School Press, Boston, MA

Cascio, Wayne F (2005) From business partner to driving business success: the next step in the evolution of HR management, *Human Resource Management* 44(2), pp 159–63

Cascio, Wayne F (2006) The economic impact of employee behaviors on organizational performance, in *America at Work: Choices and challenges*, ed Edward E Lawler III and James O'Toole, Palgrave Macmillan, New York

Casner-Lotto, Jill and Barrington, Linda (2006) *Are They Really Ready to Work? Employers' perspectives on the basic knowledge and applied skills of new entrants to the 21st Century US workforce*, research report of The Conference Board, Inc, the Partnership for 21st Century Skills, Corporate Voices for Working Families and the Society for Human Resource Management

Chambers, Elizabeth G, Foulton, Mark, Handfield-Jones, Helen, Hankin, Steven M and Michaels III, Edward G (1998) The war for talent, *McKinsey Quarterly*, 3, pp 44–57

Coffman, Curt and Gonzalez-Molina, Gabriel (2002) *Follow this Path: How the world's greatest organizations drive growth by unleashing human potential*, Warner Books, New York

Conlin, Michelle (2006) Smashing the clock, *Business Week*, 11 December, pp 60–68

Corporate Leadership Council (CLC) (2004) *Driving Performance and Retention Through Employee Engagement*, Research Summary, Corporate Executive Board, CLC, Washington, DC

CLC (2006a) Competitive employment value propositions, *Executive Board Insight*, 4th Quarter, CLC, Washington, DC

CLC (2006b) *Attracting and Retaining Critical Talent Segments, Vol II: Best Practices for Building and Managing a Competitive Employment Value Proposition*, CLC, Washington, DC

Crispin, Gerry and Mehler, Mark (2006) *The CareerXroads Fifth Annual Sources of Hire Survey*, February

Curtis, Bill, Hefley, William E and Miller, Sally A (2002) *The People Capability Maturity Model*, Software Engineering Institute, Addison-Wesley, Boston, MA

DataMonitor (2006) BP plc Company profile [online] www.DataMonitor.com (accessed 1 May 2006)

Davenport, Thomas (2005) *Thinking For a Living*, Harvard Business School Press, Boston, MA

Davenport, Tom and Prusack, Larry (2000) *Working Knowledge*, Harvard Business School Press, Boston, MA

Davenport, Thomas and Cantrell, Susan (2002) The mysterious art and science of knowledge-worker performance, *MIT Sloan Management Review*, Fall

Davenport, Thomas H, Thomas, Robert J and Cantrell, Susan (2002) The mysterious art and science of knowledge-worker performance, *MIT Sloan Management Review* **44**(1), pp 23–30

Drucker, Peter (1959) *Landmarks of Tomorrow: A report on the new 'post-modern' world*, Harper, New York

Economic and Social Research Council (ESRC) (2005) Knowledge economy fact sheet, ESRC, Swindon, UK

Economist (2006a) The battle for brainpower, survey, 7 October

Economist (2006b) The new organization, January

Economist Intelligence Unit (EIU) (2006) *The CEO's Role in Talent Management: How top executives from ten countries are nurturing the leaders of tomorrow*, EIU in cooperation with Development Dimensions International (DDI), London

Ederer, Peer (2006) *Innovation at Work: The European Human Capital Index*, Lisbon Council Policy Brief, in conjunction with Deutschland Denken! eV Zeppelin University GmbH, Brussels

European Commission (2005) *Green Paper: Confronting Demographic Change: A new solidarity between the generations*, 16 March

European Industrial Relations Observatory Online (EIRO) (2006a) *Employment relations in SMEs: Belgium*, February [online] http://www.eurofound.europa.eu/eiro/links/belgium.html (accessed 18 May 2007)

European Industrial Relations Observatory Online (EIRO) (2006b) *Employment relations in SMEs: Germany*, February [online] http://www.eurofound.europa.eu/eiro/2006/02/word/de0511104s.doc (accessed 18 May 2007)

European Social Survey (2002) [online] http://ess.nsd.uib.no/ (accessed 24 July, 2007)

Eurostat (2003) *Statistics in Focus: Graduates in tertiary education*

Forbes (2006) The telework coalition, 26 June

Frauenheim, Ed (2006) Valero Energy: Optimas award winner for innovation, *Workforce Management*, 13 March, p 23

Freeman, Richard (2005) What really ails Europe (and America), *The Globalist*, 3 June

Friedman, Thomas (2005) *The World is Flat*, Farrar, Straus, Giroux, New York, NY

Gallup (2001) What your disaffected workers cost, *Gallup Management Journal* (*GMJ*), 15 March [online] http://gmj.gallup.com/default.aspx (accessed 21 May 2007)

Garelli, Stephane (2006) Winning in a new world of competitiveness, IMD, AOC Annual Conference, Birmingham, UK, 23 November 2006

Gartner (2005) Gartner says skills shortage in India's call centers has negative impact on service delivery, press release, 12 September

Gibbons, John (2006) Employee Engagement: A review of current research and its implications, The Conference Board

Giordani, Pattie (2005) 'Y' recruiting: new generation inspires new methods, *NACE Journal*, 65(4)

Government of China (2006) China to raise education expenditures to 4% of GDP, Ministry of Education of the People's Republic of China, 6 March, [online] http://english.gov.cn/2006–03/06/content_219838.htm (accessed 17 May 2007)

Gratton, Lynda (2003) *The Democratic Enterprise*, Pearson, Harlow

Guardian (2005a) It doesn't add up, *Guardian Education*, 24 October

Hammonds, Keith H (2005) Why we hate HR, *Fast Company*, August

Handy, Charles and Handy, Elizabeth (1999) *The New Alchemists*, Arrow, London

Hansen, Fay (2006) One world, one workforce, *Workforce Management*, 15 May

Harris Interactive (2006) The Harris Poll® #58, 26 July [online] http://www.harrisinteractive.com/harris_poll/index.asp?PID=685 (accessed 17 May 2007)

Heise Online (2006) IT industry lobby group says Germany lacks specialists, 16 October, [online] http://www.heise.de/english/newsticker/news/79520 (accessed 17 May 2007)

Henley Media Group (2007) *Chief Talent Officer* (Accenture-sponsored publication) London, UK

Henry, Dan (2006) The theory and practice of employee engagement: lessons and questions, presentation at the SHRM Foundation 2006 Thought Leaders Retreat, Scottsdale, Ariz, 3–4 October 2006

Hewitt (2003) *Best Employers in Asia 2003 Regional Report*, Hewitt Associates, April, Hong Kong, China

Hollis, E (2004) UPS: delivering lifelong learning, *Chief Learning Officer*, March, pp 46–48

HR.COM (2006) Work–life experts launch new web-based training to help employers battle the costs of stress and build a resilient workforce, February [online] http://www.hr.com/servlets/sfs?&t=/Default/gateway&i=1116423256281&b=1116423256281& application=story&active=no&ParentID=1119278060936&StoryID= 1139067747063&xref=http%3A//www.google.com/search%3Fhl%3 Den%26q%3DWork%25E2%2580%2593life+experts+launch+new +webbased+training+to+help+employers+battle+the+costs+of+ stress+and+build+a+resilient+workforce&xref= (accessed 21 May 2007)

Hugo, Graham (2006) Australian experience in skilled migration, in *Competing for Global Talent*, International Labour Office, Geneva

Huselid, Mark A (2005) The impact of human resource management practices on turnover, productivity, and corporate financial performance, *Academy of Management Journal* 38, pp 635–72

Huselid, Mark A, Beatty, Richard W and Becker, Brian E (2005) A players or A positions? Strategic logic of workforce management, *Harvard Business Review*, 83(12), December, pp 110–17

IDC (2005) *Networking Skills in Europe: Will an increasing shortage hamper competitiveness in the global market?*, White Paper commissioned by Cisco Systems, September, Framingham, MA

International Herald Tribune (2006) Chinese paradox: a shallow pool of talent, 25 April [online] http://www.iht.com/articles/2006/04/ 24/news/talent.php (accessed 17 May 2007)

ISR (2004) Creating competitive advantage from your employees: a global study of employee engagement, White Paper, Chicago, IL

ISR (2006a) Retired on the job: how to recognize and recharge the complacent employee, White Paper, ISR, Chicago, IL

ISR (2006b) *ISR Employee Engagement Report*, Research Report, ISR, Chicago, IL

Japan Institute of Labour (1995) Working conditions and the labour market, *Japan Labour Bulletin* 34(1), 1 January

Kahn, William A (1990) Psychological conditions of personal engagement and disengagement at work, *Academy of Management Journal* 33, p 692–724

Kaplan, Robert S and Norton, David P (2004) *Strategy Maps: Converting intangible assets into tangible outcomes*, Harvard Business School Press, Boston, Mass

Karaevli, Ayse and Hall, Douglas T (2004) Career variety and executive adaptability in turbulent environments, in *Leading in Turbulent Times: Managing in the new world of work*, ed R J Burke and C L Cooper, pp 54–74, Blackwell, Malden, Mass

Kiger, Patrick J (2006) Flexibility to the fullest, *Workforce Management* 1 (25 September), pp 16–23

Kippen, Rebecca and McDonald, Peter (2000) Australia's population in 2000: the way we were, and the ways we might have been, *People and Place* 8(3), pp 10–17

KPMG Special Services and EIM Business & Policy Research in the Netherlands (in cooperation with European Network for SME Research (ENSR) and Infomart) (2003) *SMEs in Europe 2003*, Observatory of European SMEs 2003, no 7, Office for Official Publications of the European Communities, Luxembourg

Lewis, Jane (2006) Building a healthy work environment, presentation by organizational effectiveness consultant at the SHRM Foundation 2006 Thought Leaders Retreat, Scottsdale, Ariz, 3–4 October 2006

Lewis, Robert E and Heckman, Robert J (2006) Talent management: a critical review, *Human Resource Management Review*, **16**(2), pp 139–54

Management Issues News Online (2006) Employee engagement gives big boost to the bottom line, 7 June [online] http://www.managementissues.com/2006/8/24/research/employee-engagement-gives-big-boost-to-the-bottom-line.asp (accessed 21 May 2007)

Maslach, Christina and Leiter, Michael P (1997) *The Truth about Burnout: How organizations cause personal stress and what to do about it*, Jossey-Bass, San Francisco, CA

Maslow, Abraham H (1943) A theory of human motivation, *Psychological Review* 50, pp 370–96

McKinsey (2005) *Addressing China's Looming Talent Shortage*, report, October

Minton, Andrew (2006) *Business Week European 50 Research Survey*, CriticalEYE (Europe) Ltd

Morton, Lynne (2005) Talent management value imperatives: strategies for execution, Conference Board Research Report R-1360-05-RR, New York

New Strategist (2004) *The Millennials: Americans born 1977 to 1994*, New Strategist Publications, Ithaca, NY

OECD (2006a) *OECD Indicators: Education at a glance 2006*, OECD, Paris

OECD (2006b) *Planning for the Direct Assessment of PIAAC: Program for the International Assessment of Adult Competencies*, OECD, Paris, August

Parker, Simon (2006) *Explaining the Nature of Work and the Labour Supply of the Self-employed*, Research Report, Economic and Social Research Council (ESRC), London [online] http://www.esrc-societytoday.ac.uk/ESRCInfoCentre/ViewAwardPage.aspx?AwardId=2251 (accessed 21 May 2007)

Peters, Tom (1994) *The Leadership Alliance*, video, Enterprise Media, Cambridge, MA

Pink, Daniel (2002) *Free Agent Nation: How America's new independent workers are transforming the way we live*, Warner Business Books, New York

Ridderstrale, Jonas and Nordstrom, Kjell (2002) *Funky Business: Talent makes capital dance*, 2nd edn, Financial Times Management, London

Robison, Jennifer (2005) This HCA hospital's healthy turnaround, *Gallup Management Journal*, January

Rockliff, Sue, Peterson, Mary, Martin, Kath and Curtis, Dorothy (2005) Chasing the Sun: a virtual reference service between SAHSLC (SA) and SWICE (UK), *Health Information and Libraries Journal* 22(2), pp 117–23

Schettler, Joel (2002) Successful sabbaticals, *Training* 39(6), p 26

Schaufeli, Wilmar B, Salanova, Marisa, Gonzales-Roma, Vincente and Bakker, Arnold B (2002) The measurement of engagement and burnout, *Journal of Happiness Studies* 3, p 72

Schneider, Craig (2006) The new human-capital metrics, *CFO Magazine*, 15 February

Schwartz, Tony and Loehr, Jim (2004) *The Power of Full Engagement*, Free Press, New York

Scott-Jackson, William, Cook, Petra and Tajer, Randal (2006) *Measures of Workforce Capability for Future Performance, Vol 1: Identifying the measures that matter most*, Chartered Management Institute Research Report (supported by Oracle and Oxford Brookes University), July

Senge, Peter M (1990) *The Fifth Discipline: The art and practice of the learning organization*, Currency, New York

SHRM Foundation (2005) *Human Resources Trends in China*, report, SHRM, Alexandria, VA

SHRM Foundation (2006) The theory and practice of employee engagement: lessons and questions, Executive Summary, SHRM Foundation 2006 Thought Leaders Retreat, Scottsdale, Ariz, 3–4 October 2006

Soupata, Lea (2005) Engaging employees in company success: the UPS approach to a winning team, *Human Resource Management* **44**(1), p 95

Spitz-Oener, Alexandra (2006) Technical change, job tasks and technical demand: looking outside the wage structure, *Journal of Labor Economics*, **24**(2), pp 235–70

Stanford (2006) Internal branding at Yahoo!: crafting the employee value proposition, Stanford Graduate School of Business, case HR-25 B, p 14

Statistics Canada (2006) *Labour Force Survey*, April

Tapscott, Don (1997) *Growing Up Digital: The rise of the next generation*, McGraw-Hill, New York, NY

Thomas, Robert J (2005a) *Constellation Energy: creating a winning mindset*, Accenture Institute for High Performance Business Case Study, August.

Thomas, Robert J (2005b) *Harrah's Entertainment: instilling a customer-focused mindset*, Accenture Institute for High Performance Business Case Study, October

Thomas, Robert J (2006) *Marriott: Building a winning mindset, brand and organization*, Accenture Institute for High Performance Business Case Study

Thomas, Robert J (2008) *Crucibles of leadership: How to learn from experience to become a great leader*, Harvard Business School Press, Boston, MA

Thomas, Robert J, Linder, Jane C and Dutra, A (2006a) Inside the values-driven culture at UPS, *Outlook* 3: 19–29

Thomas, Robert J, Linder, Jane C and Pham, Chi T (2006b) UPS: mastering the tension between continuity and change, Accenture Institute for High Performance Business Case Study, July

Tichy, Noel (2004) *The Cycle of Leadership: How great leaders teach their companies to win*, Collins, New York, NY

Towers Perrin (2003) *Working Today: Understanding what drives employee engagement*, Towers Perrin US Talent Report

Towers Perrin (2005a) *2005 Global Workforce Study*, Towers Perrin

Towers Perrin (2005b) Largest single study of the workforce worldwide shows that employee engagement levels pose a threat to corporate performance globally, press release, 15 November

Treacy, Michael and Wiersema, Fred (1997) *The Discipline of Market Leaders*, Perseus Book Group, New York, NY

Treinen, James J and Miller-Frost, Susan L (2006) Following the sun: case studies in global software development, *IBM Systems Journal* **45**(4), pp 773–83

United Nations (2002) population report

Wagner, Rodd and Harter, James K (2006) *12: The Elements of Great Managing*, Gallup Press, New York

Wattenberg, Ben (2004) *Fewer: How the new demography of depopulation will shape our future*, Ivan R Dee, Chicago

Weatherly, Leslie A (2003) The value of people: the challenges and opportunities of human capital measurement and reporting, *HR Magazine*, **48**(9), 2003 Research Quarterly (Special Section), pp 1–10

Wee, Heesun (2002) Can oil giants and green energy mix? *Business Week Online*, 25 September [online] http://www.businessweek.com/bwdaily/dnflash/sep2002/nf20020925_4724.htm?chan=search (accessed 17 May 2007)

Wenger, Etienne (1999) *Communities of Practice: Learning, meaning and identity*, Cambridge University Press, Cambridge, UK

Whelan, David (2004) The slipper solution, *Forbes* **173**(11), 24 May

Whyte, William (1956) *The Organization Man*, Simon and Schuster, New York

Wiley, George (2002) Day for night: the development of long-distance reading, *Imaging Economics*, November

Index

NB: page numbers in *italic* indicate cartoons, figures or tables